# Easy Steps to Summary Writing and Note–Making

## By Nirmala Bellare
© 2020

Easy Steps to Summary Writing and Note-Making
Copyright © 2020 Nirmala Bellare

All rights reserved. No part of this book may be reproduced or used in any manner without written permission of the copyright owner except for the use of quotations in a book review.

*This book is dedicated to*

*my husband Gurudutt and my daughter Priya*

*for their valuable encouragement and guidance*

*and*

*to my students who were the source of my inspiration.*

# Table of Contents

INTRODUCTION .................................................................................................................. 1

WHAT IS SUMMARIZING? ................................................................................................. 5

UNIT I-A: FINDING THE OVERALL TOPIC ........................................................................ 7

UNIT I-B: SELECTING A TITLE ......................................................................................... 13

UNIT II: THE TOPIC SENTENCE ....................................................................................... 17

UNIT III: THE MAIN IDEA AND LENGTH REDUCTION STRATEGIES ............................ 23

UNIT IV: GIST WRITING .................................................................................................... 32

UNIT VA : THE MAIN IDEA AND SUPPORTING INFORMATION: PATTERNS OF ORGANIZATION ................................................................................................................ 40

UNIT V-B: SUPPORT ......................................................................................................... 47

UNIT VI : PATTERNS OF INFORMATION ORGANIZATION: THE PARAGRAPH AND SHORT PASSAGES .......................................................................................................... 57

UNIT VII : COHERENCE IN TEXTS: THE PARAGRAPH AND LONGER PASSAGES ...... 61

UNIT VIII: SUPERFLUOUS INFORMATION ..................................................................... 72

UNIT IX: PRACTICE WITH A VARIETY OF STYLES IN EXPOSITORY TEXTS ............... 86

| | |
|---|---|
| UNIT X: NOTE MAKING | 116 |
| EXERCISES | 122 |
| ANSWERS | 168 |
| ACKNOWLEDGEMENTS | 204 |

# INTRODUCTION

There have been quite a few publications of complete writing courses covering topics like letter and report writing, paragraph and essay writing together with summary or précis writing. However, these courses have not quite succeeded with students and teachers probably because each topic has been dealt with in an abrupt or superficial manner. This may be due to constraints of space or time (for coverage in the allotted academic term/ schedule). The summary writing skills are basic to all kinds of writing. Imbibing these is catalytic to improvement in other kinds of writing. The reading involved in the summarizing activity further helps in the same way.

This work was inspired by my research, which investigated how students process text while reading for summarizing. It yielded valuable insights into the problems faced by students in the summarizing operation. These included mainly the following:

i) Discriminating the more important from the less important information
ii) Perceiving the logical relationships between the two so that the essential focus may be retained in the summary, and
iii) Getting distracted by information that was interesting but not important to the summary.

To summarize successfully, students need both reading and writing skills. They need to use those reading strategies that are appropriate to the particular type of source-text, to arrive at the important substance of the passage. That is, read with an ability to identify the important information and to scan the text for the suitable detail that would need to be incorporated in the summary depending on the type of text being summarized and the purpose for which it is being done. For example, an engineer summarizing a feasibility study will need to use the appropriate detail of technical, financial and other figures and quantities required to give an idea of the feasibility status of the project. Summarizers also need to use the production skills of expression and writing, to state the important information with whatever necessary detail, as briefly as possible, without losing the appropriate focus and style of the source-text.

The **reading sub-skills** include a) selection of important ideas in the source text, b) identification and perception of the overall focus of the passage/ text, and c) deletion of redundant material in the source text that seems superfluous to the summary.

The **writing sub-skills** which get incrementally challenging may range from what Brown, Day and Jones (1983) call the simple "copy – delete" strategy to the more sophisticated one of what Hare & Borchardt (1985) call the "polishing" and rewriting strategy. Along the way the student would, also, sometimes, need to generate super-ordinate or overall terms for a list of terms or groups of ideas or again to generate topic sentences if they are not already included in the text. In addition, it is necessary for him/ her to perceive and retrieve the overall focus of the text, or what Kintsch and van Dijk (1978) call the "macro proposition", which finally gets encapsulated in the 'title' of the passage and the summary.

While the reading and writing sub-skills cannot be compartmentalized in the summarizing process, the initial units in the book (Units I – IV) focus more on the reading sub-skills of identifying the overall topic or picking or formulating the topic sentence and/ or the main idea of the passage provided. The student is also initiated into vocabulary building practice. Gradually, through Units V – IX, the student is led on to looking for patterns in which the information in the passage is organized in different kinds of expository texts. This is explained through a purview of and practice with Coherence Signals that link the discourse in the text. It is hoped that an appraisal of the pattern of the discourse organization should make it easier to link appropriately the important ideas selected, to form a summary with a focus that is true to the original. The penultimate unit helps revise the various sub-skills that have already been practised, with different kinds of texts including pieces of semi-scientific and reflective writing that become more challenging to summarize. The Note Making unit (X) seeks to build up on the summarizing skills and introduces strategies for grouping the material into an easy-to-store-and-retrieve format of notes or a diagrammatic representation of information in the form of charts, tables, tree- diagrams etc. These would be particularly useful for classroom and reference study which forms the bulk of academic work at the college and university level.

Some **special features** of this book are as follows:
A step-by step training in the sub-skills of summarizing and note-making, beginning with simple easy passages proceeding to more difficult ones and finally to unaided summarizing and note-making of a variety of texts.
While the early passages are short ones of 50 –100 words, the length and complexity gradually grow, leading finally to passages ranging between 500 and 1,500 words. (The number of words mentioned at the end of each passage/ summary is approximate.)

An attempt is also made to select passages that make interesting reading for college and university level entrants

A variety of expository texts in the argumentative, narrative, informative, reflective and semi-scientific/ semi-technical styles have been included. Several passages are authentic pieces of text taken from newspapers, magazines, journals, textbooks and other reference materials.

While designing the tasks, emphasis has been laid on 'performability' of the tasks by the students to engender in the students a sense of achievement when the task is completed. Beginning with word/ phrase answers and blank-filling items, the exercises lead on to gist-writing and short answers and gradually proceed to completely free composition of summaries.

Answers are also provided for all the exercises in the earlier units and to the initial exercises in the later units so that immediate feedback is available to students working on the exercises. The 'model' summaries, wherever provided, are of course mere guidelines and, therefore, only suggestive in intent. Infinite variations on these are possible and that is why, with several exercises in the later units, no model summary is offered but a discussion of the exercises and answers is encouraged between students and teachers.

The Note Making unit builds on the summarizing skills and adds on components like layout of notes or a diagrammatic representation of information in the form of charts, tables, tree diagrams etc.

The user of the book is advised to proceed with the units in the given order as much thought has gone into grading the exercises from easy to difficult. With the completed use of the book, it is hoped that the student should be reasonably able to summarize or make notes on any texts (s)he encounters in the real world.

A question has often been asked: how long should a summary be? Well, there is no sacred rule on the length of a summary. It would depend on the purpose for which, or the reader for whom it is written. It could also depend on the style of writing or the kind of message. For example, a scientific passage, like the 'Chromosomes' passage in this book, calls for more of the scientific detail to be included in the summary, whereas a literary passage could do with less of the stylistic detail while conveying the main message of the literary extract. The summaries in this book, therefore, range from 1/5 to 1/2 of the length of the source passage. Where examination tasks are concerned, the general requirement is for a précis or summary to be about a third of the original passage. However curtailing length is, definitely, an important aspect of the summary. Exercises in vocabulary building are, therefore, also provided and further practice recommended in Unit III of this course.

Regarding the use of the first, second or third person while writing the summary, it is generally expected that with all expository writing the third person would be the normal format to use. However, if a first-person account is being summarized, I would go with using the first-person or the third-person reporting for the summary, depending on the emotional involvement in the experience being recounted, as is done here with Passages 100 and 101.

# What is Summarizing?

Summarizing, as an informal activity comes quite naturally and easily to us, whether orally or in writing. For example, we talk briefly about a book or a film or something seen or heard, or write about it in a letter, diary or a school composition. There are different kinds of more formal summary-writing like activities such as, abstracts, synopses and outlines; and there are activities like making or writing a gist, paraphrasing, note making and précis writing. Often, summaries are written for varied purposes and for the benefit of a specific audience. For example, summaries may be written as a classroom exercise or as an examination task for a school or college teacher. You may, also, by using your summarizing skills, make notes from a textbook or reference material for study and examination purposes. You might, sometimes, need to summarize a story or novel, or a part of it to illustrate or exemplify a point you are making while answering a question on a literary text. A summary may, again, be submitted as an outline or a research proposal to a university professor. A boss at work may require it in the form of a feasibility report or an appraisal report or he may want a summary of a government circular or a legal notification. You may need to send an abstract for review by the editorial committee of a journal or publishing company or you may simply be reviewing or reporting a book, a film or an interesting happening to the readers of a newspaper or journal. Summary writing is, therefore, a particularly useful skill. In any case, any such summary involves picking out and condensing accurately the important ideas of a given text Before producing such a summary, we need to read through the text a couple of times or more, and then produce a summary based on the whole text or large chunks of it. We also need to worry about grammatical construction and cohesion and conform to limitations of length. In this book we shall deal with summaries that are required in the English Communication classes and with note- making that proves useful in any academic programme. We shall focus on the summarizing of and note making from expository texts. Expository writing is writing that 'exposes' a topic i.e., gives us different kinds of information about it. This general kind of text is preferred as it is the sort of text contained not only in academically used material but also in newspapers journals and magazines. Students should find newspapers and magazines to be of topical interest and should be able to use them as reading material in preparing for activities like essay-writing, seminars and debates, and for presentations in the curricular programme on topics of general and co-curricular interest.

The units, which follow, take you step by step through the process of summary writing. We begin with short passages and proceed gradually to longer ones. You first learn to identify the overall topic of a passage or unified piece of text. Next, you learn to pick out the topic sentence if a paragraph has one. If not, you learn to formulate one from the information in the paragraph. As you get to deal with longer passages, you need to arm yourself with strategies to reduce the length of the original passage so that you can write a shortened summary of it. This means that you need a rich stock of vocabulary. Exercises that can help you improve your vocabulary are sampled in Unit III. But you will need more and regular practice with similar exercises. Books offering such exercises are in plenty and you can also find them in most magazines and journals. These you could easily pick in a library or anywhere else, for reading. You also learn, in the same unit and the following one, to pick out the main idea from a given piece of text and to sum up briefly any examples or explanations you might need in support of the main idea. Thus, you will have learnt to write a gist of the given passage. As you progress with longer passages, you need to understand the rhetorical argument that underlies the passage i.e., you need to get the logical thread of the argument. This is important for you to project in your summary. Units V, VI and VII, therefore, tell you about the patterns of organization that occur in expository texts and the explicit means by which we can recognize them. With the subsequent practice you learn how to weed out superfluous information and write summaries from a variety of texts. The not-making section, which now demands the use of your summarizing skills, takes you further on to using an appropriate layout of the information in brief points, numbered if and when necessary; or even better, presenting it in a diagrammatic form wherever possible. This kind of laying out also implies an understanding of the hierarchical structure of the information that you are presenting in your notes. This is demonstrated in the way you group and sub-group the information. It is hoped that by the completion of the practice in this course and with some additional practice, if necessary, you would have achieved reasonable success and confidence with these two important skills that are so crucial to any work or study in your future careers. Most answers are provided at the end of the book for comparison with your own, so that you have immediate feedback on your performance. However, if you have a variation in the answer it could be discussed with the teacher. The 'model' summaries, wherever provided, are of course mere **guidelines** as to the possible content of the summaries. Infinite variations in writing these are possible and that is why, your summaries will need to be discussed with the teacher. It is hoped that working with this book will be a happy experience in the classroom.

# Unit I-A: Finding the Overall Topic

Let us begin by looking at the general structure of expository writing. A typical expository passage, of whatever length, has an **overall topic**, which could possibly be indicated by its title. This overall topic is spelt out in the passage in terms of the **main /central idea(s)** or the **main argument** of the passage. Let us look at some examples. We shall begin with short passages of 100 – 200 words. (The numbering of sentences and underlining in the passages, henceforth, is for convenience)

1      **1 Boys and girls enjoy the performers in a circus, but they love the clown. 2 Why is that? 3 It is because everything about him is funny. 4 His jokes and stories are funny. 5 His clothes never fit. 6 His face is thickly covered with white powder, except for parts which are painted a bright red. 7 He plays musical instruments, climbs ropes, leaps merrily, and is always falling down and making silly mistakes.**

In passage 1 above, the overall topic or title could be 'Clowns' and the main idea is that children love clowns because they are funny. This idea is contained in the first three sentences while examples of the things which make the clown funny, are contained in the remaining four sentences. Let us look at another paragraph about dolphins:

2      **1The dolphin, like the porpoise and the whale, is not a fish but a mammal. 2 It is warm-blooded --- that is, its body heat 1 remains the same, whether the water is warm or cold --- and it has lungs instead of gills: this means that it cannot breathe under water like a fish, but must come to the top to breathe air. 3 Its young are born alive and suckled on milk by their mother    4 In all these things the dolphin is like other mammals and differs from the fishes.    5 The tail fin of a dolphin is also unlike that of a fish, for it is flat instead of upright.**

The overall topic or title for passage 2 is, obviously, 'Dolphins' and the main idea in the passage is that a dolphin is not a fish but a mammal. This idea is contained in the very first sentence, but the ways in which dolphins are different from fish and like mammals are illustrated in the remaining sentences of the paragraph.

**Exercise**

**I** **(A)** For each of the following passages fill in the blank spaces provided, with a suitable title indicating the overall topic of the passage in a word or a phrase. (The first example is worked out for you):

**3** The night sky has a beauty we can all enjoy. The stars sparkle like jewels on a velvet backcloth. The moon, ever changing its shape, pours its silvery light into the darkness. At first sight, the night sky appears to be filled haphazardly with stars. But, after a while, we find that we can recognize patterns of stars and thus find our way through the heavens. By studying the heavens, we become astronomers. The Chaldeans and Babylonians were skilled observers of the heavens over 5,000 years ago.

Title: The Beautiful Night Sky_____ (Encyclopaedia.-'Space')

**4** Throughout the year, the Sun, the Moon and the planets appear to travel through a narrow band of the heavens. It is called the zodiac. There are 12 constellations along this band, called the signs of the zodiac. The positions of the heavenly bodies in the zodiac are thought by some people to influence men's lives and future actions. This belief is the basis of astrology. Astrologers were very important people in ancient times and still seem important to some people in India today.

Title: _____ (Enc.-Space)

**5** Photosynthesis, the plant's food-making process, takes place mainly in the leaves. These are arranged so that they get as much sunlight as possible, for light is essential to the process. The green chlorophyll traps the light energy, which the plant then uses to combine water and carbon dioxide gas. Sugar is formed for food and oxygen is given off.

Title: _____ (Piccolo)

**6** Tides are another force that move the waters of the oceans. They are caused by gravity between the Moon and the Earth and the Sun and the Earth. The force of gravity pulls the water like a magnet and as the Earth spins, the part of the ocean pulled most strongly changes. In each 24-hour period, two high and low tides sweep around the globe rather like giant waves. Near land the difference is much greater. The highest tides occur when the Sun and Moon are in line and are pulling together.

Title: _____ (Piccolo)

**7** If you are interested in astronomy, you should go to a planetarium. There, you will see how and why the stars change from season to season; how the planets and the Moon move through the heavens; and many things besides. You sit in a chamber with a domed roof, onto which all the heavenly bodies can be projected.

Title: _____ (Enc.-Space)

**8** Lightning is a spark of electricity, which flows within a cloud, between clouds, or from a cloud to the ground. It is very hot and can start fires and tear down trees. As the lightning burns its way through the air it creates a shock wave, which is the noise we hear as thunder. So, lightning and thunder happen at the same moment. We see the lightning first because light travels faster than sound.

Title: _____ (Enc.-Space)

**(B)** For each of the following passages fill in the blank space provided below a question title to which the paragraph provides an answer. (The first example is worked out for you):

**9** The Moon is very much smaller than the Earth. Its diameter is only about a quarter that of the Earth. If the Earth were hollow, you could fit nearly 50 Moons into it. Because it is small, the Moon has a small gravity. If you went to the Moon, you could jump six times higher than you could on Earth. (Encyclopaedia – 'Space')

Title-Question: <u>How Big is the Moon?</u>

**10** Like all ordinary stars the Sun is a mass of ball of white-hot gas. Most of it is hydrogen gas. If you could cut into the Sun, you would find that it would get hotter and hotter the deeper you went. The outer surface has a temperature of 6,000 degrees centigrade. But in the centre, the temperature is as high as 15,000,000 degrees centigrade. We call the visible surface of the Sun the 'photosphere ('light-sphere') (Enc.-Space)

Title-Question: ----------------------------------------------------------------------

**11** A bird's wings hold it up in the air as well as producing the thrust to push it forward. Lift is produced as a result of the arched upper surface of the wings. The air is 'stretched out' as it flows over this surface, and the pressure is therefore reduced: upward pressure on the lower wing surface pushes the bird upwards. The downbeat of the wing is the power stroke, during which the wing-tips twist and push the air backwards. This pushes the bird forwards. The feathers are separated on the upstroke to reduce air resistance. The wings are held back, and the tail is spread to form air-brakes on landing.
(Piccolo)

Title-Question:
_____


**12** Apollo was the spacecraft American astronauts used to travel to the moon between 1969 and 1972. It had a length of about 10 metres and a maximum diameter of 3.9 metres. Apollo spacecraft were also used for Skylab missions.
(Enc.-Space)

Title-Question:
_____

**13** A Kitchen Garden, as the name implies, is the garden around or near the house. Raising a kitchen garden is a fascinating experience. The greatest satisfaction a family gets from it is dining on the harvest, which means vegetables produced in the home garden are used in their most fresh state. Besides producing food for the family, the kitchen garden beautifies the house as it also includes trees, flowering shrubs, creepers, grass and plants. The kitchen garden is not a new innovation as even in the olden days and in backward areas families grew some vegetables near the house for use by the family.

Title-Question:
_____

(C) Look carefully at the following groups of facts and fill in the blank spaces provided for each of the groups, by choosing from the titles given below:

1. Body Facts
2. World Population Explosion
3. Animal Lifespans
4. Names of The Constellations
5. The Nearest Stars
6. Speed in Nature
7. The Brightest Stars

**(7 tables follow in printed version)**

## A

| AD | millions (est.) | AD | millions (est.) | AD | millions (est.) |
|---|---|---|---|---|---|
| AD1 | 250 | 1955 | 2,713 | 1975 | 4,022 |
| 1650 | 550 | 1960 | 2,982 | 1980 | 4,457 |
| 1750 | 750 | 1965 | 3,289 | 1985 | 4,933 |
| 1800 | 950 | 1970 | 3,632 | 1990 | 5,438 |
| 1850 | 1,200 | 1971 | 3,706 | 1995 | 5,961 |
| 1900 | 1,550 | 1972 | 3,782 | 2000 | 6,493 |
| 1925 | 1,900 | 1973 | 3,860 | 2070 | 25,000 |
| 1950 | 2,486 | 1974 | 3,950 | 2100 | 48,000 |

Piccolo

## B

| | average |
|---|---|
| Antelope | 10 |
| Bear | 15–50 |
| Cat | 15 |
| Cattle | 20 |
| Deer | 10–20 |
| Dog | 12–15 |
| Donkey | 20 |
| Duck | 10 |
| Elephant | 60 |
| Fox | 10 |
| Giraffe | 10–25 |
| Goat | 10 |
| Goose | 25 |
| Hippopotamus | 30–40 |
| Horse | 20–30 |
| Kangaroo | 10–20 |
| Lion | 25 |
| Ostrich | 50 |
| Pig | 10–15 |
| Rabbit | 5–8 |
| Rhinoceros | 25–50 |
| Sheep | 10–15 |
| Tiger | 10–25 |
| Whale | 20 |
| Zebra | 20–25 |

Piccolo

## C

| | |
|---|---|
| Spine-tailed swift | 170 km/h |
| Sailfish | 109 km/h |
| Cheetah | 105 km/h |
| Pronghorn antelope | 97 km/h |
| Racing pigeon | 97 km/h |
| Lion | 80 km/h |
| Gazelle | 80 km/h |
| Hare | 72 km/h |
| Zebra | 64 km/h |
| Racehorse | 64 km/h |
| Shark | 64 km/h |
| Greyhound | 63 km/h |
| Rabbit | 56 km/h |
| Giraffe | 51 km/h |
| Grizzly bear | 48 km/h |
| Cat | 48 km/h |
| Elephant | 40 km/h |
| Seal | 40 km/h |
| Man | 32 km/h |
| Black Mamba | 32 km/h |
| Bee | 18 km/h |
| Pig | 18 km/h |
| Chicken | 14 km/h |
| Spider | 1.88 km/h |
| Tortoise | 0.8 km/h |
| Snail | 0.05 km/h |

Piccolo

## D

Blood takes about one minute to go from the heart, around the body, and back to the heart again.

The skin covering the body measures almost 2 square metres.

We have between 90,000 and 140,000 hairs on our heads.

The lungs can hold between 3 to 5 litres of air. About half a litre is taken in at each breath.

An average adult drinks about 1.5 litres of liquid and eats about 1.5 kilogrammes of food every day.

If all the blood vessels in a human body were laid end to end they would stretch for nearly 100,000 kilometres.

An adult's brain weighs about 1.5 kilogrammes.

Piccolo

## E

| Name | Constellation | Distance (light-years) |
|---|---|---|
| Proxima Centauri | Centaurus | 4.3 |
| Rigil Kent | Centaurus | 4.4 |
| Barnard's Star | Ophiuchus | 5.9 |
| Wolf 359 | Leo | 7.6 |
| Lalande 21185 | Ursa Major | 8.1 |
| Sirius | Canis Major | 8.8 |

Robin Kerrod

## F

| Name | Constellation | Distance (light-years) |
|---|---|---|
| Sirius | Canis Major | 9 |
| Canopus | Carina | 200 |
| Rigil Kent | Centaurus | 4 |
| Arcturus | Boötes | 40 |
| Vega | Lyra | 30 |
| Capella | Auriga | 50 |
| Rigel | Orion | 800 |
| Procyon | Canis Minor | 11 |
| Achernar | Eridanus | 130 |
| Hadar | Centaurus | 300 |
| Altair | Aquila | 16 |
| Betelgeuse | Orion | 650 |

Robin Kerrod

## G

| Latin name | English name |
|---|---|
| Andromeda | Andromeda |
| Antlia | Air Pump |
| Apus | Bird of Paradise |
| Aquarius | Water Bearer |
| Aquila | Eagle |
| Ara | Altar |
| Aries | Ram |
| Auriga | Charioteer |
| Boötes | Herdsman |
| Caelum | Chisel |
| Camelopardus | Giraffe |
| Cancer | Crab |
| Canes Venatici | Hunting Dogs |
| Canis Major | Great Dog |
| Canis Minor | Little Dog |
| Capricornus | Sea-Goat |
| Carina | Keel |
| Cassiopeia | Cassiopeia |
| Centaurus | Centaur |
| Cepheus | Cepheus |
| Cetus | Whale |
| Chamaeleon | Chameleon |
| Circinus | Pair of Compasses |
| Columba | Dove |
| Coma Berenices | Berenice's Hair |
| Corona Australis | Southern Crown |
| Corona Borealis | Northern Crown |
| Corvus | Crow |
| Crater | Cup |
| Crux | Southern Cross |
| Cygnus | Swan |

Robin Kerrod

# Unit I-B: Selecting a Title

Finding the overall topic or title for short and simple passages may not be very difficult. But choosing a title for longer or more complex passages needs to be done with great thought and care. The important thing is to read carefully and gain a thorough understanding of it. The title should express the exact focus of the passage. Let us look again at the following passage:

**A bird's wings hold it up in the air as well as producing the thrust to push it forward. Lift is produced as a result of the arched upper surface of the wings. The air is 'stretched out' as it flows over this surface, and the pressure is therefore reduced: upward pressure on the lower wing surface pushes the bird upwards. The downbeat of the wing is the power stroke, during which the wing-tips twist and push the air backwards. This pushes the bird forwards. The feathers are separated on the upstroke to reduce air resistance. The wings are held back and the tail is spread to form air-brakes on landing.        (Piccolo)**

While the vague overall topic, at a first reading, may apparently seem to be 'Birds' or 'A Bird's Wings' or even 'The Structure of the Bird's Wings' these only indicate one of the topics in the passage and cover only a part of the subject of the passage. Another topic that figures in the discussion on a more careful reading is the 'Movement of the Air' and this as a title, also, would not do as it has too narrow a focus, for, it once again evokes only another sub-topic of the passage. A title like 'Air and the Wings of a Bird' would have a more comprehensive coverage and yet it would not convey the exact focus of the description in the passage. What the writer wishes to convey to us is a detailed explanation of how the structure of the wings in interaction with the air helps the bird to fly. Hence a title like 'How a Bird Flies' alone becomes the appropriate one for the passage. An imaginative student may think of a title like 'Upstrokes and Down Strokes', which may sound interesting, but it bears no relation to the theme of the passage and would, therefore, be an irrelevant title.

While choosing a title, therefore, you need to make sure of the following:

The scope of the title you select comprehensively covers/ implies all the sub-topics in the passage. That means the title should not be too broad or vague. Nor should it be too narrow or partial.

The title should also indicate to us the communicative purpose of the writer, i.e., what exactly the writer wishes to convey to us through his writing.

The title should not go off at a tangent from the subject of the passage, i.e., it should not seem digressing or irrelevant.

You must, therefore, ensure that your title is not too broad or wide or too narrow in scope, and that it does not go off the point of the passage but comprehensively conveys the exact intent of the writer.

## Exercise

I       For each of the passages that follow on the next page (five passages overleaf) some possible titles are suggested below. Only one of the suggested titles is appropriate. (Sometimes an alternative title may be possible.)

(A)     For each of the passages select your chosen title.

(B) For each of the titles not selected indicate the reason, by choosing from the options given below:

i)      too broad or vague in scope
ii)     too narrow or partial (i.e., covering only part of the passage/ summary)
iii)    not in focus or not in the communicative purpose of the passage/ summary.
iv)     Inaccurate/ Irrelevant to the topic of the passage/ summary.
v)   could be an alternative title

1       a) Preying Owls
        b) Sharp Quiet Killing
        c) Nightly Active Owls
        d) The Silent Killer
        e) Killer Owls

2       a) Colours of Nature.
        b) Colours from Chemicals
        c) Vegetarian and Synthetic Colours
        d) How to Make Colours
        e) The Making of Colours

3    a) Americans vs. Russians.
      b) The Space Race.
      c) Space Flying.
      d) The Universe Beyond the Earth.
      e) Explorer Satellites.

4    a) Learning Animals.
      b) Birds: Natural Singers.
      c) All Life is Learning
      d) Untaught Spiders
      e) Trunk-heavy Elephants.

5    a) American Arrogance
      b) Irreligious Americans
      c) Virtues of Self-Reliance
      d) Opinionated Americans
      e) Unreverential Americans

**(1 - 5 Passages   Overleaf)**

## 1

The owls are supremely suited to capturing small rodents and other animals at night. Their eyes are more efficient than our own. The large 'window' at the front lets in the maximum amount of light, and the round lens produces a bright image. The eyes look forward, like our own, and the owl can judge distances very accurately. It plunges down towards its prey and thrusts out its talons to make the kill. The prey is taken by surprise because the owl flies silently. Delicate fringes on the front edges of the feathers eliminate the noise of air rushing over the wings.

## 2

From the earliest times men have searched for bright colours to make paints or dyes. Many of these colours were obtained from plants — from wood, bark, leaves, flowers or fruits. They were used for clothing, carpets, and curtains, and for painting and staining other materials.

Most of the dyes used in modern countries are made from chemicals, many of them from coal-tar, but dyes obtained from plants are still used in some lands.

## 4

Actually, all warm-blooded animals are incredibly helpless at first. Young birds and young bats must be taught to fly. Thousands of young seal and young sea lions are drowned every year. They never learn to swim "naturally"; the mother has to take them out under her flipper and show them how. Birds sing without instruction, but they do not sing well unless they have had an opportunity of hearing older and more adept members of their species. Older harvest mice build better nests than beginners. Frank Buck says that the young elephant does not seem to know at first what his trunk is for; it gets in his way and seems more of a hindrance than a help until his parents show him what to do with it. Insects, indeed, seem to start life completely equipped with all necessary reflexes, but even there the concept of "instinct" seems to require some modification, for they improve their talents with practice. Young spiders, for example, "begin by making quite primitive little webs, and only attain perfection in their art in course of time"; and older spiders, if deprived of their spinnerets, will take to hunting.

Bergen Evans, *The Natural History of Nonsense*

## 3

The contest to invent and build bigger and better military weapons drew the United States and the Soviet Union into a spectacular space race. It began with the launch of a small orbiting satellite, Sputnik I, by the Soviet Union in 1957. The USA reacted with alarm, and rushed to catch up in whatever ways possible. Initially it met with numerous setbacks, and it was the Russians who first managed to put a man in space. Yuri Gagarin, their cosmonaut, was fired aloft in 1963.

In the next few years the Americans caught up quickly, with a series of impressive space flights. In 1969, they managed to land two astronauts on the surface of the Moon. Since then, they have made a number of other Moon landings. The Russians focused their efforts on building orbiting stations, where cosmonauts could live and work for months at a time. In the 1970s, a series of robot explorer satellites were fired to other planets. They have so far provided us with the first glimpse of the Universe beyond Earth.

## 5

Religion apart, Americans are an unreverential people. [NEGATIVE DEFINITION:] I do not mean irreverent—far from it; nor do I mean that they have not a great capacity for hero-worship, as they have many a time shown. [POSITIVE DEFINITION:] I mean that they are little disposed, especially in public questions—political, economical, or social—to defer to the opinions of those who are wiser or better instructed than themselves. Everything tends to make the individual independent and self-reliant. He goes early into the world; he is left to make his way alone; he tries one occupation after another, if the first or second venture does not prosper; he gets to think that each man is his own best helper and adviser. Thus he is led, I will not say to form his own opinions, for even in America few are those who do that, but to fancy that he has formed them, and to feel little need of aid from others toward correcting them.

James Bryce "American Commonwealth"

# Unit II: The Topic Sentence

An effective paragraph usually consists of a central or main idea and enough details to put the idea across. The controlling idea is often contained in a single sentence, commonly called the topic sentence. Governing the content and the development of the paragraph, this central or topic sentence, sets the stage for every sentence and every detail used in the paragraph to support the central idea. A topic sentence often occurs at or near the beginning of the paragraph, but it may just as easily fall in the middle or at the end. Sometimes, it may also be scattered in different parts of the paragraph and may have to be put together. In some writing, especially writing of a narrative nature, it may not be stated at all, but only implied.

**Topic Sentence First**: In the following passage (14) the central idea is in the first sentence. The paragraph opens (Sentence 1) with the talk of the marvelous development of an egg into a complete animal and the rest of the paragraph traces this development through the various stages through Sentences 2 – 9.

**14    1 Frogs and toads give us an opportunity of studying the marvelous development of an egg into a complete animal. 2 This involves a metamorphosis (a complete change of shape and of way of life) that seems like magic. 3 You can watch every stage of it. 4 With the onset of the rains, in almost any weedy pond, the females lay several thousand tiny blackish eggs, each the size of a grain of sand, and covered with a coat of transparent jelly. 5 Some weeks after the tadpole emerges, and its hind legs begin to grow. 6 Up to this point, the tadpole will have lived by nibbling the green stuff, but now it begins to need animal food and if kept in an aquarium, should be given tiny pieces of cooked meat. 7 Then the front legs begin to appear, and the whole tadpole undergoes its most remarkable change: it ceases to have a two-chambered heart and gills and to live like a fish. 8 Instead it develops a three-chambered heart, and lungs, and breathes like a land animal. 9 The tail shrinks, and now we have a miniature frog that needs to come out of the water.**

**Topic Sentence Last**: In the next example, the paragraph begins (Sentence 1) with a false notion that people have of environment being something outside us, and goes on (through Sentences 2 - 10) to explain how environment is, in fact, present within us, even in the germ cell, and that it is more than a conditioning factor of life. The paragraph concludes with the central idea, in Sentence 11, that 'Life and environment are, in fact correlates'. (Imagine that this topic sentence appeared first in the paragraph. Would it change the effect?)

---

**1** If we think of our environment as simply the outside world, as something that surrounds and "environs" us, we underestimate its role. 2 The relation of life and environment is extremely intimate. 3 The organism itself, the life structure, is the product of past life and past environment. 4 Environment is present from the very beginning of life, even in the germ cell. 5 We think of our organisms as ourselves, and environment as that which lies outside us. 6 But the environment is more than a conditioning factor of life that can be conceived of apart from it. 7 Imagine that we were suddenly transported to a much larger planet. 8 Our bodies would instantly become much heavier, and that alone would involve myriad other differences. 9 We should no longer know ourselves, nor, assuming that we could exist at all, be ourselves. 10 We never know life except in an appropriate environment, to which it is already adjusted. 11 Life and environment are, in fact correlates.

---

**Topic Sentence Scattered Throughout**: A paragraph containing a somewhat complex idea frequently introduces part of the idea, then give details, and then completes the statement of the central idea, as in the following example. Here Sentence1 begins to define the central idea by describing education as development of human material to satisfy the needs of the nation. The extent and scope of this development is explained in the next three sentences and the final sentence indicates how the various factors in this development can be grouped into five main categories. The topic sentence, therefore, would have to be framed by a combination of the elements highlighted in the paragraph below to say 'Education is the development of human beings along religious, social, economic, political and external lines and using this in the service of the nation'.

16    1 Education satisfies the needs of society by developing human material and using this in the service of the nation. 2 The extent and shape of development is determined by social and cultural patterns. 3 In primitive communities social and cultural patterns were of a simple nature and the factors influencing the shape of education were few and clearly defined. 4 But in more sophisticated communities the factors are numerous and complex. 5 It is possible, however, to group these factors under five main headings so that we may more closely inspect them in the context of education of women in India: religious, social, economic, political and external.

---

**Topic Sentence Implied**: In some paragraphs, especially in narrative or descriptive writing, the topic sentence is implied rather than explicitly stated. In such paragraphs the details are arranged so that a central idea is formed in the reader's mind. In the following paragraph, the topic is the formation of Rare Earths. This is conveyed to us in the form of a story of the rocks.

17    1. Do you know that the sand of which you make castles when playing on a sea-beach might contain particles of valuable mineral substances? 2 If it does it will get the glorious name 'Rare Earths'. 3 These Rare Earths have a wonderful story behind them. 4 Once upon a time they were rocks in the range of mountains running parallel to the sea. 5 But there was the rain, bit by bit, every year. 6 The rainwater carried the Rare Rocks, as they should have been called then, into the sea. 7 But it was not an ordinary sea; it was a sea with a generous heart. 8 It took pity on the mountains, which allowed the rain to do this mischief to them and decided to give back the valuable substances it had got, and more than that. 9 The good sea ground the rocks into small particles, sorted out the different minerals it had received and deposited each type in a bed on the beach.

### Exercise

Find **the topic sentence** in each of the following paragraphs. If the central idea is not directly stated combine the important ideas to make a topic sentence or formulate your own wording of it:

**18**   A serious threat to farmers in many parts of the world is erosion. If a large area of land is cleared of trees and bushes and is then badly treated by the farmer, the rain and winds may gradually wash away, or blow away, much of the fertile top-soil. When this happens, crops of corn or grass become weaker and weaker until nothing much will grow at all. If erosion is allowed to continue, it will turn good farmland into desert.

**19**   Since 1973, the world has had to cope with soaring oil and gas prices. It has also had to face up to local shortages of all forms of energy. During this time the demand for energy has grown steadily, while many of the world's leading oil producers have raised prices and limited their output of crude oil. The rest of the world has had to find a way to pay huge fuel bills on the one hand, and to save energy and find new sources on the other. Many nations have now begun to search for forms of energy such as nuclear power and solar power, in preparation for the future.

**20**   The mountaineer continues to improve in skill year after year. A skier is probably past his best by the age of thirty, and most international tennis champions are in their early twenties. But it is far from unusual for men of fifty or sixty to climb the highest mountains in the Alps. They may take more time than younger men, but they probably climb with more skill and less waste of effort, and they certainly experience equal enjoyment.

**(7 more passages 21 - 27  follow in the original printed version)**

**21**

Each person is not only a free, single end, like the green palm leaf that unfolds, grows in a curve of beauty, and dies in its season; he is like the whole palm leaf, the part inside the trunk, too. He is the culmination of his entire ancestry, and *represents* that whole human past. In his brief individuation he is an *expression* of all humanity. That is what makes each person's life sacred and all-important. A single ruined life is the bankruptcy of a long line. This is what I mean by the individual's involvement with all mankind.

Susanne Langer, "Man and Animal: The City and the Hive"

**22**

We did sleep that night, but we woke up at six A.M. We lay in our beds and debated through the open doors whether to obey till, say, half-past six. Then we bolted. I don't know who started it, but there was a rush. We all disobeyed; we raced to disobey and get first to the fireplace in the front room downstairs. And there they were, the gifts, all sorts of wonderful things, mixed-up piles of presents; only, as I disentangled the mess, I saw that my stocking was empty; it hung limp; not a thing in it; and under and around it—nothing. My sisters had knelt down, each by her pile of gifts; they were squealing with delight, till they looked up and saw me standing there in my nightgown with nothing. They left their piles to come to me and look with me at my empty place. Nothing. They felt my stocking: nothing.

Lincoln Steffens, *Autobiography*

**23**

We spread the blankets inside for a carpet, and eat our dinner in there. We put all the other things handy at the back of the cavern. Pretty soon it darkened up and begun to thunder and lighten; so the birds was right about it. Directly it begun to rain, and it rained like all fury, too, and I never see the wind blow so. It was one of these regular summer storms. It would get so dark that it looked all blue-black outside, and lovely; and the rain would thrash along by so thick that the trees off a little ways looked dim and spiderwebby; and here would come a blast of wind that would bend the trees down and turn up the pale underside of the leaves; and then a perfect ripper of a gust would follow along and set the branches to tossing their arms as if they was just wild; and next, when it was just about the bluest and blackest—fst! It was as bright as glory and you'd have a little glimpse of tree-tops a-plunging about, away off yonder in the storm, hundreds of yards further than you could see before; dark as sin again in a second, and how you'd hear the thunder let go with an awful crash and then go rumbling, grumbling, tumbling down the sky towards the underside of the world, like rolling empty barrels down stairs, where it's long stairs and they bounce a good deal, you know.

Mark Twain, *The Adventures of Huckleberry Finn*

**24**

Indeed, the bureaucratic-industrial civilization that has been victorious in Europe and North America has created a new type of man. He has been described as the "organization man" and as *homo consumens*. He is in addition the *homo mechanicus*. By this I mean a "gadget man," deeply attracted to all that is mechanical and inclined against all that is alive. It is, of course, true that man's biological and physiological equipment provides him with such strong sexual impulses that even the *homo mechanicus* still has sexual desires and looks for women. But there is no doubt that the gadget man's interest in women is diminishing. A New Yorker cartoon pointed to this very amusingly: a salesgirl trying to sell a certain brand of perfume to a young female customer recommends it by remarking, "It smells like a new sports car."

Erich Fromm, *The Heart of Man*

## 25

The chief feature of the landscape, and of your life in it, was the air. Looking back on a sojourn in the African highlands, you are struck by your feeling of having lived for a time up in the air. The sky was rarely more than pale blue or violet, with a profusion of mighty, weightless, ever-changing clouds towering up and sailing on it, but it had a blue vigor in it, and at a short distance it painted the ranges of hills and the woods a fresh deep blue. In the middle of the day the air was alive over the land, like a flame burning; it scintillated, waved and shone like running water, mirrored and doubled all objects, and created great Fata Morgana. Up in this high air you breathed easily, drawing in a vital assurance and lightness of heart. In the highlands you woke up in the morning and thought: Here I am, where I ought to be.

Isak Dinesen, *Out of Africa*

## 26

As children become teenagers, parents often fear what the neighbors may say, and so they are unable to allow the youngster to behave in ways that might be quite temporary and very normal for him at that particular time. This fear is perhaps strongest in small communities where everyone knows everyone else. Studies have shown that small-town adolescent girls, on the average, experience more conflict with their parents than any other adolescent group, a fact that is associated with the tendencies of their fathers to be more s with them. At times and in places where the misdeeds of teenagers are magnified out of all proportion as they are in the scares of juvenile delinquency that sweep across many a community, even the most innocent mistake of a teenager may be exaggerated into a portent of ominous significance that seriously blocks communication between the generations.

## 27

Imagine, for a moment, that you have drunk from a magician's goblet. Reverse the irreversible stream of time. Go down the dark stairwell out of which the race has ascended. Find yourself at last on the bottommost steps of time, slipping, sliding, and wallowing by scale and fin down into the muck and ooze out of which you arose. Pass by grunts and voiceless hissings below the last tree ferns. Eyeless and earless, float in the primal waters, sense sunlight you cannot see and stretch absorbing tentacles toward vague tastes that float in water. Still, in your formless shiftings, the *you* remains: the sliding particles, the juices, the transformations are working in an exquisitely patterned rhythm which has no other purpose than your preservation—you, the entity, the ameboid being whose substance contains the unfathomable future. Even so does every man come upward from the waters of his birth.

Loren Eiseley, *The Invisible Pyramid*

# Unit III: The Main Idea and Length Reduction Strategies

The overall subject in a passage, as we have seen, is spelt out through the passage in terms of the main/ central idea(s) or the main argument of the passage. The main idea/ argument in a paragraph may be contained in a sentence or a clause in the passage. Other sentences around it relate to this idea directly or indirectly. These other sentences carry subordinate ideas explaining or elaborating or generally supporting the main idea. Sometimes, these explanations or elaborations may be further illustrated or exemplified. Let us look, once again, at the examples we saw earlier.

---

**A    1 Boys and girls enjoy the performers in a circus, but they love the clown. 2 Why is that? 3 It is because everything about him is funny. 4 His jokes and stories are funny. 5 His clothes never fit. 6 His face is thickly covered with white powder, except for parts which are painted a bright red. 7 He plays musical instruments, climbs ropes, leaps merrily, and is always falling down and making silly mistakes.**

---

As we saw earlier, in passage A, the overall topic or title could be 'Clowns' and the main idea is that children love clowns because they are funny. This idea is contained in the first three sentences and the supporting information is in the examples of the things, which make him funny. These are mentioned in the remaining four sentences. Let us look at the other paragraph about dolphins:

**B    1 The dolphin, like the porpoise and the whale, is not a fish but a mammal. 2 It is warm-blooded --- that is, its body heat remains the same, whether the water is warm or cold --- and it has lungs instead of gills: this means that it cannot breathe under water like a fish, but must come to the top to breathe air. 3 Its young are born alive and suckled on milk by their mother. 4 In all these things the dolphin is like other mammals and differs from the fishes.    5 The tail fin of a dolphin is also unlike that of a fish, for it is flat instead of upright.**

Again, the overall topic or title for the passage is, obviously, 'Dolphins' and the main idea in passage B is that a dolphin is not a fish but a mammal. This idea is contained in the very first sentence, and the supporting information indicating how dolphins are different from fish and like mammals is contained in the sentences that follow.

We are aware that in summarizing a passage the important ideas need to be contained in a reduced length. Thus, the ideas in a passage of 100 words needs to be compressed into a length of 30 to 40 words. How can this reduction of length be achieved? It can be done in 3 ways:

We can omit much of the less important information such as fine details, elaborations, examples/ illustrations etc. These can be easily be distinguished when we arrive at the main/ important idea(s). Discussion and practice with this kind of omission will come gradually in subsequent exercises.

Where explanations, examples/ illustrations need to be included they can be abbreviated by reducing a) information in paragraphs to sentence length or b) that in sentences to phrase length. For example, the dolphin's comparison with a mammal in the paragraph in Passage B may be briefly contained in a sentence as follows: The dolphin is warm-blooded, breathes air with its lungs, and bears and suckles its young like humans". Similarly, the illustrations in Sentences 4 –6 in Passage A above can be stated simply as 'funny jokes or stories, ill-fitting clothes and oddly painted faces.' Such a task involves being able to locate and then to transform or substitute, according to necessity, the important words at the core of the explanation or illustration. These then need to be formulated into appropriate phrases or sentences for use in the summary. Locating the important words is, as we have seen, a matter of reading, understanding and judgement. All these improve with practice. To be able to transform or substitute the words and to formulate the necessary phrases/ sentences for the summary, it is important to build a wide stock of vocabulary and to know all the various word forms. Thus, in the example of Passage A above, 'ill-fitting' (clothes) is derived from (clothes) 'that never fit'. The exercises which follow sample the kind of vocabulary you should be building, by learning as you read or by consulting dictionaries, practicing exercises in word-teaching books or playing crossword games. Also knowing the precise connotation (exact meaning) of words helps you to describe things or actions appropriately. The skills of effective expression go a long way in refining the skill of summarizing.

A whole group of ideas may be accommodated in a word or a phrase by using one word for a list of things. For example, the happy and funny 'actions' of the clown substitutes for 'He plays musical instruments, climbs ropes, leaps merrily, and is always falling down and making silly mistakes.' Once again, therefore, there is the need to build up the kind of vocabulary that helps us to substitute one word in place of many.

**Exercises**

**I**
(A) Indicate the **adjectives** from which each of the following adverbs are formed:

Feebly, visibly, hopefully, angrily, cheerily, unluckily, clumsily, coolly, increasingly, probably.

(B) Indicate the **adverbs** that are formed from the following adjectives:

easy, harmonious, tidy, accurate, gentle, merry, fast, able, disgraceful, neat.

(C)   Give the **noun forms** of the following verbs:

mumble, economize, display, approach, disembark, crawl, denounce, accelerate, stroll, strut.

**II**   (A) Place each of the verbs in I (C) above in the space provided in front of the meanings listed below :

1 _____ to increase one's speed
2 _____ to come nearer to
3 _____ to walk in a stiff, self-satisfied way.
4 _____ to speak publicly against
5 _____ to get off a ship
6 _____ to spread out to be seen
7 _____ to make do (manage) with less money
8 _____ to speak one's words indistinctly
9 _____ to walk in a quiet, unhurried way

10 _____ to move on hands and knees

B) From the following adjectives choose the one most likely to describe the thing named by the noun and write it in the space provided:

sandy, shrill, delicious, sore, cloudless, brilliant, neat, deadly, winding, luxurious.

1 a _____ sky;   2 a \_\_\_\_\_ weapon;   3 a \_\_\_\_\_ beach;   4. a \_\_\_ room;

5 a \_\_\_\_ pudding;   6 a \_\_\_\_\_ handwriting;   7 a _____ voice;   8a \_\_\_\_\_ lane;
9 a _____ diamond;   10 a \_\_\_\_\_ throat.

**III** Replacing one word for many:

(A) Choose from the following list the word for each of the parts of the body listed below:

Knuckles, eyebrow, wrist, forehead, chest, stomach, elbow, ankle, thigh, sole, nape, under-arm.

1, the joint between the hand and the arm
2. the part that joins the palm to the lower arm
3. the underside of the foot
4. the joint between the foot and the leg
5. the part of the head above the eyes
6. the back of the neck near the head.
7. the part of the leg between the knee and the hip
8. the upper front part of the body
9. the hairy ridge over the eyes
10. the part below the chest where the food is digested
11. the joints in the fingers.
12. The hollow in the underside of the shoulder

(B)  What do they do for a living? Choose from the following list the word to complete each of the sentences which follow:

Jockey, purser, ambassador, caddie, sculptor, matron, architect, mason, professor, plumber.

1.  A _____ runs a hospital or a hostel
2.  A _____ rides racehorses
3.  A _____ carves statues
4.  A _____ attends to passengers on an aeroplane
5.  A _____ fits and repairs water pipes
6.  A _____ represents his country abroad
7.  A _____ lays bricks and stones in a building
8.  A _____ teaches university students
9.  A _____ designs buildings
10. A _____ attends golfers

(C)  What are they used for? Choose from the following list the word to complete each of the     sentences which follow:

spanner, thermometer, corkscrew, bulldozer, pliers, tractor, tin-opener, telescope, scales, tongs

1   _____ are used to bend and cut wires
2   A _____ is used to pull out corks
3   _____ are used to weigh things
4   A _____ is used to measure temperature
5   A _____ is used to see distant objects
6   A _____ is used to open tins
7   A _____ is used to undo nuts
8   A _____ is used to shift earth or demolish structures
9   _____ are used to hold and lift various objects
10  A _____ is used to pull a plough

(D)  In the left-hand column are some 'heart' expressions. Match them with their meanings given in the right- hand column:

| EXPRESSION | MEANING |
|---|---|
| 1 light- hearted | A to memorize |
| 2 kind- hearted | B to be discouraged |
| 3 heartless | C cruel |
| 4 hearty | D without enthusiasm |
| 5 heart rending | E cheerful and friendly |
| 6 heart broken | F sincere |
| 7 half- heartedly | G to cheer up |
| 8 heartfelt | H generous |
| 9 to learn by heart | I very sad |
| 10 to take heart | J to work eagerly |
| 11 to lose heart | K distressed |
| 12 to put one's heart into | L happy |

**IV** For **each** of the following passages

A) provide an overall title,
B) state the main general idea in a phrase or short sentence and
C) indicate the examples or illustrations explaining the main idea, again, in a phrase or sentence only. Also indicate the sentences in which these occur as shown in **the example below:**

**28** There are so many kinds of dolphin that the list of names given to them by the experts is a long one. 2 Some kinds live in the great rivers of China, India and South America, but when most people think of dolphins they think of the kinds that live by the sea. 3 This is not surprising, for dolphins are found both in warm and in cooler seas in many parts of the world. 4 The two chief kinds are the common dolphin of the Mediterranean and the bottle-nosed dolphin. 5 The common dolphin is usually about eight feet long and is shaped like a fish. 6 The bottle–nosed dolphin is larger than the common dolphin and may reach a length of twelve feet.

(Child's First Encyclopaedia)

A) Overall Title: Kinds of Dolphins
B) Main Idea: River dolphins and Sea dolphins (Sentence 2)
C) Illustrations: Sea dolphins of two kinds: smaller common dolphins and 12-feet long bottle-nosed dolphins (Sentences 3-6)

**29** The growth of population has not been caused by a sudden increase in human fertility, and probably owes little in any part of the world to an increase in birth-rate. It has been caused almost entirely by advances in the medical and ancillary sciences, and the consequent decrease of the deathrate in areas where the birth-rate remains high. It is illuminating to consider the impact on population growth of even a single discovery in medical science. DDT is an outstanding example. The story of DDT is an adjunct to public health campaigns in 1945, when two members of the Institute of Tropical Agriculture in Trinidad spent a weekend in British Guiana. The Health Officer reported that the extremely high infant mortality rate of 250 or more was due largely to insect-borne diseases. They told him of DDT. Shortly afterwards, he was able to get enough to spray by airplane a 10 mile area, including the city of Georgetown. Results were instantaneous. By 1948, the infant mortality rate dropped to 67. As a result, that small area had one of the most rapid rate of population increase ever recorded.
(R. A. Close)
A) Overall Title: _____
B) Main Idea: _____
C) Illustrations: _____

**30** 1 How much sleep do we need? 2 It is probably true to say that up to thirty years ago not only could we not answer this question, but we could see no research tools which might eventually enable us to do so. 3 Since then there have been important developments which have changed the picture; in particular, new forms and techniques of neuro-physiological measurement have emerged, and, secondly, experimental psychology has developed better methods of evaluating human performance and behaviour. 4 Studies, for example, of body and eye movements, of sensory thresholds, and, above all, of the electrical potentials of the brain during sleep, encourage us to think that we may be able to assess with useful accuracy the depth of quality of sleep. 5 In carefully controlled experiments, also, the amount of sleep has been varied to find the effects of lack of sleep upon performance and upon physiological changes in the body, especially those which accompany the effort to maintain normal behaviour and working standards in spite of deprivation of sleep.

(R. A. Close)

    A) Overall Title: _____
    B) Main Idea: _____
    C) Illustrations: _____

**31** In the Italian region of Apulia lives a small spider called a tarantula. There is an ancient belief that the bite of this insect is very poisonous. Today we know that this is not true; the bite of the tarantula is not very harmful; but hundreds of years ago even doctors and other learned men believed the tale. In fact people who had been bitten used to dance to a special kind of music, the rhythm of which got faster and faster. This dance was called the Tarantella. It was supposed to work the poison out of their systems in three or four days.

These ancient dances, Tarantellas, are still danced today in Southern Italy. Dances rather like the Tarantella were danced in some other European countries including Belgium, France and Germany, where the tarantula or a spider very like it is found. So perhaps there is no real connection between the dance and the spider. Perhaps one can explain the name of the dance by the fact that it started near the town of Taranto.

(Child's First Encyclopaedia)

A) Overall Title: _____
B) Main Idea: _____
C) Illustrations: _____

**32** The burning of coal is very wasteful of energy. This can be realised when we remember that one pound of coal burned in the furnace of a power station will raise (=produce) enough steam to drive a generator that will produce enough current to light a one-bar electric fire for three hours. On the other hand, if all the energy in the atoms of a pound of coal could be released, there should be enough energy to drive all the machinery in all the factories in Britain for a month.

(David Le Roi in Thornley)

A) Overall Title: _____
B) Main Idea: _____
C) Illustrations: _____

Having learnt to identify and separate the main ideas from the illustration, the question may arise as to how much of the illustration we need to retain in a summary? This would depend on two factors:

1) How important does illustration become to making the main idea meaningful? If any part of the main idea seems vague or requires clarification, then it would help to use a minimum of illustration or example(s) to make the idea clear. For example, mentioning the details about the sea dolphins is not crucial to understanding that there are two kinds of dolphins – the river and the sea dolphins. On the other hand it may be important to mention briefly the Georgetown statistics to show how population increase has been greatly affected by the application of advances in medical science, because 'greatly affected' does not very effectively convey, the difference to the population increase.

2) The practical purpose for which the summary is being written could decide how much of the examples/ statistics should be included in the summary/ notes. For example, if you were making notes from a reference book or textbook to prepare for your examinations you would need illustrations/ examples/ statistics at your fingertips to answer well the examination questions/ tasks. Having these ready for reference in your notes is then very important. Or again, if you are summarizing a feasibility study of a project or proposal for your boss at work, details of figures and statistics from your data would be very important to convey through the summary.

It is important, therefore, to use your discretion to decide on how much of illustration to include in your summary. Discuss with your teacher/ friend whether and how much of the illustration you will need to include in your summaries of the passages under Ex. (IV) above and in the exercises that follow in subsequent units.

# Unit IV: Gist Writing

A gist is a very brief type of summary of a paragraph or a somewhat longer passage sometimes in only a sentence or two. Gist writing like summary writing requires you to do the following:
1) Select only the main idea(s) from the passage keeping the overall passage in view.
2) State these in a sentence or two making sure you have the exact focus or emphasis of the passage.
3) Omit from it the illustrative/ supportive information that may seem interesting to you but is not important to the gist or summary.

To understand the correct **focus** of the passage it is important to understand the relationship of the main ideas with the supporting information. This relationship is indicated by, what are called, **signals of coherence**. A well-written paragraph, therefore, has besides a central controlling idea and supporting information, coherent connections between the parts of the paragraph. This coherence is created by the use of **transitional signals, pronouns, repetitions, substitutions etc.**, which emphasize the relationship between the parts of the paragraph. For example, the words **highlighted** in the passage repeated below are the transitional signals which indicate the logical connections that create the coherence of the paragraph:

33    The burning of coal is *very wasteful of energy*. **This can be realized when** we remember that *one pound of coal* burned in the furnace of a power station will raise (= produce) enough steam to drive a generator that will produce enough current to light *a one-bar electric fire for three hours*. **On the other hand,** if all the energy in *the atoms of a pound of coal* could be released, **there should be** *enough energy to drive all the machinery in all the factories in Britain for a month.*                (David Le Roi in Thornley)

While the **italicised** expressions give us the relationship of the content of the argument, the **highlighted** expressions (i.e., the signals of coherence) establish the logical connections between the sentences or sections of the paragraph. While the relationship of the content may become easily clear, understanding the logical connections is particularly important because it helps us to put into a synopsis (or shortened version) the idea of the passage. Thus in the example above, the comparison of coal and its atoms in terms of energy generated is made clear by the expressions 'This can be realized' and 'On the other hand', It clarifies the focus of the argument, which may be seen in the summary statement: 'Burning of coal as it is for energy, is **more wasteful than** harnessing the energy in the atoms of the coal'.

**Exercises**

Carefully read each of the following passages and answer the questions below, which lead you to forming the gist of the passage. Underline the coherence signals and these should help you (The coherence signals in the first passage are highlighted for you):

**34** Many small animals including slugs and snails, woodlice, centipedes, come out **at night** because they do not have waterproof skins. The air is, always, more moist **at night**, and the animals are less likely to dry up and die than they are **in the daytime**. Hedgehogs, mice, toads, and similar creatures are also active **at night. This is because** they feed on the smaller nocturnal (night-active) animals. **The chain then** passes on to **a second tier** of predators, including foxes, badgers, stoats and owls. It is **less easy** to see why animals like rabbits should be active **at night, but it may be** a way for them to avoid eagles, buzzards, and other **diurnal (day-active)** birds of prey,' (110words)

I   Many animals are mentioned in this paragraph, but the message of the writer is not to make a list of animals but to convey a specific idea about them. What is the main distinction in their activity that the writer is talking about?

II   Among the coherence links highlighted in the paragraph, separate the transitional signals from the repetitions.

III   There are 3 reasons mentioned in this paragraph to explain why the animals are active at night. Mention them and illustrate each with two examples of the animals.

IV   Write a gist of the passage in about 60 words by combining your answers to Exercises I and III above.

**35**   The owls are supremely suited to capturing small rodents and other animals at night. Their eyes are more efficient than our own. The large 'window' at the front lets in the maximum amount of light, and the round lens produces a bright image. The eyes look forward like our own, and the owl can judge distances very accurately. It plunges down towards its prey and thrusts out its talons to make the kill. The prey is taken by surprise because the owl flies silently. Delicate fringes on the front edges of the feathers eliminate the noise of air rushing over the wings.
      (90 words)

**I**   The opening sentence makes a very general statement indicating the theme of the paragraph. Choose two factors from each of the following sets, which help make the owl an effective **night hunter.**

   A.   1. maximum light;   2. the large window;   3. round lens;   4 talons thrust out
   B.   1. judging distances accurately;   2. surprising the prey;   3. the fringe of the feathers;   4. air rushing over the wings.

**II**   Combine your chosen answers to write a gist of the passage in two sentences.

**36**   For a normal public supply of water, there are several reasons for treating the water to purify it. First, there is turbidity. Turbid water has small particles of solids suspended in it, so it will be cloudy or muddy to look at. Then there is colour, and colour is not the same as turbidity. Clear water can still have colour, if, for example, iron salts are dissolved in it; but wholesome water should be colourless. Purification should also remove taste and odour (unpleasant smell), and it may be necessary to remove the algae (water-plants of very simple form) which grow in water ----- especially in a reservoir (large storage tank).

Then, most important of all, the water must be made free from contamination from sewage, or free from pathogens --- those organisms which carry disease. This is tested by measuring the water's freedom from certain bacteria.
      (135 words)

**I**   What are the five reasons for treating water to purify it?
**II**   Which words /expressions are used to signal the different sections of the paragraph containing these reasons?
**III**   Put these reasons together very briefly in a gist of not more than 20 words.

**37** 1 The synthesis of carbohydrate is usually referred to as photosynthesis or carbon assimilation and occurs in all green plants in sunlight. 2 In most plants the completion of this process is indicated by the appearance of starch in the leaf-cells, though a few species never synthesize starch. 3 It is probably preceded by a sugar such as glucose, but this does not accumulate.
4 It has been generally recognized that the synthesis of carbohydrate is dependent on the presence of light, the green substance chlorophyll and a supply of carbon dioxide and water, together with other factors that probably affect the rate of synthesis but do not actually control it.

**I** Read the following statements carefully and indicate whether they are 'True' or 'False' according to the passage:
    a) Photosynthesis is a synthesis of carbon.
    b) It occurs in green plants only.
    c) All plants show starch in the leaf-cells when photosynthesis is complete.
    d) Some plants do not show any starch.
    e) Photosynthesis is the making of carbohydrates in green plants.

**II** a) Which of these statements will help to formulate a gist of the first paragraph?
    b) Which sentences in the paragraph become superfluous to the gist?
    c) What are the transitional signals in the sentences that indicate this?

**III** a) What are the three conditions on which photosynthesis depends? Where do these occur in the paragraph?
    b) Which transitional signals mark off the information superfluous to a gist of the paragraph?
**IV** Prepare a gist of the passage in 30 words.

**38** 1 The important thing about laser light is that it is coherent (= holding together: working as one thing). 2 The individual light rays are all of the same wavelength or colour, and are all in step i.e., moving at the same rate as each other. 3 A laser beam differs from a beam of ordinary light in both character and effectiveness, in the same way that a platoon of well-drilled soldiers differs from a disorganized mob.

4 When light waves from a laser march in step, they can perform amazing feats. 5 The reason is that their energy is not dissipated (= scattered) as the beam spreads out. 6 This makes for an intense concentration of energy at a very sharply defined point. 7 It also greatly extends the range of a light source i.e., the light can reach great distances to the target or objective.

8 Three of the many spectacular achievements of the laser demonstrate how the properties of coherent light can be put to work:

9 Because its light does not spread out even at great distances, a laser can illuminate the surface of the moon with a two-mile-wide circle of light.

10 Because its energy is concentrated at a fine point, it can send a short searing pinpoint of light into the human eyeball to weld a detached retina back into place and restore sight.

11   And since its radiation is so intense, it can burn holes in a steel plate 0.125 inches thick at a distance of several feet. 12 A laser can weld metals as well as retinas. 13 But here, too, its use is for precise work, as in making micro-electronic circuits. 14 Nevertheless, large lasers mounted atop high mountain peaks are being developed to provide a defence against intercontinental ballistic missile warheads

## Exercises

I   a) What is meant by the coherence of laser light?
b) Which sentences contain the explanation?
c)   Is there an illustration to clarify this explanation? In which sentence?
II   a) What are the three great properties of laser light? In which sentences are these mentioned?
b)   Which words signal a statement of these properties?
III   a) What are the three special ways in which these properties help?
b)   With which words are these signalled in the text?
IV   Write a summary of the passage, using scientific vocabulary, in about 90 words.


(B)   Read carefully each of the five pieces of text (39 – 43) that follow overleaf. **For each** (Famous Lives) text, attempt the **Exercise I** and **II** which follow on the next page.


**(Passages 39 – 43 + 'Famous Lives' follow)**

## 39

**SIDDHARTHA GAUTAMA** (563–484 BC) was an Indian prince who became world famous under the name of Buddha. The name means the 'awakened' or 'enlightened one'. According to legend, he left his wife and child to become a wandering religious beggar. He meditated for a long time, until he worked out ideas about freedom and self-knowledge. These ideas have become known as the 'way'. He spent most of his life preaching, and teaching his disciples and followers. Buddhism, the way of life taught by Buddha, became especially widespread in China.

## 40

**ALEXANDER THE GREAT** (356–323 BC) was a famous Greek general. In 336 BC he became the king of Macedon, a state to the north of Greece, and consolidated his control over the other Greek states conquered by his father, Phillip.

He then went on to conquer the empire of the Persians. He took Egypt, where he founded the great city of Alexandria. His army finally pushed as far east as India. Alexander died in Babylon, at the age of 33. His empire did not last long after he died, but it did much to spread the learning and way of life of the Greeks throughout the Middle East.

## 41

**CLEOPATRA** (69–30 BC) was a queen of Egypt. She was famous for her beauty and her political cleverness. At first she ruled jointly with her brother, who was also her husband, until she was driven out by him. Later she gained the support of the Roman leader Julius Caesar, who defeated her brother. She became Caesar's mistress, and lived with him in Rome until returning to Egypt and taking up power again. Later she won the love of Mark Antony, another ruler of Rome. When she and Antony were defeated by Romans she killed herself, rather than be paraded in defeat through Rome. Legend claims that she died by being bitten by an asp, although it is more likely that she took poison.

## 42

**LEONARDO DA VINCI** (1452–1519) was one of the most gifted men of the Renaissance. He is famous for his paintings, especially the portrait of *Mona Lisa* and the fresco called *The Last Supper*. But he also did sculpture and architecture, and was a skilled engineer and builder. He designed plans for tanks, submarines and flying machines that were centuries ahead of his time. He also made studies of the weather, the human body and mathematics. These contributed greatly to the knowledge of the time.

## 43

**LUDWIG VAN BEETHOVEN** (1770–1827) lived most of his life in Vienna, where he worked as a composer and studied briefly with Mozart. He refused to be supported by a patron, and lived by teaching, performing and composing music. He had trouble with his hearing, and became totally deaf by 1819. Nevertheless, he continued to compose music until his death eight years later.

Unit IV

# FAMOUS LIVES

I. In each of the following groups choose the sentence which best sums up the achievements that have made the following people famous:

A) Siddhartha Gautama

1) Siddhartha Gautama was an Indian prince who became a religious beggar
2) Siddhartha Gautama was the founder of Buddhism which teaches about freedom and self-knowledge.
3) Siddhartha Gautama's fame spread far and wide especially in China.
4) Siddhartha Gautama left his wife and child and spent most of his life preaching and teaching his disciples.

B) Alexander the Great

1) Alexander became the king of Macedon and controlled the Greek states.
2) He founded the city of Alexandria.
3) He established the Greek empire far and wide by the age of thirty three.
4) He spread the Greek way of life throughout the Middle East.

C) Cleopatra

1) Cleopatra was known for her beauty, her pride and her political acumen
2) She ruled Egypt jointly with her brother who was also her husband.
3) The Queen of Egypt was helped by the famous Roman leaders like Jullius Caesar and Mark Antony.
4) Cleopatra killed herself with the poison of an asp bite.

D) Leonardo Da Vinci

1) Leonardo Da Vinci was a gifted man of the Renaissance
2) The beautiful paintings 'Mona Lisa' and 'The Last Supper' were painted by him.
3) He proved his versatility as a painter, architect, engineer, builder and scholar.
4) He studied the weather, the human body and mathematics.

E) Ludwig van Beethoven

1) Ludwig van Beethoven was a deaf musician
2) He studied music with the famous Mozart in Vienna.
3) He continued to compose music in spite of his deafness.
4) Ludwig van Beethoven was a proud and brilliant music composer and performer.

II    In each of the above groups consider the sentences (1, 2, 3, 4) which you did not select as your answer to Ex. I above. Say whether each of these
a)    states no achievement.
b)    states a less important achievement.
c)    states the result and not the cause of the fame.
d)    gives a partial account of the achievement.
e)    states a wrong/ partially true achievement.

# Unit V-A : The Main Idea and Supporting Information: Patterns of Organization

We have seen that supporting information develops the main or controlling idea in a paragraph in order to make it convincing and effective. This supporting information need not be only illustration and examples as we have already seen. There are broadly two general methods by which the controlling idea may be developed, and the supporting information gets organized. The first is an **analysis** of the total idea into its component parts (such as a definition or an explanation of a term or phenomenon, a classification of types, or a sequence of stages in a process). A second method of development is **support** that is, confirming or clarifying the idea of the topic sentence through some kind of elaboration or explanation (through details, evidence, examples, illustrations, or reasoning).

The paragraphs that follow illustrate how general methods of analysis and support are used to develop a central idea. Following these we shall show how various patterns of logical connection may be used in developing not just a paragraph but also a whole theme over a longer passage, which could be useful in perceiving the essential focus of the summary. The **signals of coherence** include pronouns, repetitions, substitutions and sentence connectors or signals of transition (showing logical, time or space connections). We shall focus in this unit on the transitional signals. These are **italicised** in each of the passages for you. Observe these carefully as these will help you to identify the organizational focus of the passage.

## A
### Analysis of the Main Idea

The idea in the topic sentence of a paragraph can be analysed or explained in different ways(Note the italicised words/ ideas in each passage, also underlined for you in the first passage)

## 1. *Definition/ Description*

At some point a key term with an unfamiliar meaning needs to be defined. So, also, a term that one needs to give one's own meaning to. In scientific texts a definition places a term in a class and then gives details to distinguish it from other members of the class. But in simple expository prose, a term can be defined or described or explained in different ways. Thus, as in an earlier passage, a dolphin is very simply described in terms of how it is similar to a porpoise or whale and how it is different from fish, as follows:

---

**2**   1 *The dolphin, like* the porpoise and the whale, *is not a fish but a mammal.* 2 It is warm-blooded --- *that is*, its body heat remains the same, whether the water is warm or cold --- *and* it has lungs instead of gills: this means that it cannot breathe under water like a fish, but must come to the top to breathe air. 3 *Its young* are born alive and suckled on milk by their mother. 4 *In all these things* the dolphin is like other mammals and differs from the fishes. 5 The tail fin of a dolphin is *also unlike that of a fish*, for it is flat instead of upright.

---

Or, again, a Kitchen Garden, to reproduce an earlier passage, is explained a little differently as follows:

---

**13**   A KITCHEN GARDEN, as the name implies, is the garden around *or near the house. Raising a kitchen garden is a fascinating experience.* The greatest satisfaction a family gets from it is dining on the harvest, *which means* vegetables produced in the home garden are used in their most fresh state. *Besides* producing food for the family, the *kitchen garden beautifies the house* as it also includes trees, flowering shrubs, creepers, grass and plants. *The kitchen garden* is not a new innovation as even in the olden days and in backward areas families grew some *vegetables near the house for use by the family.*

---

## 2. *Classification of Kinds or Parts*

Classification is a process of taking a jumble of things and ideas and arranging them into groups or classes according to their common characteristics. For example, in the following paragraph, used earlier, the various parts of clocks are classified into two important groups of mechanisms:

**44**     Ordinary clocks have *two important parts*. 2 *One part* consists of a mechanism, which moves regularly second by second. 3 *The other part*, which is connected to the mechanism, tells us the hours, and minutes, of the day.

Or again, in the following paragraph, the kinds of dolphins are classified in terms of two broad kinds, the river and sea dolphins, and two sub-varieties: the common and the bottle-nosed kind.

**45**     There are *so many kinds of dolphin* that the list of names given to them by the experts is a long one. 2 *Some kinds live in the great rivers of* China, India and South America, but when most people think of dolphins, they think of the *kinds that live by the sea*. 3 This is not surprising, for dolphins are found both in warm and in cooler seas in many parts of the world. 4 The *two chief kinds* are the *common dolphin* of the Mediterranean and the bottle-nosed dolphin. 5 The common dolphin is usually about eight feet long and is shaped like a fish. 6 The *bottle–nosed dolphin* is larger than the common dolphin and may reach a length of twelve feet.
(Child's First Encyclopaedia)

*3. A Sequence of Ideas:*

A paragraph can develop a progression or sequence of ideas with each following another in a necessary order. The order may be one of space as in a physical description, or one of time as in a narrative. This structure may also be used to list a sequence of details of description, or a variety of concrete or situational examples to make the phenomenon in the central idea clear. Or it may also be used for relating a chain of causes or consequences or for describing a reasoning process. To cite an earlier passage, the paragraph below indicates a sequence of stages in the development of a frog, which follow both a time and a space order. The coherence signals of **time** are indicated in **italics** and those of **space** are **underlined**:

**14**   1 *Frogs and toads give us an opportunity* of studying the marvellous development of an egg into a complete animal. 2 *This* involves a metamorphosis (a complete change of shape and of way of life) that seems like magic. 3 You can watch every stage of it. 4 *With the onset of the rains,* in almost any weedy pond, the females lay several thousand tiny blackish eggs, each the size of a grain of sand, and covered with a coat of transparent jelly. 5 *Some weeks after* the tadpole emerges, and its hind legs begin to grow. 6 Up to this point, the tadpole will have lived by nibbling the green stuff, but *now it begins* to need animal food and if kept in an aquarium, should be given tiny pieces of cooked meat. 7 *Then* the front legs begin to appear, and the whole tadpole undergoes its most remarkable change: it ceases to have a two-chambered heart and gills and to live like a fish. 8 Instead it develops a three-chambered heart, and lungs, and breathes like a land animal. 9 The tail shrinks, *and now* we have a miniature frog that needs to come out of the water.

---

## Exercises

**A**   **1)** Identify the patterns of organization of the ANALYSIS kind used in the following paragraphs. Also, underline the coherence signals that indicate the pattern. Discuss these signals with your teacher or a partner.

**2)** Write a summary of the passage using a pattern similar to the original. Compare the coherence signals in **both**. (The first exercise is worked out for you):

**46**   Lacquer is got from the lacquer tree in the summer by making cuts in the bark, or by cutting off one or two small branches. The sap that flows from the cuts is white in colour, but it soon turns first grey and then black. It is allowed to dry partly, but before hardening completely it is formed into cakes and sent to the market. The sap is boiled and carefully strained through a cloth to make it fit for use.

*Pattern:* Process.   *Transition Signals:* underlined.

*Summary:* The white sap collected from cuts made in the lacquer tree soon turns black. It is then allowed to dry but is formed into cakes before it hardens. It is *then* boiled and strained to make it fit for use. *(Coherence signals underlined.)*

**47**    There are three kinds of book owners. The first has all the standard sets and bestsellers ---- unread, untouched. (This deluded individual owns wood pulp and ink, not books.) The second has a great many books --- a few of them read through, most of them dipped into, but all of them as clean and shiny as the day they were bought. (This person would probably like to make books his own, but is restrained by a false respect for their physical appearance.) The third has a few books or many --- every one of them dog-eared and dilapidated, shaken and loosened by continual use, marked and scribbled in from front to back. (This man owns books.)

**48**    Most insects start life as eggs. The baby insects that hatch out have no wings and often look very different from adults. Butterflies, for example, go through a caterpillar stage and young bluebottles are maggots. The big change of the adult stage takes place in the pupa or chrysalis. Young earwigs and grasshoppers, on the other hand, resemble the adults quite closely. They gradually acquire wings as they grow up.

**49**    A tree in the forest, old with too many springs (= years), is conquered by flourishing fungal parasites; on a day of high wind it falls. The saprophytes slowly devour the log's tissue. Gradually they themselves decay and become food for other saprophytes. The bacteria then take over. There are many linked species, each reducing the dead stuff to forms more elemental. At last, the nitrifying bacteria, both by their living and their multitudinous dying, release nitrates into the soil. Rain and soil water dissolve them. The roots of bracken, spring where the old tree grew. They absorb the nitrates, and they are life again.

## [7 more passages 50 – 56 follow ]


Exercises may be discussed with the teacher (All answers are not provided)

## Unit V (A)

### 50

In 1650, an Irish churchman named Bishop Ussher worked out the date when the world and all its plants, animals and people, were created. From his studies of the Bible, he concluded that life began at 9 am on October 23, 4004 BC.

In fact, the bishop was nowhere near the truth. The world is a much more ancient place than he ever imagined. Signs of very ancient civilizations abound in the Middle East. The ruins of Jericho show that a thriving town existed there as early as 7000 BC. Even a thousand years before that, people in the same region were farming wild grain, and herding cattle, sheep and goats.

Tens of thousands of years before the first civilizations, human beings were already living in small groups. They hunted game and fished, dug for roots, and gathered nuts, berries, fruit and insects. Their tools were made of wood, bone and stone. They used fires, built rough homes, spoke languages and worshipped many different gods.

These prehistoric people, who already looked very much the way we do today, evolved from ape-like ancestors about 100,000 years ago. But the very first signs of human beings are older still; they go back well over two million years.

*Piccolo*

### 51

Some centuries after the rise of the Sumerian city-states, a great civilization sprang up in the narrow valley of the Nile river in Egypt. Here, flanked on both sides by arid desert and to the north protected by the sea, dozens of bustling villages and towns grew up.

Over the years the Egyptians built a vast system of dams and canals to deal with the yearly floods of the Nile, and to bring water to their crops. The river also served as the main highway of the area. It was the only reliable link between the towns that dotted the riverbanks for hundreds of kilometres. Regular winds guided the boats up river. Rowers, helped by the current, brought them downstream again.

Around 3100 BC a strong king, named Menes, united all of Egypt for the first time under his rule. In the centuries that followed, the kings (or pharaohs as they were called) became extremely powerful. Under their leadership Egyptian civilization flourished in splendour for almost 2000 years.

*Piccolo*

### 52

That man, I think, has had a liberal education who has been so trained in youth that his body is the ready servant of his will, and does with ease and pleasure all the work that, as a mechanism, it is capable of; whose intellect is a clear, cold, logic engine, with all its parts of equal strength, and in smooth working order; ready, like a steam engine, to be turned to any kind of work, and spin the gossamers as well as forge the anchors of the mind; whose mind is stored with a knowledge of the great and fundamental truths of Nature and of the laws of her operations; one who, no stunted ascetic, is full of life and fire, but whose passions are trained to come to heel by a vigorous will, the servant of a tender conscience; who has learned to love all beauty, whether of Nature or of art, to hate all vileness, and to respect others as himself.

Thomas Huxley, "A Liberal Education"

### 53

And the rain now seemed to have made the heat more intense. Before the rain the air had at least been dry and the perspiration evaporated and brought some relief, but now with the brassy sun striking full on the wet rocks and the bare muddy fields, the steam rose up, enveloping houses, cattle, laborers, even the moving train itself, until the whole of the vast Deccan plateau was like one gigantic Russian bath. In the train, windows were closed again because the air which entered was more suffocating than the air inside. In the ditches along the tracks the flood water flowed blood red, diminishing almost as you watched it into a fine trickle, swallowed up altogether presently by the heat of the sun and the greedy thirst of the hot, red earth. Louis Bromfield, "Night in Bombay"

Unit V (A)

### [54]

What is civilization? It is a set of rules by which most men abide, of promises to which most men adhere. It is a set of institutions, of homely customs, which express the experience of centuries. It has its roots in cultural disciplines, religious and humanistic, which give life its meaning. Man creates these disciplines and supports them, to foster what is good in his nature and control what is bad. When he begins to break his own rules and ignore his customs (instead of making them ever more subtle and humane with the passing decades) civilization sickens at the roots.[11]

Herbert Agar 'The Truth Is Good News'

### [55]

This, then, is how one might define jazz: it is a new music of a certain distinct rhythmic and melodic character, one that constantly involves improvisation—of a minor sort in adjusting accents and phrases of the tune at hand, or a major sort in creating music extemporaneously, on the spot. In the course of creating jazz, a melody or its underlying chords may be altered. The rhythmic valuations of notes may be lengthened or shortened according to a regular scheme, syncopated or not, or there may be no consistent pattern of rhythmic variations so long as a steady beat remains implicit or explicit. The beat is usually four quarternotes to the bar, serving as a solid rhythmic base for the improvisation of soloists or groups playing eight or twelve measures, or some multiple or dividend thereof.

Barry Ulanov, *The History of Jazz in America*

### [56]

It is time to rewrite those physics textbooks. Our solar family has expanded. Seventy-four years after Pluto was discovered, scientists have spotted a 10th planet, Sedna, which is the "most distant object ever detected orbiting the Sun", according to NASA. A large cold ball of icy rock situated deep in space, 10 billion km from earth, the new planet did not reveal itself easily. The hunt began about a year ago, with the launch of an Outer Solar System project at the California Institute of Technology. In August 2003, NASA launched the Spitzer Space telescope. It took the piercing infrared rays of Spitzer, analysed by astronomer Michael Brown of the CIT, to home in on Sedna. After a nailbiting wait, this was verified at the Tenegra Observatory in Arizona.

(courtesy: India Today)

# Unit V-B: Support

A central idea may get supported in one or more of several different ways (words/phrases italicised in each passage):

## 1. Details / Examples / Illustrations / Evidence:

You will have observed by now that the use of details, examples, and illustrations is almost indispensable to all kinds of paragraph organization. Complex ideas cannot become clear without details or examples to support the argument or illustrate a point. Debatable ideas cannot be convincing without evidence. Abstract ideas are intangible without specifics. Generalizations without support are empty. To illustrate, look at the passage of the clowns, which lists examples of why the clown is loved by children:

---

1  1 Boys and girls enjoy the performers in a circus, but they love the clown. 2 Why is that? 3 It is because everything about him is funny. 4 His *jokes and stories are funny.* 5 His clothes *never fit.* 6 His face is *thickly covered with white powder, except for parts which are painted a bright red.* 7 He *plays musical instruments, climbs ropes, leaps merrily, and is always falling down and making silly mistakes.*

---

Or again, look at the evidence supplied to validate the statement that the growth of population is almost entirely due to advances in medical and ancillary sciences:

**57**   *The growth of population* has not been caused by a sudden increase in human fertility, *and* probably owes little in any part of the world to an increase in birth-rate. *It has been caused* almost entirely by advances in the medical and ancillary sciences, *and* the consequent decrease of the death-rate in areas where the birth-rate remains high. *It is illuminating to consider* the impact on population growth of even a single discovery in medical science. *DDT is an outstanding example. The story of DDT* as an adjunct to public health campaigns in *1945, when two members* of the Institute of Tropical Agriculture in Trinidad spent a weekend in British Guiana. *The Health Officer* reported that *the extremely high infant mortality rate* of 250 or more was due largely to insect-borne diseases. *They* told him of DDT. *Shortly afterwards*, he was able to get enough to spray by airplane a 10 miles area, including the city of Georgetown. *Results* were instantaneous. *By 1948, the infant mortality rate dropped* to 67. *As a result*, that small area had one of the most rapid rate of population increase ever recorded.
(R.A.Close)

---

## *2. List of Causes /Reasons /Conditions:*

An idea may be analysed in terms of the causes or reasons which give rise to the phenomenon described in the idea. Thus, we have a list of reasons for treating water for its purification in the following passage:

---

**58-A**  For a normal public supply of water, *there are several reasons* for treating the water to purify it. *First,* there is turbidity. Turbid water has small particles of solids suspended in it, so it will be cloudy or muddy to look at. *Then* there is colour, and colour is not the same as turbidity. Clear water can still have colour, if, for example, iron salts are dissolved in it; but wholesome water should be colourless. Purification *should also* remove taste and odour (unpleasant smell), and it may be necessary to remove the algae (water-plants of very simple form) which grow in water ----- especially in a reservoir (large storage tank).
*Then, most important of all*, the water must be made free from contamination from sewage, or free from pathogens --- those organisms that carry disease. This is tested by measuring the water's freedom from certain bacteria.

(J. H. Stephens)

## 3. Description:

Description is often required in expository writing – writing designed to expose (to set forth or recreate) its non-fictional subject. It is also needed in narrative writing. Expository description is used to portray a subject, giving concrete details and specifics to make it come alive. The central idea usually expressed in a topic sentence, guides the selection of details and their arrangement so that the paragraph yields either a single dominant impression or several features of a more diverse or complex impression. Look at the simple description of the beauty of the night sky in a passage used earlier:

---

3   The night sky has a beauty we can all enjoy. *The stars sparkle* like jewels on a velvet backcloth. *The moon*, ever changing its shape, pours its silvery light into the darkness. *At first sight, the night sky appears* to be filled *haphazardly* with stars. *But, after a while*, we find that we can recognize *patterns of stars* and thus find our way through the heavens. By *studying the heavens*, we become astronomers. The Chaldeans and Babylonians were skilled *observers of the heavens* over 5,000 years ago.

---

## 4. Narration:

Expository writing frequently contains a retelling of an incident or a series of incidents. But unlike fiction where narration is used primarily to advance a story, exposition uses narration to make a point or establish some generalization. It makes use of chronological order not to tell an event but to explain a process. The following paragraph used earlier, tells us how rare earths were formed over billions of years:

---

**24**   1 Do you know that the sand of which you make castles when playing on a sea- beach might contain particles of valuable mineral substances? 2 *If it does it will* get the glorious name 'Rare Earths'. 3 *These* Rare Earths *have a wonderful story* behind them. 4 *Once upon a time* they were rocks in the range of mountains running parallel to the sea. 5 *But there was* the rain, *bit by bit*, every year. 6 The rain water *carried the Rare* Rocks, as they should have been called then, *into the sea*. 7 *But it was not an* ordinary sea; *it was a sea* with a generous heart. 8 *It took pity* on the mountains, which allowed the rain to do this mischief to them and decided to give back the valuable substances *it had got, and more than that*. 9 The good sea ground the rocks into small particles, sorted out the different minerals *it had received* and deposited each type in a bed on the beach.

## 5. Comparison and Contrast:

Comparison and Contrast are usually used to clarify a central idea. Likenesses or differences between two or more items are pointed out in order to define one or both items more clearly, as in the case of fish and mammals in the passage of the dolphins above (Passage 2 in Unit I-A).

## 6. Cause and Consequence:

Expository writing often deals with causes and results. The question *Why?* or *How?* or *What will be the outcome?* is answered in any of several patterns. It may be a list of causes or effects. It may describe the causal connection between two single events. Or the events may be multiple. Or a whole series of causal links may be involved. Look at the causal connection between tides and the force of gravity of the Sun, Moon and Earth explained in the following paragraph used earlier:

**58-B** Tides are *another force that move* the waters of the oceans. *They are caused* by gravity between the Moon and the Earth and the Sun and the Earth. The force of gravity *pulls the water* like a magnet and as the Earth spins, the part of the ocean pulled most strongly changes. *In each 24-hour period, two high and low tides sweep* around the globe rather like giant waves. Near land the difference is much greater. *The highest tides* occur when the *Sun and Moon are in line* and are *pulling together.*
### (Piccolo)

## 7. Reasoning /Argument:

Very often a statement made in a piece of writing may need an explanation or argument to make the statement convincing. This may call for a line of reasoning or a sequence of ideas presented in a logical progression. In the following paragraph, used earlier, the intimate relationship between life and the environment, from its earliest beginnings and through every moment of our lives (how we would no longer be ourselves if we were transported to another planet) leads up convincingly to the statement that life and environment are, in fact correlates.

---

**59**  1 *If we think* of our environment as simply the outside world, as something that surrounds and "environs" us, *we underestimate* its role. 2 *The relation of* life and environment is extremely intimate. 3 The *organism itself,* the life structure, is the product of past life and past environment. 4 Environment is present *from the very beginning of life,* even in the germ cell. 5 *We think of* our organisms as ourselves, and environment as that which lies outside us. 6 *But* the environment is more than a conditioning factor of life that can be conceived of apart from it. *Imagine* that we were suddenly transported to a much larger planet. 7 *Our bodies would* instantly become much heavier, and that alone would involve a myriad of other differences. 8 *We should no longer* know ourselves, nor assuming that we could exist at all, *be ourselves.* 9 *We never know life except* in an appropriate environment, to which it is already adjusted. 10 Life and environment *are, in fact correlates.*

---

### 9. Problem & Solution:

The central idea may present a problem and the rest of the paragraph(s) offer or suggest the solution, as shown in the mini text below.
'Pollution *is a problem*; polluted seas and rivers *are health hazards. One solution* is *to ban the* dumping of industrial wastes.'
However, it is more likely that the problem may extend over a whole paragraph or two and the solution may follow in subsequent paragraph(s). In the following passage, the problem of the common cold is outlined in the first two paragraphs, while the solution and its evaluation are offered in the subsequent paragraph:

**60**     The most common of all diseases are colds. *For a long time*, scientists have been *trying to discover the* cause of colds, *but* they have *only partially* succeeded. When we have a test, *many kinds of bacteria* are found in the nose, mouth and throat. *But* the same bacteria are also found in the same places when we do not have a cold.

It is now believed that colds *are caused by* very small living things called viruses. Viruses are much smaller than bacteria. *When we* catch cold the viruses *start to grow* on the smooth linings of the mouth, nose and throat, and cause little breaks or openings in these smooth linings. Different kinds of bacteria *then break through* the linings *and begin to grow. The growing* bacteria then make the linings very sore *and give off* the poisons which make us feel sick.

Many medicines *for the cure of* colds are sold, *but few of them* work very well. *The best way to cure* a cold *is to go to bed.* Rest gives the body a chance *to fight* the harmful bacteria, *and often prevents* the more serious diseases *that sometimes follow* colds.


**Exercise**

**A)** Identify the **patterns of organization** of the SUPPORT kind used in the following paragraphs. Also, **underline the coherence signals** that indicate the pattern. Discuss these signals with your teacher or a partner
1.
**B)** Write a **summary** of the passage using the pattern of the original. Compare the coherence signals in both. (The first exercise is worked out for you):

*Example:*

**61**    Cotton grows best on well-drained soils, but it needs plenty of water, especially in the growing season. The climate has to be fairly hot. The best places for cotton growing are countries where the rain falls in frequent but not too heavy showers and there is plenty of sunshine between. Cotton plants are easily hurt by frost and need a growing season of about two hundred days. A hard frost kills them, and if frost comes after the seeds have been planted it usually means that the farmer has to replant his fields. A frost at harvest time injures the top of the plant and so makes the yield poor. After the flowers have blossomed, cotton does best in dry, sunny weather, which makes the bolls burst open. Cotton-picking can then begin.


*Pattern:* 'List of Conditions'.
The paragraph lists the conditions in which **cotton grows best.** These are indicated by coherence signals(underlined) like: *but it needs, has to be hot, where,* etc., and are traced right up to the point of the picking of the cotton bolls. It also mentions conditions **harmful to cotton growing** like: *but not too heavy showers, A hard frost kills,* etc.

*Summary:* <u>*Cotton grows best on*</u> well-drained soils, <u>*in*</u> a hot climate *with frequent* <u>*but not too*</u> heavy showers/ rains *and* plenty of sunshine in between. <u>*Frost*</u> is extremely <u>*harmful to the*</u> cotton plant. Dry, sunny weather <u>*after the*</u> flowers have blossomed helps the bolls burst open <u>*and then*</u> cotton picking <u>*can begin.*</u>
(Coherence Signals italicised & underlined)


**(10 Passages 62 - 71 follow in print)**

[62]

In medical research this country has done noble work. An American, William T. G. Morton, gave suffering humanity the boon of anaesthesia. His priority in this great discovery has been disputed, it is true, but all the other claimants were also natives of the United States. Theobold Smith is the founder of one of the most important branches of bacteriology—for it was he who first discovered the part played by insects in conveying infectious diseases. It was Doctor Smith, also, who conquered that scourge of childhood—diphtheria—by his discovery of toxin-antitoxin. Equally important was the work of the American Federal Commission, under Doctor Walter Reed, in demonstrating that a certain species of mosquito is the agent for spreading yellow fever. But it is only within the past few decades that the United States has taken its place as the undisputed leader in medical research. The founding of the Rockefeller Institute has not only brought to this country some of the world's greatest investigators but it has organized and financed preventive work in almost every part of the world. The headquarters of the scientific army which is warring against disease is now in the United States.⁶

Thomas J Nortenbaker "What's Wrong with the United States"

[63]

[TOPIC:] In contrast with our old attitude of tolerance for social assassination, however, we are now beginning an energetic campaign of human conservation. [SPECIFIC DETAILS:] We are instituting excellent and, in many places, free hospital and dispensary service. We are making nurse and doctor public servants, and are introducing them into the public schools. We are fighting typhoid fever with uncontaminated water supplies, and tuberculosis not only by direct attack but with improved housing and factory conditions. We are improving city and state Boards of Health, and are striving for a National Board of Health, which shall supervise the general health conditions of the nation. In our cities we are providing public recreation centers, public baths. Our city and state authorities are doubling the protection of the milk, meat, and other foods of the people. Our factory legislation and our laws regulating dangerous occupations have resulted in a considerable saving of life, while our laws against child labor have had an enormously beneficial effect. All of these changes, together with a rapid advance in sanitary science and a vast improvement in the standards of living of the people, have resulted in a rapid decline in the death rate, especially in the city.⁸

W. E. Weyl, "The New Democracy"

Unit V (B)

[64]

Women in our society complain of the lack of stimulation, of the loneliness, of the dullness of staying at home. Little babies are poor conversationalists, husbands come home tired and sit reading the paper, and women who used to pride themselves on their ability to talk find on the rare evening they can go out that their words clot on their tongues. As the children go to school, the mother is left to the companionship of the Frigidaire and the washing machine. Yet she can't go out because the delivery man might come, or a child might be sent home sick from school. The boredom of long hours of solitary onesided communication with things, no matter how shining and streamlined and new, descends upon her. Moreover, the conditions of modern life, apartment living, and especially the enormous amount of moving about, all serve to rob women of neighborhood ties. The better her electric equipment, the better she organizes her ordering, the less reason she has to run out for a bit of gossipy shopping at the corner store. The department stores and the moving-picture houses cater to women—alone—on their few hours out. Meanwhile efficient mending services and cheap ready-made clothes have taken most sensible busy work out of women's hands and left women—still at home—listening to the radio, watching television.¹⁷

Margaret Mead, "What Women Want"

A corollary of American optimism was tolerance. This tolerance, which was half-part indifference, extended to slavery, slums, piratical business, and political corruption. The presence on the continent of a great community of unlike, free, and nominally equal men stimulated this toleration, as did also the fluidity of American life, the facile escape from local evil conditions, the easy association in business and society of diverse elements, and the free exchange of goods and ideas between different sections. Prosperity, too, made for tolerance. To a well-fed, well-housed, suitably mated man, few beliefs, opinions, or prejudices are intolerable; and the ready humor of America, tinged with the joy of mere well-being, was both an antidote and an alternative to intolerance.⁸

[65]

W. E. Weyl, "The New Democracy"

66

I had never been on the Lahore-Delhi bus before, and for me it was an amazing experience. It reconfirmed my belief that there are more similarities between the two sides than real differences. All along the over 500-km route from Lahore to Delhi, the bus passed through several big and small towns in the Indian states of Punjab and Haryana. The people—mostly farmers—were no different from their counterparts across the international border. Their language was the same, as was their lifestyle. Perhaps they only differed in their religious beliefs and, of course, the headgear. One visible difference was that on the Indian side of Punjab, the billboards and hoardings were in Gurmukhi—the script that's been long forgotten in Pakistani Punjab. My misfortune was I was unable to read the wall-chalking or ads. Even in Delhi, it was only the script which prevented me from reading Hindi, otherwise the spoken word on the streets was not that different from my Urdu—the official attempt to further Sanskritise Hindi in offices and media notwithstanding. Other similarities included lazy officials, inefficient police, broken roads, chaotic traffic, absence of basic infrastructure, and poverty.

Zaffar Abbas
(courtesy: Outlook)

Unit V (B)

67

YOUNG children are most accident-prone immediately after returning home from the creche or play-school, shows research done by the National Center for Injury Prevention and Control in the US. Kids who have been away from home and parents are extra-cranky upon arrival and let off steam by moving about the house in agitation. This coincides with a time when parents are busy preparing the meal or settling in after a day's work. Result? A greater risk of falls, burns, cuts or poisoning immediately upon arrival. Difficult though it is, experts advice parents to watch over youngsters till they work off their homecoming excitement.

Kalpana Deuskar
(courtesy: The Sunday Review)

[68]

I remember the smell of sea and seaweed, wet flesh, wet hair, wet bathing-dresses, the warm smell as of a rabbity field after rain, the smell of pop and splashed sunshades and toffee, the stable-and-straw smell of hot, tossed, tumbled, dug and trodden sand, the swill-and-gaslamp smell of Saturday night, though the sun shone strong, from the bellying beer-tents, the smell of the vinegar on shell cockles, winkle-smell, shrimp-smell, the dripping-oily back-street winter-smell of chips in newspapers, the smell of ships from the sundazed docks round the corner of the sandhills, the smell of the known and paddled-in sea moving, full of the drowned and herrings, out and away and beyond and further still towards the antipodes that hung their koala-bears and Maoris, kangaroos and boomerangs, upside down over the backs of the stars.

Dylan Thomas, *Quite Early One Morning*

[69]

Happiness is not to be secured by politics alone, but there are certain political conditions without which, in our modern world, happiness must be precarious and temporary. The first of these is that all the major armaments should be under the control of one single authority, so that great wars should no longer be possible. The second is that there should be a continual approach in the poorer parts of the world towards that level of prosperity which has already been achieved in the West. And the third is that the habits of populations everywhere should be such as to prevent a rapid increase of population.

Bertrand Russell, *Fact and Fiction*

[70]

Kitsch is everywhere and surrounds us all. Kitsch is hideous hordes of plaster reindeer and bow-tied footmen defiling the front lawns of Middle America. It is the Rose Bowl Parade, the Eiffel Tower, the Nuremberg stadium, Disneyland, wax museums, heroic statuary, miniature castles, musical wedding cakes, cuckoo clocks and artificial flowers. It is a well coiffed Charlton Heston leading the people of Israel through a huge vat of quivering Jell-O on the way to the promised land, or a dainty coffee cup emblazoned with a swastika. Kitsch, in brief, is bad taste in every conceivable form—and the modern world is its most prolific creator.

*Newsweek*, "The World of Bad Taste"

Unit V (B)

Kalpona Deuskar
(Courtesy: The Sunday Review)

[71]

IF someone is regularly stressed-out on the job, psychologists begin to suspect that it is not the work, but the worker who may be responsible for a large part of the stress. It has been observed that people with stress-prone personalities behave worked-up even in relatively low-pressure positions.

What makes a person stress-prone? People who want predictability at all times are the ones who feel stressed more often, say psychologists. Continuity-loving workers feel out-of-control and upset when something requires them to change their thinking or routine, even if there is no threat. To minimise the stress-effect, specialists suggest we expect something unforeseen every working day and expect some changes to the planned order of work.

Another stress-prone type is the perfectionist. People who cannot bear to ever make a mistake should remember that there are uncontrollable factors also acting on their work. Those who translate "I made a mistake today" into "I am no good" are mistaking a hiccup for a heart attack.

Always pushing one's own personal needs to the back also builds up a sense of stress. The likeliest candidates for this are working mothers. Experts suggest that you put your own needs in a fair "queue" with all the jobs to be done. And when it is time to meet those needs, do them full justice, without guilt. Psychologists now believe that it is not so much what happens that causes emotions -- it is what we tell ourselves about them.

# Unit VI : Patterns of Information Organization: The Paragraph and Short Passages

Paragraphs and patterns, therefore, as we have seen, do not always operate on a one to one basis. Sometimes, a pattern may extend beyond a single paragraph to two or even three paragraphs depending on the instalments of information or the kinds of ideas grouped together. For example look at the following definition of 'Lifts' extending over two paragraphs, the <u>first</u> describing <u>what a lift is</u>, in terms of how the machine works and the <u>second</u> tells you <u>where these are generally found</u> or <u>the purposes for</u> which they are <u>used</u>:

72 **A LIFT is a power-driven machine which can raise or lower a platform or a car inside a shaft called a "hoistway". The car may carry either passengers or goods, and usually moves between steel guide rails.**
**Lifts are usually found in tall buildings, but are also used, of course, in mining and other work underground.**

On the other hand, as in all skillful writing, a paragraph may use a **combination of organizational patterns.** In the following paragraph the topic is developed with a specific example, which is then explained in terms of cause and effect. The phenomenon of every society carrying within itself the seeds of life and its own potential death (topic) is explained with a specific example of the United States. It explains how the progress of the country within a democratic pattern carried the seeds, of its potential death: i. e., the progress was also the cause of its potential death:

73	Every system of society carries within itself the seeds of life and its own potential death. Democracy in the United States had a favoured childhood. The continent was there to conquer, and opportunity beckoned to all who had the strength to reach out for it. The land was stored with riches, which were recklessly and lavishly spent and, though the wealth was not distributed equally, it did provide for the majority of Americans the highest standard of life to be found in the world. Under such circumstances, democracy could thrive, and the potentialities of its death be kept down. But the economic system has changed to the disadvantage of the individual. Industrialism and concentrated finance shifted power to the relatively few, and political power has not been able to restore to the individual his full economic initiative. Indeed, it may never achieve this restoration. The old birthright may already be lost in its original form. And this may be the potentiality of death within our democracy, a postulation which deserves the most searching thought.

Such combinations may be used over shorter and longer passages. It is important, therefore, to understand these organizational patterns in order to be able to retrieve the essential argument/ focus of the passage.

### Exercise

Read each of the following passages carefully, observing the pattern(s) of organization used. Write a brief summary of each passage trying to retain the correct focus of the passage. Discuss your answers with your teacher /or friend.

**(5 passages 74 - 78 follow in print)**

## 74

The cuckoo does not build a nest of its own, but uses the nests of other birds, especially those of the meadow pipit, pied wagtail, reed warbler, hedge sparrow and robin. It puts its eggs in the borrowed nests and leaves it to the birds who own the nests to hatch them and rear the young. It is said that the cuckoo often lays its eggs on the ground and carries them in its beak to the nests it has chosen. Only one egg is put into each nest.

When the young cuckoo is about thirty hours old it begins to clear the nest for itself. It throws out all the other eggs and young birds, using its strong back to tip them over the side of the nest. For the first twelve days of its life, the young cuckoo has a hollow in the small of its back that helps it to do this.

The young cuckoo is now fed by the birds who own the nest. They do not seem to notice that there is anything wrong, or that the rest of their eggs have gone. The cuckoo grows quickly, and it may soon be bigger than the foster-parents who are feeding it. When it is old enough it leaves the nest and flies away.

The cuckoo has a bad name because of its habit of making other birds care for its eggs, but it also helps the farmer by eating harmful insects and their grubs.

## Unit VI

## 75

### A Judge Rules on Whiskey

**Kenneth Vinson**

If when you say whiskey you mean the devil's brew, the poison scourge, the bloody monster, that defiles innocence, dethrones reason, destroys the home, creates misery and poverty, yea, literally takes the bread from the mouths of little children; if you mean the evil drink that topples the Christian man and woman from the pinnacle of righteous, gracious living into the bottomless pit of degradation and despair, and shame, and helplessness, and hopelessness, then certainly I am against it.

But if when you say whiskey you mean the oil of conversation, the philosophic wine, the ale that puts a song in their hearts and laughter on their lips, and the warm glow of contentment in their eyes; if you mean Christmas cheer; if you mean the stimulating drink that puts the spring into the old gentleman's step on a frosty, crispy morning; if you mean the drink which enables a man to magnify his joy, and his happiness, and to forget, if only for a little while, life's great tragedies, and heartaches, and sorrows; if you mean that drink, the sale of which pours into our treasuries untold millions of dollars, which are used to provide tender care for our little crippled children, our blind, our deaf, our dumb, our pitiful aged and infirm; to build highways and hospitals and schools then certainly I am for it.

This is my stand. I will not retreat from it. I will not compromise.

## 76

While the pioneer was felling the forest, the city had been growing apace.
The city, which all over the world was becoming the new home of civilization, had developed in America more rapidly than elsewhere. It grew with the progress of the pioneers; it grew even faster after the pioneer period ended. [CAUSE:] As the supply of free western farms ceased, as the settlers, with no further place to go, began to exploit what they had, the alternative which the frontier once offered to the city disappeared. The progress of agriculture enabled one farmer to perform what two had performed before, and the surplus rural population moved to the up-growing cities. The immigrants, finding the new lands pre-empted, remained at the ports of entry. The new opportunities, the chances which the pioneer had sought among the trees, on the plains, or in the sands of California's rivers, were now sought in the mysterious, congested, surcharged life of the city."

W. E. Weyl

## 77

"'It's not my fault! it's not my fault! Nothing in this lousy world is my fault, don't you see that? I don't want it to be and it can't be and it won't be." This outcry comes from Kerouac's Sal Paradise, but it expresses the deep conviction of multitudes of irresponsibles in the age of self-pity. It is a curious paradox that, while the self is the center of all things, the self is never to blame for anything.

The fault is always the fault of someone or of something else. This is implicit in all the letters which are addressed to Abigail Van Buren. "Dear Abby: This is my problem . . . My husband . . ." "Dear Abby: Here is my problem . . . My wife . . ." Or it may be my son, my daughter, my mother-in-law, my neighbors. It is never Me.

Blame it on God, the girls, or the government, on heredity, or on the environment, on the parents, on the siblings, on the cold war, on the pressures toward conformity, on being unloved and unwanted. But don't blame it on me, the very center around which the whole universe revolves. This me is like the innocent and apparently unmenacing Dennis, who stands before an accusing mother, in the middle of the parlor, with his body twisted about as he looks back on the carpet at some curious mud tracks which lead right up to his heels. Says Dennis, in bewilderment, "I don't know what that stuff is . . . it just keeps following me."

Robert Eliot Fitch, *Odyssey of the Self-Centered Self*

Machines were made to be man's servants. Yet man has grown so dependent on them that they are in a fair way to become his master. Already most men spend most of their lives looking after and waiting upon machines. And the machines are very strict masters. They must be fed with coal and given petrol to drink and oil to wash with, and they must be kept at the right temperature. And if they do not get their meals, they refuse to work, or burst with anger and spread ruin and destruction all around them. This brings us to the question; "What do we do with all the time which machines have saved for us and the new energy they have given us?" For the most part we use our time and energy to make more and better machines; but more machines will give us still more time and still more energy and what are we to do with them?

The answer is that we should try to become more civilized. For the machines themselves and the power which machines have given us are not themselves civilization; they only make civilization possible. Being civilized means making and liking beautiful things, between man and man. Man has a better chance today to do these things than he ever had before. He has more time, more energy, less to fear, and less to fight against. If he gives this time and energy which his machines have won for him to making more beautiful things, to finding out more and more about the universe, to removing the causes of quarrels between nations to discovering how to prevent poverty, then I think our civilization would certainly be the greater, as it would be the most lasting that there has ever been.

# Unit VII: Coherence in Texts: The Paragraph and Longer Passages

A paragraph is coherent when the relationships between parts of the paragraph are clear, smooth and logical. The reader moves easily from one sentence to the next and from one idea to the next, seeing their connection to one another and to the paragraph's central idea. There are two means commonly used to achieve this flow of thought: 1) a logical sequence of ideas, and 2) the use of functional transition devices. The sequence of ideas is contained in the key words while the logical linking of the ideas is done with devices like repetition, restatement, parallel structures and transitional signals. Once the coherence pattern is clear, a well-focused summary becomes easier and the transitional devices serve as guidelines. We shall look more closely, through illustrations, at how this happens.

## 1    Ideas in Logical Sequence

We have seen, in the preceding units, that the relationship between the central or controlling idea and the supporting information follows a plan or pattern of development such as exemplification, classification, definition, comparison and contrast, reasoning and so on. The following paragraphs illustrate some of the arrangements of ideas within the total paragraph structure.

*1.    Idea Sequence: A Logical Progression*

In the following paragraph, as explained earlier, **the italicised phrases** indicate the sequence of ideas while **the highlighted transitional signals** trace the logic of the argument.

---

**33**    The *burning of coal is very wasteful* of energy. **This can be realised when** we remember that *one pound of coal* burned in the furnace of a power station will raise (= produce) enough steam to drive a generator that will produce enough current to light *a one-bar electric fire for three hours*. **On the other hand, if all** the energy in *the atoms of a pound of coal* could be released, **there should be** *enough energy to drive all the machinery in all the factories in Britain for a month.*

(David Le Roi in Thornley)

In the summarized version this would read as:

*The burning of coal, in its natural form, is **more** wasteful than harnessing the energy in the atoms of the coal.* The underlined expression indicates the crux of the argument.

### 4. Idea Sequence: Space /Time Order

An order of visual space is used when something is being physically described or a time order may be used when the history or progress of a process or development is being described. We saw this in the example of the 'Frogs and Toads' passage (21) in Unit V above, where a sequence of stages in the development of a frog was described following both a time and a space order. Another description of fishes follows, which uses a **time order** to describe their evolution in the **first three sentences** (note the underlined words), while the remaining four sentences, in the italicised expressions, describe their physical makeup beginning with their scale-covered bodies and ending up with the tail fin and other fins:

**79**   1 The fishes were the first *animals with backbones* on earth. 2 The early forms, many of them without jaws, have long since become extinct, but there are about 20,000 species alive *today*. 3 About 5,000 of these live in fresh water and the rest are found in the seas. 4 Almost all have *scale-covered bodies*, and they generally have *two pairs of fins*, which correspond to the limbs of land-living vertebrates. 5 These paired fins are generally concerned with steering and braking. 6 The *tail fin* provides the driving force as the body moves from side to side in the water. 7 The *other fins* provide stability.

(CFC)

### 5. Idea Sequence: Only Relevant Ideas:

An effective paragraph will have no irrelevant ideas creeping in. Look at the following short paragraph used earlier, describing nocturnal animals and giving reasons (in italics) why they are active at night. There is no extra irrelevant information in the passage.

**34** Many small animals including slugs and snails, woodlice, centipedes, come out at night because they *do not have waterproof skins*. The *air* is always more *moist at night*, and the animals are *less likely to dry up and die* than they are in the daytime. Hedgehogs, mice, toads, and similar creatures are also active at night. This is because *they feed on the smaller nocturnal (night-active) animals*. The chain then passes on to a second tier of predators, including foxes, badgers, stoats and owls. It is less easy to see why animals like rabbits should be active at night, but it may be a way for them *to avoid eagles, buzzards, and other diurnal (day-active) birds of prey,*'

(Piccolo)

### 6. Idea Sequence: A Single Impression

Sometimes it is a single tone that binds all the details in a paragraph. For example, all the italicised details in the following paragraph, used earlier, describe the perennial heavenly beauty and the majesty of the stars which attracted man to study them:

The night sky has *a beauty* we can all enjoy. The stars *sparkle like jewels* on a *velvet* backcloth. The moon, ever changing its shape, pours its *silvery light* into the darkness. At first sight, the night sky appears to be filled haphazardly with stars. But, after a while, we find that we can recognize *patterns of stars* and thus find our way through the heavens. By *studying the heavens*, we become astronomers. The Chaldeans and Babylonians were *skilled observers of the heavens over 5,000 years ago*.

## Devices for Transition & Coherence

Together with a coherent sequence of ideas in a paragraph, transitional devices provide an additional guide to understanding the focus of the passage. These devices are more explicit than the organic structure of the thought pattern. They are of *five* kinds and may be illustrated through the following paragraph. Three of these devices are indicated separately by highlighting, italics and underlining and the other two are independently explained below.

**80** 1 **Why** am I so bent on *conversation*? 2 For pleasure **first**, pure selfishness, **but also because** *conversation* is a school for thinkers and should be a school for democrats. 3 <u>When one finds</u> supposedly educated people *arguing* heatedly over matters of fact and shying away from matters of *opinion*: <u>when one sees</u> one's hosts getting nervous at a difference of *views* regarding politics or the latest play; <u>when one is</u> formally *entertained* with *information games* or queries cut out of the paper about the number of geese in a gaggle; <u>when the dictionary</u> and the encyclopaedia are regarded as final arbiters of *judgement* and not as fallible repositories of fact; <u>when intelligent youth</u> is *advised* not to go against the accepted *belief* in any circle because it will startle, shock and offend --- **it is time to recognize, first**, that the temper of democratic culture is tested at every dinner table and in every living room ---- just as much as at school, in the pulpit, or on the platform; **and second**, that by this test and despite our boasted freedom of opinion, we lack men and women whose minds have learned to move easily and fearlessly in the perilous *jungle of ideas*.

(200 words)                    Jacques Barzun

---

*1. Repetition of Key Words:*

Repetition keeps the central idea before us as we read through successive sentences. Barzun's repetitions fall along two lines: those having to do with the idea of "conversation" and those having to do with the idea of "opinion" as shown by the **italicised** expressions in the paragraph above.


*2. Restatement:*

All repetition acts as a connection, but restatement of aspects of the central idea makes for more effective coherence Thus, the idea that free thinking, even in little everyday matters, becomes conducive to building up a democratic culture is stressed by the following restatements:

"-- conversation is a school for thinkers and should be a school for democrats" in Sentence 2, is **restated** near the end of the long Sentence 3 as "that the temper of democratic culture is tested at every dinner table and in every living room"

### 3. *Pronouns and Demonstratives:*

Pronouns and pointer words like "this" and "these" act as connecters by **referring back** to the same idea in another sentence. Thus, we have "by this test" in the second last line of Sentence 3 referring back to "democratic culture is tested" used a little earlier.

### 4. *Parallel Structure:*

Repeated sentence patterns connect ideas by adding new thoughts to an already established context. The parallel structure also points up a similarity shared by the ideas. Thus, look at the **underlined** structures beginning with "when –" in the passage above, showing the various instances of a lack of democratic temper.

### 5. *Transitional Wording:*

Transitional words and phrases carry the reader smoothly from one idea to another and show a special relationship between the ideas. These transitional signals are **highlighted** in the passage for you. Observe them carefully. As mentioned earlier, they are good indicators of the focus of the passage. Thus, these become useful in making a summary which might read as follows (Note the concomitant transition signals being used in the summary, which again, have been highlighted for you. You could try matching these with the signals in the original passage):

Conversation, **besides** being pleasurable to me, *is* important **because** it is a school for thinkers and democrats. **The democratic culture is tested** at the dinner table and in the living room, **as our** experience with arguments over politics or cultural matters shows. **So also**, our experience with information entertainment and games and our advice to young people on not going against accepted belief **shows that** we lack men and women who can really boast of freedom of opinion.

(75 words)

A transitional device, as we have seen, is used **between or even within sentences** if it is needed to make the relation in thought clear to the reader. Thus, when the summary paragraph above is written as shown below without important transition devices [e.g., *The democratic culture, besides,* and *because* (within the sentence) and *So also* (between sentences)], the relations in thought are not clear:

Conversation, being pleasurable to me, is important for thinkers and democrats. This is tested at the dinner table and in the living room with arguments over politics or cultural matters. Our experience with information entertainment and games, and with advice to young people on not going against accepted belief is there. We lack men and women who can really boast of freedom of opinion.

Some other **commonly used transitional words** and phrases may be listed as follows:

*Cause and Consequence:* then /as a result /consequently /therefore /accordingly.

*Addition*: and /also /next /second, third, etc /another /further /likewise /additionally /one could also cite /furthermore /in addition.

*Comparison*: Likwise / similarly /in the same way /by the same way /by the same token.

*Contrast*: but /however /on the other hand /on the contrary /in contrast /yet /nevertheless /regardless of.

*Example and Illustration*: for example, / for instance /specifically /that is.

*Concession:* after all, / though /although this may be true /even though /of course /despite the fact that /that is not to say.

*Conclusion or Summary*: in brief /to sum up /in short /to summarize /in conclusion /hence /in as much as /this being so.

## Longer Passages

In longer passages a transition device should be used **between paragraphs** whenever it is needed to show logical sequence of thought. For instance, if a paragraph presents a contrast to the thought of the preceding one, the writer shows this relation by some connective like *However, But, Yet or Nevertheless*. If a paragraph indicates a result following from the discussion in the preceding paragraph, the writer may use *Therefore, Consequently, Accordingly*, or some similar connective. These devices serve as guideposts for the reader to show him/her the course the theme is taking. Connection may also be made by means of pronouns, parallel structures, repetition of words /phrases /statements or restatement of an idea. These become valuable guidelines in identifying the sequence of ideas and the pattern of organization in the paragraph/ passage and, therefore, also in writing a summary with the appropriate focus.

## Exercises

A) Find the **devices for coherence** in the following paragraphs/ passages in subsequent units; that is, pick out the transitional words /phrases, repetitions, parallel phrasing, pronouns and so on. (Use different codes to indicate these as shown in the example below.)

B) Use these, if necessary, to identify the overall **pattern of organization.**

C) Make a brief **summary** of the passage and compare the transitional devices used in the summary with those used in the original passage. Discuss your answers with your teacher. Two sample exercises are worked out for you:

## Two Examples :

81    *Our world* is becoming ever more crowded and filled with machines and gadgets. Making *these* things requires vast amounts of <u>raw materials</u>. *We* **also** need vast amounts of energy <u>to drive</u> machines, <u>to provide</u> <u>heat and light</u>, and <u>to power</u> all forms of transport.

<u>Some raw materials</u> needed for manufacturing and energy are grown. <u>Trees provide</u> wood for *fuel*, furniture, building, paper and so on. <u>Plants and animals provide</u> materials such as wool, cotton and leather. **But today** <u>most of the raw materials and fuels</u> we use come from the ground such as iron and other metals, coal, oil and gas.                    (90 words)

**A)** *Key to Answers*: Italics without underlining for Pronouns; Italics with underlining for Repetitions; Underlining only for Parallel Structures; Highlighting for Transitional Devices.

**B)** *Pattern of Organization*: Problem and Solution

**C)** *Summary:* Our modern world of machines requires vast amounts of raw materials to make them **and** to provide heat light and energy. Some materials are grown e.g., trees that provide the wood for building and fuel, animals that provide wool and leather. **But** many materials like metals, oil and gas come from under the ground.          (50 words)

---

**82** The main places in which *diamonds* <u>are found</u> are in South Africa, in the region around Kimberley, **but** *they* <u>are also found</u> in the Congo, Brazil and India. **At** Kimberley, *they* are in a curious kind of rock called "blue ground". ***This is*** like a very stiff clay composed of ground up rocks and containing many minerals. **Mixed with** *it* are sharp stones and boulders of very heavy rocks. <u>*The blue ground*</u> is found in deep pits, which may be 700 yards across.

**After** <u>*the rock*</u> has been dug or quarried it is left out in the weather to soften and crumble. *It* <u>is</u> **then** <u>crushed, washed and sifted</u> --- that is, shaken over small holes to let the dust drop out --- **until** *it* consists of clean sand and small stones. *This* <u>is</u> **next** <u>scattered</u> over greasy boards, *which* are <u>made to shake</u> by machinery. The <u>*diamonds*</u> <u>get stuck</u> in the grease **while** the other stones <u>remain loose</u> **and** are <u>washed away</u>. **After** *that* the grease is <u>*washed off*</u> in a liquid and the <u>*rough diamonds*</u> are collected.

A <u>*rough diamond*</u> looks like a very dull, shapeless pebble: it has to be cut and polished **before** *it* will sparkle. **Since** *it* is a crystal, it splits easily in directions parallel with the faces of the *crystals* of which it is made up, **and the first thing to do** is to "cleave" in one or more of *these directions*. This <u>is done</u> by experts who use a blade of steel and strike it with a wooden mallet.

**Though** *it* will <u>split</u> in certain <u>directions</u>, a <u>diamond</u> is very hard. *It* cannot be scratched <u>or cut</u> **except** with another <u>diamond</u> or with <u>diamond dust</u>. The cutting <u>is usually done</u> with <u>another diamond</u>, which is made to turn at a high speed. **When** the main <u>faces</u> <u>have been cut</u>, smaller *faces* or <u>"facets"</u> <u>are produced</u> by grinding the <u>diamond</u> on a soft iron wheel with <u>diamond dust</u> and olive oil. The sparkle of a <u>cut diamond</u> depends on the positions of <u>the facets</u>. Most <u>diamonds</u> are very small but a few large ones <u>have been found.</u>

(350 words)

**A)** *Key to Answers*: Italics without underlining for Pronouns; Italics with underlining for Repetitions; Underlining only for Parallel Structures; Highlighting for Transitional Devices.

**B)** *Pattern of Organization*:   Process (Time Order)

**C)** *Summary*: <u>The diamonds</u> in Kimberley <u>are found</u> in deep pits in a clay like rock, called "blue ground', composed of ground up rocks, stones and minerals. *The quarried rock* <u>is left</u> in the open to crumble **and then** <u>crushed, washed and sifted</u> **to let** the dust drop out. **The remaining** clean sand and stones <u>are scattered</u> over greasy boards, **which** <u>are shaken</u> by the machinery so that the stones (diamonds) <u>get stuck</u> in the grease. The grease **is then** washed away and the dull shapeless looking diamonds <u>are cut and polished</u> *to sparkle*. **The** <u>crystal (diamond)</u> **is** <u>cut</u> by experts with another *diamond,* **which** <u>is made to turn</u> at high speed. ***After*** *the 'facets' or faces* <u>are produced</u> the grinding or polishing *is done* on a soft iron wheel with diamond dust and olive oil. <u>*The sparkle*</u> **depends on** the positions of the facets.
(140 words)

---

**(More passages 83-89 follow in print)**

## Unit VII

### 83

The birth of a volcanic island is an event marked by prolonged and violent travail: the forces of the earth striving to create, and all the forces of the sea opposing. The sea floor, where an island begins, is probably nowhere more than about fifty miles thick—a thin covering over the vast bulk of the earth. In it are deep cracks and fissures, the results of unequal cooling and shrinkage in past ages. Along such lines of weakness the molten lava from the earth's interior presses up and finally bursts forth into the sea. But a submarine volcano is different from a terrestrial eruption, where the lava, molten rocks, gases, and other ejecta are hurled into the air through an open crater. Here on the bottom of the ocean the volcano has resisting it all the weight of the ocean water above it. Despite the immense pressure of, it may be, two or three miles of sea water, the new volcanic cone builds upward toward the surface, in flow after flow of lava. Once within reach of the waves, its soft ash and tuff are violently attacked, and for a long period the potential island may remain a shoal, unable to emerge. But, eventually, in new eruptions, the cone is pushed up into the air and a rampart against the attacks of the waves is built of hardened lava.

Rachel Carson, *The Sea Around Us*

### 84

Teenagers feel differently about their parents than they did as children, or than they will as they become adults. A child's love for his or her parents is a dependent, appreciative, even enthusiastic kind of devotion. Adolescent feeling for parents is normally less vocally affectionate, and more openly critical than it has been before or will be again. Mark Twain observed that when he was sixteen he could not understand how his father could be so stupid; by the time he reached twenty-one, he was amazed at how much the old man had learned in the past five years!

### 85

The station buildings were long, low huts, made of sun-dried, mud-colored bricks, laid up without mortar (*adobes*, the Spaniards call these bricks, and the Americans shorten it to '*dobies*'). The roofs, which had no slant to them worth speaking of, were thatched and then sodded or covered with a thick layer of earth, and from this sprung a pretty rank growth of weeds and grass. It was the first time we had ever seen a man's front yard on top of his house. The buildings consisted of barns, stable-room for twelve or fifteen horses, and a hut for an eating-room for passengers. This latter had bunks in it for the station-keeper and a hostler or two. You could rest your elbows on its eaves, and you had to bend to get in at the door. In place of a window there was a square hole about large enough for a man to crawl through, but this had no glass in it. There was no flooring, but the ground was packed hard. There was no stove, but the fireplace served all needful purposes. There were no shelves, no cupboards, no closets. In the corner stood an open sack of flour, and nestling against its base were a couple of black and venerable tin coffee-pots, a tin tea-pot, a little bag of salt, and a side of bacon.

Mark Twain, *Roughing It*

Easy Steps to Summary Writing and Note-Making

Unit VII

86. The stage in Shakespeare's time was a naked room with a blanket for a curtain; but he made it a field for monarchs. That law of unity, which has its foundations, not in the factitious necessity of custom, but in nature itself, the unity of feeling, is everywhere and at all times observed by Shakespeare in his plays. Read *Romeo and Juliet*: all is youth and spring; youth with its follies, its virtues, its precipitancies; spring with its odors, its flowers, and its transciency. It is one and the same feeling that commences, goes through, and ends the play. The old men, the Capulets and the Montagues, are not common old men; they have an eagerness, a heartiness, a vehemence, the effect of spring; with Romeo, his change of passion, his sudden marriage, and his rash death, are all the effects of youth; whilst in Juliet, love has all that is tender and melancholy in the nightingale, all that is voluptuous in the rose, with whatever is sweet in the freshness of spring; but it ends with a long deep sigh like the last breeze of the Italian evening. This unity of feeling and character pervades every drama of Shakespeare.

Samuel Taylor Coleridge, *Lectures on Shakespeare*

87. It was a cheerless morning when they got into the street; blowing and raining hard; and the clouds looking dull and stormy. The night had been very wet; large pools of water had collected in the road and the kennels were overflowing. There was a faint glimmering of the coming day in the sky; but it rather aggravated than relieved the gloom of the scene: the sombre light only serving to pale that which the street lamps afforded, without shedding any warmer or brighter tints upon the wet housetops, and dreary streets. There appeared to be nobody stirring in that quarter of the town; the windows of the houses were all closely shut; and the streets through which they passed, were noiseless and empty.

Charles Dickens, *Oliver Twist*

88. In psychology behavior refers to any overt action on the part of an animal organism. The action may be simple or complex. At one extreme, it may be blinking an eye, flexing a finger, tilting the head, swallowing some water, taking a step, uttering a sound, or putting a mark on an answer sheet. At the other extreme, it may be singing a song on a television show, attempting a ten-foot putt on the eighteenth hole of a golf tournament, bargaining for an automobile on a used car lot, taking a final examination in a freshman history course, painting a still life in an attic studio, or piloting an ocean liner from New York to Liverpool. In psychology behavior is used to designate an overt action.

William S. Ray, *The Science of Psychology: An Introduction*

89. My confidence in the future of our species is not due to ignorance of its failings. My confidence is based on two different but related sets of facts. First, the human species has exhibited for at least 100,000 years certain traits which are uniquely and pleasantly human and which are more interesting than those that account for its bestiality. Second, the human species has the power to choose among the conflicting traits which constitute its complex nature, and it has made the right choices often enough to have kept civilization so far on a forward and upward course. The unique place for our species in the order of things is determined, not by its animality, but by its humanity.

René Dubos, "The Humanizing of Humans"

# Unit VIII: Superfluous Information

The relationship between the main and subordinate ideas in expository writing may sometimes be indicated very obviously and clearly. The text of such a passage may be well sign-posted to help us follow the argument. Look at passage 44, used earlier:

---

**44  Ordinary clocks have two important parts. 2 One part consists of a mechanism, which moves regularly second by second. 3 The other part, which is connected to the mechanism, tells us the hours, and minutes, of the day**

---

The 'two' parts of the clock, in the main idea in Sentence1, are clearly indicated with 'One part ---' and 'The other part ---' in the subordinate ideas in Sentences 2 and 3. A longer, similarly obviously organized passage (43) could read like this:

Now look at the following passage:

## 90    Causes of Disease

1 For many centuries it was thought that diseases were caused by evil spirits.  2 Modern medical science, however, has made great advances in the scientific investigation of the causes of disease, and these causes are now grouped into a few general categories.  3 The following are some of the main categories.
1      *Congenital causes of disorders*:   4 These causes act within the womb and result in disorders which are usually obvious at birth such as mongolism, abnormalities of the nervous system and deformities of the heart. 5 These disorders are caused either by a fault in the chromosomal structure of the fertilized egg or by damage caused to the developing embryo in the womb. 6 A developing embryo can be affected by a disease of the mother.  7 For example, during the early months of pregnancy, German measles can lead to abnormalities of the heart and ears.  8 The smoking of more than ten cigarettes a day by a pregnant woman may retard the normal growth of the foetus in the womb. 9 Deformities may also be due to drugs taken during pregnancy.

2   *Infection:* 10 An enormous number of living things enter the body's tissues, grow there and cause disease. 11 Infectious agents act in different ways. 12 Viruses act inside the cells. 13 The polio virus, for example, causes paralysis by growing in and destroying a particular type of nerve cell in the spinal cord. 14 Bacteria, on the other hand, are mainly extracellular. 15 Malaria, which is still one of the world's greatest killers, destroys the blood's red cells. 16 It is caused by a tiny parasite, which is carried by mosquitoes. 17 Its symptoms are a high fever, headache and violent shivering. 18 It can result in chronic ill health or death.

3   *Nutrition:* 19 The effects of nutrition on health are both direct and indirect as health depends in many ways on the quantity and quality of diet. 20 Large numbers of people suffer from chronic starvation, and devastating famine can result from floods, droughts and poor harvests. 21 Even a diet, which is quantitatively sufficient, can lead to disease if it is deficient in vitamins. 22 A diet, which consistently lacks a sufficient quantity of a particular vitamin, is certain in time to give rise to the corresponding vitamin deficiency disease.
(300 words)

In passage **90** above, the categories of the causes of disease are clearly paragraphed with titles and numbering. Each paragraph contains an explanation of the causes of disease under each category. Examples of the diseases are also mentioned clearly. But, on the whole, in comparison with passage **44** above, the information is less tightly organized. For writing a summary of the passage, a good amount of the information would be **superfluous** i.e., the information seems naturally useful and interesting in the passage, but becomes unnecessary when you are trying to give briefly the main intent of the passage to make a *gist* or *summary*. Such superfluous information could distract us from the main idea of the passage. Let us see how this happens:

Look at the first three sentences. What is the most important idea here that would appropriately summarize the little extract? Which of the following four options would seem to provide a good summary of the three sentences?
a)   Categories of causes of disease
b)   Modern medical science of diseases
c)   Evil spirits - the cause disease
d)   Scientifically investigated causes of disease

If option d) best summarizes the important idea in the first three lines let us see what is wrong with the other three options. Option a) seems too narrow and specific an idea and leaves out the concept of a scientific perspective. Option b), on the other hand, seems too wide in scope to form an appropriate condensation of the extract from the text, for it covers the whole area of medical science of diseases. 'Evil spirits cause disease', or the c) option, constitutes an interesting idea but does not convey the appropriate focus of the subject because it talks about the view of people in a pre-scientific era. Thus, while the opening sentence of the passage makes an interesting introduction to the subject and therefore could distract us while writing a summary, the main idea is contained in Sentence 2. Sentence 1, therefore, becomes superfluous to the summary.

However, information that seems superfluous to the summary is not at all superfluous within the passage. It is related to the main ideas of the passage in different ways. The main idea may be rephrased or paraphrased for better understanding or clarity. Sometimes the background of the idea may need mention, or additional details or elaborations may be required. Often illustration or exemplification might become necessary. For example, the talk about 'evil spirits' in Sentence 1 of passage **90** informed us of how people in ancient times believed diseases to be caused, a view that surprises and intrigues us because of the medical awareness that people today have. The first sentence, therefore, gives us a historical perspective on the causes of disease (i.e., a background of the earlier understanding of disease).

Let us examine another instance of superfluity. Look at the second paragraph, which talks about the 'Congenital Causes of Disorders'. This main idea, that also titles the paragraph, is further **explained** in Sentence 5 as including two kinds of causes of the disorders. The resulting diseases are named in Sentences 4, 7, 8 and 9. What, then, does the opening Sentence 4 of the paragraph do? It tells us that 'congenital' means 'act(ing) within the womb'. This explanation is implied in the word 'congenital' (a rephrasing) and could possibly be deleted from a summary of the passage, to avoid **redundancy** or repetition.

The hierarchical information of the two congenital causes of disease in the paragraph (of about 100 words) can be **diagrammatically** represented as follows:

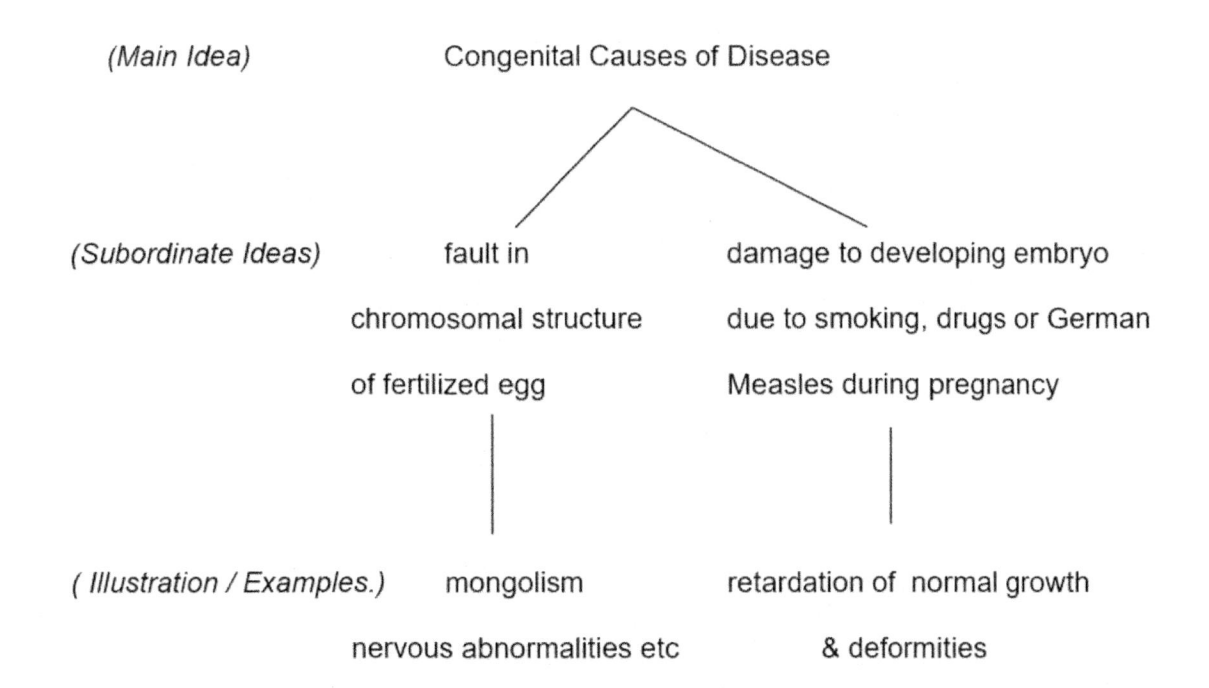

```
(Main Idea)              Congenital Causes of Disease
                                  /\
                                 /  \
                                /    \
(Subordinate Ideas)       fault in           damage to developing embryo
                          chromosomal structure   due to smoking, drugs or German
                          of fertilized egg       Measles during pregnancy
                               |                       |
                               |                       |
(Illustration / Examples.)  mongolism           retardation of normal growth
                          nervous abnormalities etc    & deformities
```

The **verbal version** of this representation i. e., the **summary** could read as follows:

*The congenital group of causes of disease include a) a fault in the chromosomal structure of the fertilized egg leading to mongolism, nervous abnormalities etc., and b) damage to the embryo because of smoking, drugs or German Measles during pregnancy leading to retardation of normal growth and deformities.*
*(46 words)*

The condensation of the 100+ words paragraph to a length of 46 words is achieved in two ways:

1) **Deletion of fine details**: The very fine details in the subordinate ideas such as a '(damage to the embryo) *during the early months of pregnancy*', or again, '(smoking) *of more than 10 cigarettes a day*', and yet again, '(retardation of normal growth) *of the foetus in the womb*' etc., are omitted. These very fine details do not affect the meaning and focus of the summary. Their deletion is, therefore, helpful in summarizing.

2) The **combination of ideas across sentences** 4-9 to form a single sentence helps avoid repeated use of function words like articles, prepositions and verbs or verbal phrases like 'affected by', 'caused by' 'may also be due to' etc. This also becomes possible because of the use of the active voice instead of the passive used in the original text.

Now read again Passage **90** carefully and try to fill in the numbered blanks in the diagrammatic representation (below) of the passage and the verbal summary: (You can later check back with the Answers)

### Diagrammatic Representation Of ('Causes of Disease') Passage 90

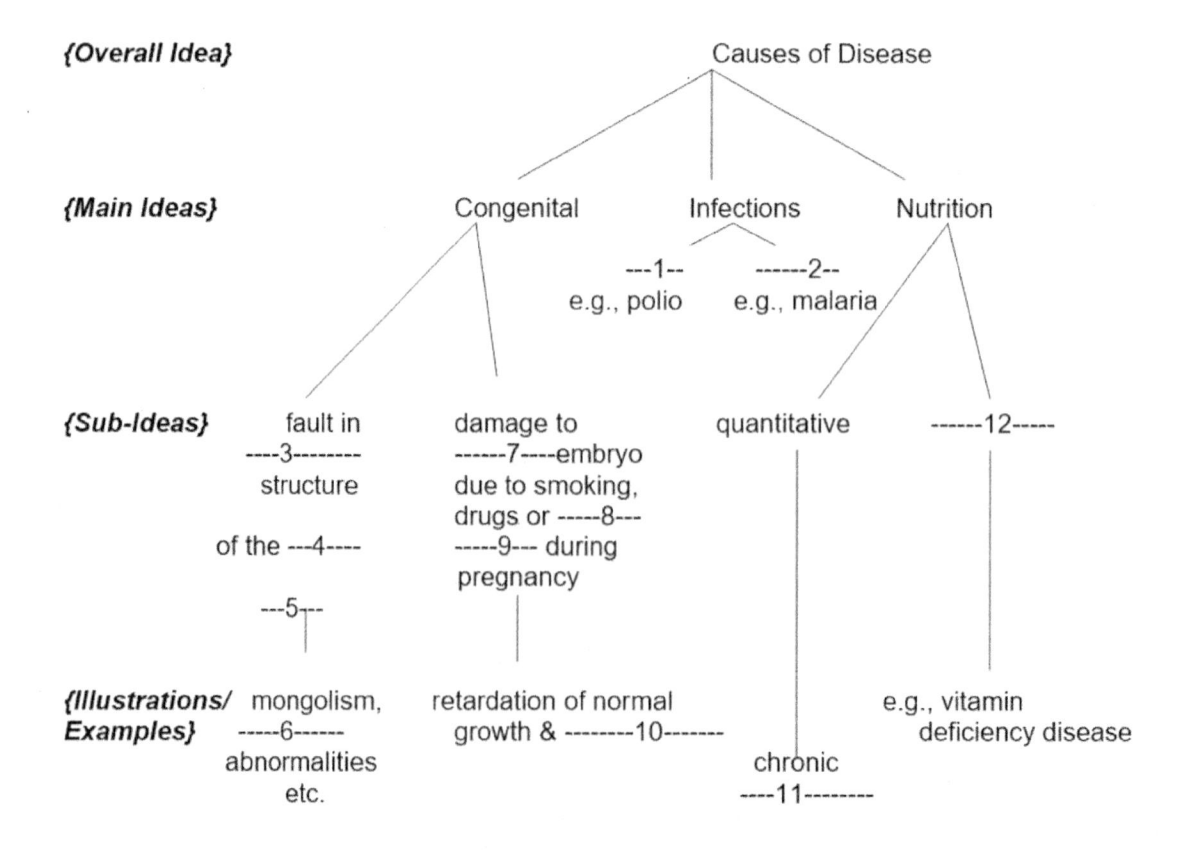

```
{Overall Idea}                          Causes of Disease
                                 /             |              \
{Main Ideas}              Congenital       Infections        Nutrition
                                             ---1--      ------2--
                                          e.g., polio   e.g., malaria

{Sub-Ideas}    fault in          damage to        quantitative      ------12-----
              ----3--------      ------7----embryo
              structure          due to smoking,
                                 drugs or -----8---
              of the ---4----    -----9--- during
                                 pregnancy
                  ---5---

{Illustrations/  mongolism,      retardation of normal              e.g., vitamin
 Examples}       -----6------    growth & --------10-------         deficiency disease
                 abnormalities                        chronic
                 etc.                                ----11--------
```

## Verbal Summary of Passage

The causes of ---1---- can be grouped into three categories. The congenital cause can ----2----- a fault in the chromosomal structure of the ------3----- ---4-- leading to mongolism, nervous abnormalities etc., or damage to the ---5-- because of ---6---, drugs or German Measles during pregnancy leading to -------7---- of normal growth and deformities. ----8-- infection in the second category can lead to diseases like polio and an example of bacterial infection is ----9--. Under-nutrition in the ---10--- category can lead to starvation while qualitatively inadequate ----11--- can cause vitamin or some other ----12-- disease.

(94 words)

(You may check your answers in the summary by referring to the completed diagrammatic representation above)

## Exercises

Each of the following passages is followed by exercises on picking out the main ideas and identifying related information. However, all the related information need not necessarily be included in the summary.

**91** The earthworms are amongst the commonest of animals. There are a great many in all fertile soils. An acre of old grassland may have three million earthworms beneath its surface, weighing up to 610 kilograms. This is about the weight of the cattle that can live on the grass on the same area.

Earthworms live below ground. They push their pointed end between the bits of soil, making a space through which they can move. If the soil is too tightly packed to allow this, the earthworms eat their way forwards, swallowing soil in front of them and passing it out behind them as they go.

The hole made by an earthworm is called its burrow. It is often made in the form of a "U", passing down into the soil and then up again. The opening of the burrow is usually filled with leaves or twigs. Some earthworms come to the surface to feed, usually at night, for earthworms do not like strong light. The worm keeps its tail in its burrow, ready to draw back quickly if danger threatens. With the front end of its body it seeks any plant material that may be within reach. Some earthworms like meat and some are very fond of chocolate.

Earthworms also feed on tiny bits of plant and animal matter in the soil. Much soil is swallowed and passed through the body of the worm as it burrows, and any small pieces of food that the soil contains are used up as it does so. Some earthworms feed below the ground all the time.

Earthworms are a great help to the farmer and the gardener. They mix up the soil and make it full of holes so that air and water can pass freely into it. By passing soil through their bodies they help to turn some of the substances in it into a sort of manure. Roots of plants often grow down the burrows made by worms.

(-adapted from CFE)    (250 words)

I     Stated below are some of the ideas that seem to be expressed in the passage.
A)    Select the statement(s) that best **help(s) to summarize** the passage.
B)    Indicate whether each of the **remaining** statements is
    i.    repetitive of the main idea,
    ii.    inaccurate or incorrect (according to the passage),
    iii.    too general (broad in scope) to summarize the paragraph,
    iv.    too narrow or specific in detail to be important for the summary.

**(The exercises on the first paragraph are worked out for you).**
*Paragraph 1*
a)    The earthworms are the commonest animals.
b)    There are many earthworms in fertile soils.
c)    The earthworms weigh 610 kilograms.
d)    The cattle on the land are as heavy.
{Example:
Answer: A) – b.
        B) a- iii; c- ii; d- iv.}

*Paragraphs 2 & 3:*
a)    Earthworms always live below the ground
b)    They burrow through all kinds of soils.
c)    Some earthworms come out to feed on leaves and twigs.
d)    Earthworms feed on the soil in the ground.
e)    Earthworms stay underground to avoid dangers.
f)    The burrows they make are U-shaped.
g)    They feed on meat and chocolates in our homes.
h)    Earthworms feed above and below ground.
*Paragraph 4: & 5:*
a)    Earthworms are useful to the farmer and the gardener.

b) They provide passage for the roots of the plants.
c) They make the soil porous and fertile.
d) They provide air and water for the plants in the soil.
e) They provide manure for the plants.
f) They feed on the food contained in the soil.

II    Fill in the blanks to complete a summary of the whole passage (The blanks are numbered for your convenience):
Earthworms are very ---1--- in fertile soils. They burrow through loose as well as ----2---- packed soils and leave the soil ---3----- and fertile. They generally stay --4---- the ground to avoid strong -----5---- and feed on the food in the --6-----. The soil passed through their ---7-- provides a kind of ---8---- for the plants and the --9------ provide a passage for the ---10-- of plants.
(64 words)


**92**    The diamond is one of the most valuable precious stones, yet it is made up entirely of the common element carbon, which we all know in the form of coke, soot, charcoal and lamp-black. The difference between a clear, sparkling diamond and these dirty black substances lies in the way their atoms are packed together. In the common forms they are not arranged in a special way but are just heaped together anyhow.
Graphite, or black lead (the lead in pencils), is a form of carbon in which the atoms are loosely arranged to form small plates, each with six sides, but these are easily broken because the spaces between the atoms are so wide. In a diamond, the atoms are packed as tightly as possible. They thus form a crystal, which is usually shaped like two pyramids joined base to base.
It takes a very great deal of pressure and heat to force the carbon atoms so closely together, but it has been done by man. Diamonds made in this way are very tiny and badly coloured. All the good diamonds, suitable for making jewels for people to wear, are found in the earth. At some time or other the rocks in which they were formed must have been deep below the surface, where the heat is always great and the pressure is far greater than man can produce.

(230 words)                              (adapted from CFE)

**Exercises**
**I**    Stated below are some of the ideas that seem to be expressed in the **I** passage.92
   A) Select the statement(s) that best **help(s) to summarize** the passage.

B) Indicate whether each of the remaining statements is
   i. repetitive of the main idea
   ii. extraneous(=outside) the passage or incorrect (according to the passage),
   iii. too general (broad in scope) to summarize the paragraph
   iv. too narrow or specific in detail to be important for the summary.

*Paragraph 1*
a)   Diamonds are made up of carbon.
b)   Carbon is found in coke, soot, charcoal and diamonds.
c)   Their atoms are packed in a special way in coke, soot and charcoal.
d)   In common diamonds the atoms are heaped anyhow.
e)   Coke, soot, charcoal and lamp-black are dirty substances.

*Paragraph 2*
a)   In graphite the atoms form plates.
b)   In a diamond these plates are loosely packed.
c)   In a diamond the atoms loosely form a crystal shaped like two pyramids joined base to base.
d)   The atoms are tightly packed in a diamond.

*Paragraph 3*
a)   Man makes the best diamonds.
b)   Diamonds are extracted from the earth.
c)   Good diamonds are judged by their size and colour.
d)   The heat and pressure in the diamond mine makes the best diamonds.
e)   Good diamonds are used for making jewellery.

**II**   Fill in the blanks to complete a summary of the whole passage (The blanks are numbered for your convenience):

Diamonds are made of ----1---- atoms, which are ----2---- packed to form a crystal ---3---- like two pyramids joined ----4---- to base. The best ----5---- come from deep under the ---6------- where the heat and -----7---- is far greater than ----8----can produce.
                                             (44 words)

**93**   Most young people enjoy some type of physical activity. It may be walking, cycling or swimming. It may be a game of some kind – football, hockey, golf or tennis. It may be mountaineering.

Those who have a passion for climbing high and difficult mountains are often looked upon with astonishment. Why are men and women willing to suffer cold and hardship and to take risks on high mountains? This astonishment is caused probably by the difference between mountaineering and other forms of activity to which men give their leisure.

Mountaineering is a sport and not a game. There are no man-made rules as there are for such games as golf or football. There are, of course, rules of a different kind which it would be dangerous to ignore but it is this freedom from man-made rules that makes mountaineering attractive to many people. Those who climb mountains are free to use their own methods.

If we compare mountaineering and other more familiar sports, we might think that one big difference is that mountaineering is not a 'team game'. We should be mistaken in this. There are, it is true, no matches between teams of climbers but when climbers are on a rock face linked by a rope on which their lives may depend, there is obviously team-work.

The mountaineer continues to improve in skill year after year. A skier is probably past his best by the age of thirty, and most international tennis champions are in their early twenties. But it is far from unusual for men of fifty or sixty to climb the highest mountains in the Alps. They may take more time than younger men, but they probably climb with more skill and less waste of effort, and they certainly experience equal enjoyment. (300 words)

## Exercises

I  Stated below are some of the ideas that seem to be expressed in the passage.
  A) Select the statements that **together** best help to **summarize** the passage.
  B)  Indicate whether each of the **remaining** statements is
     i. repetitive of the main idea
     ii. inaccurate or incorrect (according to the passage)
     iii. too general (broad/ vague in scope) to summarize the paragraph/passage
     iv. too narrow/ specific in detail to be important for the summary.

a)  Young people enjoy physical activity.
b)  Mountaineering is a good physical activity.
c)  Some people love mountaineering.
d)  Some other people are astonished by this.
e)  Climbing high and difficult mountains can be high and risky and full of hardship.
f)  Mountaineering is a sport not a game.
g)  There are man-made rules in mountaineering.
h)  Mountaineers can use their own methods.

i) There are unwritten rules for ensuring the safety of mountaineers.
j) Ignoring these rules can be dangerous.
k) Mountaineering does not require teamwork.
l) There is no competition in mountaineering.
m) Mountaineering is not for people past their thirties.
n) Mountaineering skills can improve with practise and increase enjoyment.
o) Older people can climb with more effort than younger men and women.
p) Old and young can enjoy mountaineering.

**II** Fill in the blanks to complete a summary of the whole passage (The blanks are numbered for your convenience):
Mountaineering is not a ---1---- like hockey or tennis but a valuable ---2---- and physical activity. -----3----- are looked upon with astonishment because of the --4---- and hardships they face at the sport. ----5----- is different from other games because there are no man-made ----6---- and one can use one's own ----7----. However, teamwork is important because as they climb in ---8-- the mountaineers depend on the co-operation among ------9----. If other games can be played best --10--- the age of thirty mountaineering skills improve with ---11--- and both young and old can --12-- the sport.

**94** The origin of many place names in Mumbai have become obscure with time. The area of Lalbagh, in the heart of the former "Girangaon" or "village of textile mills", is one such example. Parel-Lalbagh was once among the most affluent localities in the city, primarily due to its proximity to Government House, the residence of the governors of Bombay (now the Haffkine Institute at Parel).

Several prosperous citizens constructed palatial mansions here, including Lowjee Castle and the house known as Lalbaug, built in 1972 on 10,000 square yards by Pestonjee Bomanjee Wadia, a descendant of the master-craftsman Lowjee Nusserwanjee, whose name will always be connected with the Bombay Dockyard and shipbuilding. Eventually, V. Shantaram, the renowned film producer-director-actor, purchased the land and the house was demolished to construct the Rajkamal film studios.

There are many who believe that it was the stately Wadia mansion, Lalbaug, that lent its name to the area. Not so it seems, according to the older residents of Lalbagh Industrial Estate, who aver that both the house and the area, Lalbagh, were named after the 14th century dargah of a Muslim pir, Lal Syed Shah. The dargah has a well located just outside its compound, which is used by local Hindu and Muslim families who have lived in harmony for many decades. During the riots of 1993, the dargah was set on fire but was quickly repaired by local residents who state that it was "outsiders with vested interests" who caused the destruction.

On the dargah is an inscription in Urdu, which, together with the names of the donors of the marble platform, states, "Yeh Lalbagh yaadgar Lal Shah Baba ka mandir hai" (This is the temple of Lalbagh in memory of Lal Shah Baba). Close to this is the dargah of Lal Shah Baba's brother, Chand Syed Shah, also a pir.

(Sarada Dwivedi)

Exercises

**I**     Stated below are some of the ideas that seem to be expressed in the passage.
   **A)** Select the statement(s) that best **help(s) to summarize** the passage.
   **B)** Indicate whether each of the remaining statements is
      i. repetitive of the main idea,
      ii. inaccurate or incorrect (according to the passage),
      iii. too general (broad/ vague in scope) to summarize the passage
      iv. too narrow or too specific in detail to be important for the summary.

a)     The origins of many place names in Mumbai have been forgotten
b)     Lalbagh was one of the most affluent localities in Mumbai.
c)     Lalbagh is named after a sprawling mansion built by Pestonjee Wadia in 1792.
d)     He was also associated with the Bombay Dockyard and shipbuilding.
e)     Older residents maintain that Lalbagh was named after a 14th century dargah of a Muslim pir named Lal Syed Shah.
f)     The dargah was partially destroyed during the 1993 riots.
g)     Local residents rebuilt it.
h)     An inscription on the dargah mentions the reason for its name.
i)     Close by is the dargah of Lal Shah Baba's brother.
j)     Lal Shah Baba donated the marble platform.

**II**     Write a summary of the passage in about 40 words. Which details would you add to Option e) to make a fuller summary?

**95**     'Not so long ago ... from their children' (Passage overleaf)
**I**     Stated after the passage overleaf are some of the ideas that seem to be expressed in the passage.
   A) Select the statement(s) that best help(s) to summarize the passage.
   B) Indicate whether each of the remaining statements is
      i     repetitive of the main idea,
      ii     inaccurate or incorrect (according to the passage),
      iii     too general (broad/ vague in scope) to summarize the paragraph/ passage,

iv    too narrow or too specific in detail to be important for the summary.

### (Passage 95 follows)

Unit VIII

## 95

Not so long ago, children were brought up on homely advice and instinct. By listening to the mother or the mother-in-law and going with the flow. Today, though, the rules of the game have changed. According to the 2001 Census, there are 3.5 crore children under the age of six in urban India behind whom are double the number of anxious parents. Urban India is changing faster than ever. There are more sources of information, better communication and better technology. The remote control has replaced the rattle, the PlayStation is the new play pen.

Indian parents are faced with a multitude of complicated choices. Can a child really learn more between the ages of one and six than it can ever again in its whole life? Is TV good or bad? How much is too much? Should they first learn to swim or sing? Parenting has grown from being a full-time preoccupation to an investment-centric science, not unlike campaign or portfolio management. The expert advice is coming in from all corners, as counsellors, classes and cyberspace promise the path to effective parenthood and the superachieving child of our dreams.

Grandmother's remedies and nightly story-reading session are no longer seen as enough. An entire industry has been built on the fragile self-confidence and the guilt of the modern Indian parent. There are books and workshops on effective parenting, classes in dance and music for children as young as four years to websites promising all the answers. At one level this has made the Indian parent a more responsive one in contrast to the traditional, unbending disciplinarian. At another it has created pressures on parents who have high expectations of their own efforts and demand high achievement from their children.

Aroon Purie
(Courtesy India Today June 8-14, 2004)

a)    Children were brought up on homely advice and instinct.

b)    Advice came from the mother or mother-in-law.

c) Anxiety among parents has grown today.

d) There are more sources of information.

e) There is better communication and better technology.

f) The remote control has replaced the rattle.

g) Plenty of complicated choices for modern Indian parents.

h) Parenting – an investment-centric science.

i) Can a child really learn more before the age of six than it can ever again in his whole lifetime?

j) Is TV good or bad for the child?

k) Should he first learn to swim or sing?

l) Advice available from books, counsellors, classes and cyberspace.

m) Grandma's remedies and story-telling no longer enough.

n) Parents today are more responsive than the traditional unbending disciplinarian of earlier years.

o) Parents have high expectations from children.

p) Children are pressured to show achievements, sometimes, beyond their scope.


**II** Summarize the passage in about 80 words by combining your chosen points and including the examples as briefly as possible.

# Unit IX: Practice with A Variety of Styles in Expository Texts

Read through each of the following passages a couple of times and do the exercises that follow, re-reading when necessary.

## Argumentative Writing

**96** The prophecies that the opening of the railways would bring ruin and disaster upon landlords and farmers did not in the end prove true. The agricultural communications, so far from being "destroyed" as had been predicted, were immensely improved. The farmers were enabled to buy their coals, lime and manure for less money, while they obtained a readier access to the best markets for their stock and farm produce. Notwithstanding the predictions to the contrary, their cows gave milk as before, their sheep fed and fattened, and even skittish horses ceased to shy at the passing locomotive. The smoke of the engines did not obscure the sky, nor were farmyards burnt up by the fire thrown from the locomotives. The farming classes were not reduced to beggary; on the contrary, they soon felt that, so far from having anything to dread, they had very much good to expect from the extension of the railways.

Landlords also found that they could get higher rents for farms situated near a railway than at a distance from one. Hence, they became clamorous for "sidings". They felt it would be a grievance to be placed at a distance from a station. After a railway had been once opened, not a landlord would consent to have the line taken from him. Owners who had fought the promoters before Parliament and compelled them to pass their domains at a distance at a vastly increased expense on tunnels and deviations, now petitioned for branches and nearer station accommodation. Those who held property near towns and had extorted large sums as compensation for the anticipated deterioration in the value of their building land, found a new demand for it springing up at greatly advanced prices. Land was now advertised for sale, with the attraction of being "near a railway station".

**Exercises** (see next page)

'The prophecies of the opening of the railways ...near a railway station'
**I.** What is the central idea of the passage? In which sentence is it stated?
**II.** Which sentences elaborate the idea? Do they extend over one or both paragraphs?
**III.** How are the points in Paragraph 1 different from those in Paragraph 2?
**IV.** Writ a summary in about 100 words.

**V**   **A**. From the following options choose the **most appropriate title** for your summary:
   a) The Advantages of the Railways
   b) Railway Prophecies
   c) The Opening of the Railways
   d) Disadvantages of Railways

   **B**. For each of the options **not chosen** indicate the reason by choosing from the options indicated below, to say whether the title was
   i. too broad in scope
   ii. too narrow (i.e., covering only part of the passage/ summary)
   iii. not in the spirit of the passage/ summary
   iv. irrelevant to the topic of the passage/ summary.
   v. too vague

**97** '1.Children approaching adulthood sometimes begin to regard the adult both as a parent and as a symbolic representative of the adult world. 2. Much adolescent rebellion is a defiant "emancipation proclamation" against any, and all adult authority, as such. 3. In response to this, adults are apt to mobilize against youth as youth. The little incident of freshness by a son, suddenly isn't Johnny being confused at all; it becomes "one of those things modern youth want to do and we better show them where to get off". 5.Child and adult then view each other not as familiar persons, but as symbolic representatives of a hostile group.

6, As children become teenagers, parents often fear what the neighbours may say, and so they are unable to allow the youngster to behave in ways that might be quite temporary and normal for him at that particular time, 7, This fear is perhaps strongest in small communities where everyone knows everyone else. 8. Studies have shown that small-town adolescent girls, on the average, experience more conflict with their parents than any other adolescent group, a fact that is associated with the tendency of their fathers to be stricter with them. 9. At times and in places where the misdeeds of teenagers are magnified out of all proportion as they are in the scares of juvenile delinquency that sweep across many a community, even the most innocent mistake of a teenager may be exaggerated into a portent of ominous significance that seriously blocks communication between the generations.

11. Teenagers feel differently about their parents than they did as children, or than they will as they become adults. 11. A child's love for his or her parents is a dependent, appreciative, even enthusiastic kind of devotion. 12. Adolescent feeling for parents is normally less vocally affectionate, and more openly critical than it has been before or will be again. 13. Mark Twain observed that when he was sixteen he could not understand how his father could be so stupid ; by the time he reached twenty-one, he was amazed at how much the old man had learned In the past five years!'

**Exercises** (on 97 above)
**I**
<u>Paragraph 1</u>
1) Is there a topic sentence in the first paragraph? If so, which one is it?
2) Which sentences develop the idea in the topic sentence?
3) How is Sentence 4 related to the topic sentence?
4) What is the pattern of organization in paragraph 1?
5) Summarize the paragraph in about 30 words.
<u>Paragraph 2</u>
6) Does Paragraph 2 have a topic sentence? If so, which one is it?
7) Is the idea in it elaborated before or afterwards? In which sentences?
8) What is the relationship of Sentence 6 with the text around it?
9) What is the pattern of organization in paragraph 2?
10) Summarize the paragraph in 30-40 words.
<u>Paragraph 3</u>
11) Is there a topic sentence in Paragraph 3? If so, which one is it?
12) Is Sentence 13 important to a summary of the paragraph? Why?
13) What is the pattern of organization in paragraph 3?
14) Summarize the paragraph in about 30 words.

15) Combine your answers to Questions 4, 8 and 11 to make a summary of the entire passage.

**II** **A.** From the following options choose the **most appropriate** title for your summary:
a) Parents and Adolescents
b) Attitudes of Teenagers and their Parents
c) The Generation Gap
d) Understanding Mark Twain's Experience

**B.** For each of the options **not chosen** indicate the reason by choosing from the options indicated below, to say whether the title was
i. too broad;
ii. too narrow (i.e., covering only part of the passage/ summary)
iii. not in the spirit of the passage/ summary
iv. irrelevant to the topic of the passage/ summary.
v. too vague

## 98

To begin with, in a primitive society, men satisfied their wants by means of barter, which was the simple exchange of goods between two individuals. This method involved two men meeting, each of whom had something to offer which the other wanted. The chances of such a meeting taking place were poor, and a society which lived by barter was poor. Its economy made little progress, and the variety of goods available was narrow. Man studied this problem and eventually invented money. So, the first function of money is to act as a medium of exchange. That, after all, is the purpose of all work by men: to build up a surplus of goods and services which they do not want to consume themselves, in order to exchange them for other goods and services which they do want and the sellers do not want. In other words, money has no intrinsic value. There may be such a person as a real miser who gets pleasure out of counting his money and gloating over it, but the ordinary man wants money merely to enable him to buy the things he needs to make life worth living.

Let us repeat that very important remark. Money has no value in itself. It is what money will buy that matters. That is what we mean by the purchasing power of money. If our money buys us only a few of the things we want, we are poor. If it buys us a lot of these things, we are relatively well off. These remarks may seem statements of the obvious, but many people do not appreciate their significance. That is why economists speak of the monetary illusion or the veil of money. Most men measure their wealth by the number of pounds which are contained in their pay-packets or which stand to their credit at the bank, and not by the goods and services which they can purchase with their money.

One of the biggest and most important tasks that the economists has, is to educate the general public in the true function and meaning of money. If we can get people to understand what money really is, we have a background on which there is a direct change of building up a stable economy.

## Exercises

I       What are the patterns of organization in the three paragraphs?

II      Expand the following outline of the passage into a summary of about 135 words.

Barter in primitive society ------ Money a medium of exchange ------ No intrinsic value ----- worth only the goods and services it can buy -------- The purpose of all work: to produce surplus goods and services which can be exchanged for goods and services needed ------- a good credit in the bank a monetary illusion ---- proper understanding of the function of money by the public important to establishing a stable economy.

III     A. From the following options choose the **most appropriate** title for your summary:

a)     Money and Barter
b)     The Meaning of Money
c)     Money makes the Mare Go!
d)     The Importance of Money

    **B.** For each of the options **not chosen** indicate the reason by choosing from the options indicated below, to say whether the title was

i.     too broad in scope.
ii.    too narrow (i.e., covering only part of the passage/ summary).
iii.   not in the spirit of the passage/ summary.
iv.   irrelevant to the topic of the passage/ summary.
v.    too vague.

# Narrative Writing

**99**     The silence of the Reference Library was broken only by an occasional cough and now and then by the scarcely audible sound of pages being turned over. There were about twenty people in the room, most of them with their heads bent over their books. The assistant librarian who was in charge of the room sat at a desk in one corner. She glanced at Philip as he came in, then went on with her work.

Philip had not been to this part of the library before. He walked around the room almost on tiptoe, afraid of disturbing the industrious readers with his heavy shoes. The shelves were filed with thick volumes: dictionaries in many languages, encyclopaedias, atlases, biographies and other works of reference. He found nothing that was likely to interest him, until he came to a small section on photography, which was one of his hobbies. The books in this section were on a high shelf out of his reach, so he had to fetch a small ladder in order to get one down. Unfortunately, as he was climbing down the ladder, the book he had chosen slipped from his grasp and fell to the floor with a loud crash. Twenty pairs of eyes looked up at him simultaneously annoyed by this unaccustomed disturbance. Philip felt himself go red as he picked up his book, which did not seem to have been damaged by its fall.

He had just sat down when he found the young lady assistant standing alongside him. "You must be more careful when you are handling these books", she said severely. Satisfied that she had done her duty, she turned to go back to her desk. Then a sudden thought struck her. "By the way, how old are you?" she asked Philip. "Thirteen," he told her. "You're not allowed in here under the age of fourteen, you know?" the assistant said. "Didn't you see the notice on the door?" Phillip shook his head. He expected the assistant to ask him to leave, Instead, in a more kindly tone, she said: "Well, never mind. But make sure that you don't disturb the other readers again, otherwise I shall have to ask you to leave."

## Exercises

I     For each of the paragraphs in the passage, pick out the actions or ideas from those listed below, that are important to include in a summary of the passage. (Select a total **of about ten** points only.):

*Paragraph 1:*
a)     There was silence in the Reference Library.
b)     Somebody coughed.
c)     Twenty people were busy reading.
d)     The assistant librarian sat in a corner.
e)     She glanced at Philip.

*Paragraph 2:*
a) Philip was new to the library.
b) He walked on tip - toe.
c) He tried not to disturb the readers.
d) The library was full of reference books.
e) There was a section on photography.
f) Philip liked photography.
g) He used a ladder to reach the books.
h) The book he had chosen fell with a crash.
i) Philip was embarrassed.
j) The book was not damaged.

*Paragraph 3:*
a) The assistant librarian scolded Philip.
b) She asked him his age.
c) Children under fourteen were not allowed to use the library.
d) Philip had not read the notice.
e) She did not ask him to leave.
f) She spoke to him kindly.
g) She was happy that he showed interest in reading.
h) She asked him not to disturb the readers again.

**II** Use the selected points to write a summary of not more than 100 words.

**III** **A.** From the following options choose the **most appropriate** title for your summary:
a) The Silence in the Library
b) Philip in the Reference Library
c) Philip's Interest in Photography
d) Breaking the Rules of the Library

**B.** For each of the options **not chosen** indicate the reason by choosing from the options indicated below, to say whether the title was
i. too broad in scope.
ii. too narrow (i.e., covering only part of the passage/ summary).
iii. not in the spirit of the passage/ summary.
iv. irrelevant to the topic of the passage/ summary.
v. too vague.

**100**      Although I had ridden in many international races, I had never been so excited as I was at the thought of this village competition. Every year there was a big show at the village which included all sorts of competitions-from a beauty competition to horse racing. It was extremely popular, and among the competitors were people of all ages.

My host had offered to lend me his horse. Although it was not trained, it had speed and I liked riding on it. For me the race had an added attraction. A neighbour of my host's was also competing, and he had said that his horse would beat mine.

When we arrived at the racecourse, a running race was in progress. Half a dozen runners were running round the course. There had been some delay, and we were told that our race would begin after some time. I went to look at my horse. While I was looking at it the neighbour came up, riding his horse. His horse looked like a real racehorse, and I felt he would easily beat me.

Soon it was time for our race. Eight horses with riders came up to the start. We all started faultlessly. Before we had covered half the course, the neighbour was in the lead; I was third. At the end of the second round-we had to do four-the neighbour still had the advantage. But soon it was clear that his horse had given of its best and was now tired. With every step it seemed to slow down. Now the probability of the neighbour beating me was not so high. In the meantime, I had shortened the distance between me and the rider in front, and by the end of the third round the neighbour had fallen into second position. Soon he and I were running second, with the leader a few metres ahead of us. Now I knew that I would beat the neighbour, and with luck I might even win the race. I had already improved my position further, with the neighbour now coming third, and my horse just a couple of metres behind the first horse. Bending low in my saddle, I just touched my horse with the stick, and it shot forward. I could now hear the horse in front breathing hard. As we straightened after the last curve, we were running neck and neck. Then, before I knew what had happened, I was ahead, with the finishing line rushing to meet us. I had won the race.

## Exercises
I      Combine your answers to the following questions to write a summary of the passage in about 100 words:
a) What made the author participate in the village race?
b) How many riders competed with him?
c) What was the author's position at halfway?
d) When and why did the author feel more confident of beating his neighbour in the race?
e) What happened in the final lap of the race?

II    **A.** From the following options **choose the most appropriate title** for your summary:
- (A) The Village Race
- (B) A Horse Race
- (C) Slow and Steady Wins the Race
- (D) Steady Wins the Race

**B.** For each of the options **not chosen** indicate the reason by choosing from the options indicated below, to say whether the title was

a. too broad in scope.
b. too narrow (i.e., covering only part of the passage/ summary).
c. not in the spirit of the passage/ summary.
d. irrelevant to the topic of the passage/ summary.
e. too vague.

**101** It was already late when we set out for the next town, which according to the map was about fifteen miles away on the other side of the hills. There we felt sure that we would find a bed for the night. Darkness fell soon after we left the village, but luckily, we met no one as we drove swiftly along the narrow winding road that led to the hills. As we climbed higher, it became colder and rain began to fall, making it difficult at times to see the road. I asked John, my companion, to drive more slowly.

After we had travelled for about twenty miles, there was still no sign of the town which was marked on the map. We were beginning to get worried. Then, without warning, the car stopped. A quick examination showed that we had run out of petrol. Although we had little food with us, only a few biscuits and some chocolate, we decided to spend the night in the car.

Our meal was soon over. I tried to go to sleep at once, but John, who was a poor sleeper, got out of the car after a few minutes and went for a walk up the hill. Soon he came running back. From the top of the hill he had seen, in the valley below, the lights of the town we were looking for. We at once unloaded all our luggage and, with a great effort, managed to push the car to the top of the hill. Then we went back for the luggage, loaded the car again and set off down the hill. In less than a quarter of an hour we were in the town, where we found a hotel quite easily.

### Exercises
I    Write a summary of the passage by identifying the following:
- the expectation of the travellers
- their problems
- altered expectations
- chance solution

**II**    **A.** From the following options **choose the most appropriate title** for your summary:

a) Journey in the Hills
b) An Adventurous Night
c) Adventure across the Hills
d) An Exciting Journey

**B** For each of the options **not chosen** indicate the reason by choosing from the options below, to say whether the title was

i.   too broad in scope.
ii.  too narrow (i.e., covering only part of the passage/ summary).
iii. not in the spirit of the passage/ summary.
iv.  irrelevant to the topic of the passage/ summary.
v.   too vague.

## Informative/ Reflective Writing

**102**     1.There are certain birds which show preference for the society of man and take advantage of his curious activities to make their habitations in the neighbourhood of his own. 2. Of these the robin is the most intimate. 3. The reason for the universal recognition of the robin in England is not merely his friendships or indifference to the presence of man but his strong personality. 4. He is striking in his way of coming into the open, in the jubilance and forthrightness of his song when other birds are silent, in his staccato (jerky) movements, in his bold and colourful dress and in his character to match it. 5. It is his original departure from the timidity characteristic of the race of small birds which endears him to us and invites us to woo him ---- especially with the irresistible bait of the meal worm --- to familiarities which we can achieve with no other species. 6. His alarm note is as explosive as his nature and sounds like the tocking of a grandfather clock. 7. The song is unlike that of any other singing bird, and follows no set pattern, being at once ringing, exultant and full of timbre, but at the same time a kind of thoughtful recitative, with a beautiful undersong. 8. The robin nests almost anywhere and in anything from a tin kettle to a hole in a tree or bank. 9. Five or six eggs, white in ground colour, with freckles of light red, are id in a roughish nest of dead leaves, grass and moss interwoven with hair and a few feathers.
(260 words)

**Exercises**

1.    A What is the overall topic of the passage? Choose **any one** from the following answers:
a)    Certain birds
b)    All about the robin
c)    The robin's strong personality
d)    The habits of the robin

2.    B In the exercise above consider the answers which you **did not** select. Say whether each of these
i)    was too general a phrase.
ii)    stated an unimportant aspect.
iii)    was irrelevant.
iv)    gave a partial theme.
v)    stated an incorrect theme.

3.    Considering that the passage is about the robin, which sentence introduces the bird?

4.    What does Sentence 2 say about the robin? That it is
a)    loved by all
b)    the tiniest bird
c)    the cleverest bird
d)    the most playful bird

5    How is the idea in Sentence 1 related to the idea in Sentence 2? Is Sentence 1
a)    an example of the robin's intimateness?
b)    an introduction to the robin's popularity
c)    an elaboration of the robin's popularity

6.    Express Sentence 1 briefly within 10 words.
7.    Now express the ideas in Sentences 1 and 2 together in about 15 words.
8.    What is the main point of S. 3? Express it as briefly as possible (in about 10 words).
9.    Can any of Sentences 1, 2 or 3 be called the topic sentence? Or would they help in formulating the topic sentence?
10.    Which other sentences give more information about his "strong personality"?

**11.** Which word in Sentence 4 describes a quality of the robin's character, which is reflected in the following instances of his description/ behaviour:
- His way of coming into the open
- The forthrightness of his song
- His bold and colourful dress
- His staccato movements
- His character to match
- His alarm note as explosive as his nature

**12.** Combine the important ideas in Sentences 4 – 7 as briefly as possible.

**13.** What are the important ideas in Ss.8 – 9. Underline 5 crucially important words which indicate these ideas. Choose the words carefully.

**14.** Which details in Ss. 8 – 9 are interesting to read about but not important for the summary?

**15.** Combine the important ideas in the last two sentences within 20 words.

**16.** What is the pattern of organization in the paragraph ?

**17.** Combine your answers to Questions 7, 8, 11 and 14 to form a summary.

**18.** Fill in the blanks in the following model summary of the passage and compare this completed passage with your own:
Of the birds which enjoy ----1---- society the robin is the most ---2--- in England because he has a ---3--- personality, revealed in his ----4----. He is colourful in dress and ---5--- and fearless in song and ---6---. His song is free and vibrant with a ---7--- undersong. His warning note is explosive like his ---8---. He lays freckled ---9--- in a rough nest which he builds almost ----10---.


**103** 1. War is a terrible evil, and it is right that a sense of the miseries it brings upon the earth should be constantly present to our minds.
2. There are, however, evils, such as slavery or oppression, which are greater still, and in our country any man of courage and spirit would rather die than submit to a foreign yoke. 3. We would no more think of admitting an invader to our shores than of allowing a burglar or murderer to force a way into our homes. 4. We feel strongly the duty and necessity of self-defence against attack, no matter what the odds against us.

5. It may, again, be necessary to fight a preventive war, to go out and attack our enemy while he is still far off, not waiting till he is knocking at our gates, to keep our country safe from him. 6. We must never let our innate love of peace be an excuse for indolence, or wavering of purpose, or a shirking of the burden we must bear to assure ourselves of the blessings of freedom.

7. Finally, we have often fought, and must inevitably fight again, to assist the weak and oppressed, even when we ourselves remain unmolested with no storms looming ahead. 8. When some signal crime or wickedness is disgracing the civilized world, we must gird on our armour and go forth like the knights of olden times in defence of the weak, in singleness of purpose, not counting the cost. 9. Such a cause, when we are entirely disinterested in the material sense, is surely the noblest of all in which to take up war.

(266 words)

## Exercises

1. Which **one** of the following statements **best** conveys the gist of the passage?
a) War is a terrible evil that we should avoid.
b) Wars are fought for many reasons.
c) We have fought many wars.
d) War is terrible but sometimes necessary.
e)

2. In the exercise above consider the statements that you **did not select**. Say whether each of these
i. was too general a statement.
ii. stated an unimportant point.
iii. was irrelevant.
iv. gave a partial summary.
v. made an untrue statement.

3. What are the two important ideas in the gist of the passage and which sentences in the express these ideas elaborately?

4. What are the three greater evils mentioned than the miseries of war? Mention each in a word or phrase. Which transitional devices are used to demarcate them?

5. Is there a pattern of organization used for the whole passage? What is it?

6. What is the overall term expressed in Sentence 2 that includes all these three reasons justifying war? Mention in one word only.

7. What kind of war becomes necessary to maintain our freedom?
8. What excuse is used to avoid this kind of war?
9. What are the real reasons for avoiding it? Express these in your own words.
10. Which are the noblest reasons for fighting a war?
11. Why is such a war noble?
12. Summarize the passage by combining your answers to Questions 3, 5, 6, 7, 9 and 10
13. Mention some of the colourful ideas in the second, third and fourth paragraphs that become superfluous to the summary.
14. Fill in the blanks in the following model summary of the passage and compare this completed passage with your own under Ex. 12:

War is a great evil but --1--- and oppression under a foreign yoke are ---2-- and we should prefer death to either. ---3----- in self-defence at any cost is necessary. We may, ----4-----, need to go to war to prevent an enemy --5----. Avoiding such a war by making an ----6----- of our love for peace is wrong for our ------7---- is most precious. Again, fighting for the ----8--- and the downtrodden when outraged, irrespective of ---9----- or material advantage is the noblest of all ---10----.

**104** There are two kinds of popularity which I will call intimate and long distance- popularity, and the first is Far more real than the second. A man who is intimately popular is liked by those who know him; a man who is popular at long distance has, by some means, succeeded in propagating a favourable notion of himself among those who do not know him. The two kinds of popularity may go together, but often they are separate, and the man who enjoys long-distance popularity is disliked at close quarters.

Intimate popularity is always a proof of some virtues. If a man is disliked by those who meet him, he may have many defects and even vices, but still he is liked for a cause, even though it be unknown to those who like him. His society gives pleasure and it does so because he himself takes pleasure in the society of others, which means that he is disposed to like rather than dislike them. It is to him a pleasure to meet those he has never met before; he expects to find them good company and therefore is good company himself. He is ready to take risks in social intercourse and will not wait to discover whether you are a bore before he opens out to you. He is, in fact, sanguine about human nature, and we like those who are sanguine especially about ourselves, more than those who despond; they fill us with their own vitality and make us sharers in their own enjoyment.

may say that this easy instinctive liking is slight virtue; but it is a virtue, for it makes you happy. It is better to like people for no particular reason than to like them without reason, better to make them happy than to make them miserable. The man who is intimately popular may be vain, but he is not an egotist – he is more interested in others than in himself; he enjoys, no doubt, the exercise of his social arts, but that is worth enjoying; he is a hedonist, but one who gives pleasure to others.

**Exercises**

I    What patterns of organization are used in each of the three paragraphs?

II    Combine your answers to the following questions into a summary of about 100 words:

What are the two kinds of popularity?

Which one is preferred and why?

What are the seven reasons given to justify the virtues of intimate popularity?

# Semi-Scientific/ Semi-Technical Writing

Articles in daily use which are made of 'plastics' are familiar to all; for example combs, toothbrushes, beer-bottle stoppers, picnic cups and saucers, the telephone, films, ashtrays and toys. In addition, the industrial uses of these materials are widespread, since they take their place in the manufacture of electrical instruments and accessories, radio sets, gears, bearings, lacquers and varnishes. The name 'plastics' is, at first sight, something of a paradox, since the characteristic property of the articles made from these materials is that they retain their shape and are by no means 'plastic' as we know and handle them. However, in the course of manufacturing the article, the material from which it is made is capable of being made to flow, under the influence of heat and pressure; hence under suitable conditions it was once plastic, but it retains its shape permanently when restored to natural conditions.

As may be gathered from this, the bulk of plastic articles is made by the process known as moulding. This operation is carried out in special presses, such that the moulds can be heated as the pressure is applied, followed by cooling after moulding is completed.

The wide range of industrial plastics can be broadly divided into two categories, the thermo-plastic and the thermo-setting products. Thermo-plastic materials can be softened and re-softened repeatedly by the application of heat and pressure, provided they are not heated to such an extent that chemical decomposition takes place. Thermo-setting plastics undergo chemical change when subjected to heat and pressure. This converts them into an infusible and insoluble condition, so that they cannot be further re-formed by the application of more heat and pressure.

*Knight & MacAlpine*

The planet we live on is not just a ball of inert material. During past ages dramatic changes have taken place inside the earth. Indeed, it is likely that without these changes life could never have originated on the earth. And changes are still going on today. They show themselves in the occurrence of earthquakes, in the outbursts of volcanoes, and in the uplift of mountain ranges.

In outward appearance, the earth is a nearly spherical ball with a radius of 6,350 kilometres. Internally the earth consists of two parts, a core and a mantle. An essential difference is that the core consists mainly of liquid and the mantle mainly of solid rock. The core extends outwards from the centre to a distance of some 3,450 kilometres. The mantle, as its name shows, is an outer covering extending from the core to the surface of the earth.

Judged by ordinary standards, the core is made of rather dense stuff. The material at the centre of the earth is at least thirteen times as heavy as ordinary water, while in the outer parts of the core the material is about ten times as heavy as ordinary water.

The mantle possesses a thin outer crust that is exceptional in being composed of[1] a particularly light kind of rock, with a density about 2·7 times that of water. (Compare this with a density of 13 at the centre of the earth.) Over the continents of the world this crustal rock is about thirty-five kilometres thick, while over the oceans it is at most only two or three kilometres thick. Below the crustal layer comes a different, denser rock, probably of a basic silicate variety.[2] Indeed it seems likely that, apart from the thin outer crust, the rocks of the whole mantle are of a basic silicate variety right down to the junction with the core, at a depth below the surface of about 2,900 kilometres.

*Fred Hoyle*

## Exercises (on 105)
I       What is the overall topic? What would be a suitable title for the passage?
II      What are the topic sentences in each paragraph? (These may be stated in the passage or you may need to formulate them.)
III     What patterns of organisation are used in each paragraph? (The transitional signals will help you to confirm your answers.
IV      Summarize the passage in about 120 words by combining your answers to the following questions:
a)      What is the paradox about plastic materials?
b)       briefly the moulding process.
c)      Describe briefly the two kinds of industrial plastics.


## Exercises (on 106):
I       What is the overall topic? What would be a suitable title for the passage?
II      What patterns of organisation are used in each paragraph? (The transitional signals will help you to confirm your answers.)
III     What are the topic sentences in each paragraph? (These may be stated in the paragraph or you may need to formulate them.)
IV      Expand the topic sentences to combine into a summary of about 120 words


## Exercises on 107 (overleaf)
I       What is the overall topic? What would be a suitable title for the passage?
II      What patterns of organisation are used in each paragraph? (The transitional signals will help you to confirm your answers.)
III     Summarize the passage in about 250 words by combining your answers to the following questions:
a)      What makes chromosomes carriers of heredity?
b)      How do DNA molecules carry the code for the vital functions of cells?
c)      What are the three properties of DNA?
d)      How did Crick and Watson explain the process of self-duplication?
e)      Explain briefly the process of self-reproduction within the organism in terms of DNA molecules?

## (Passage 107 overleaf)

In recent years some *insight* has been gained into the chemical composition and structure of the *chromosomes*; for the first time, consequently, we have an *inkling* of how they *function* as carriers of *heredity*. Apparently the most important *constituent* of the chromosome is an extraordinary chemical substance known as *DNA* (Deoxyribonucleic Acid). The *molecules* of this substance are long stringlike *fibers*. Because they are bundled into chromosomes, these fibers can be *apportioned* in an orderly way at each cell division; in the absence of such *packaging*, the cell nucleus would resemble a thread factory operated without *spools*. DNA molecules are frequently compared to the *tapes* that control modern business machines, because it is almost certain that the physical structure of DNA fibers does indeed carry the code for all of the *vital functions* performed within living, growing and dividing cells.

The incredible efficiency of the DNA coded tape can be illustrated by saying that all of the chromosomes present initially in the *fertilized* eggs from which the present population of the world (some two and a half billion people) developed would occupy a volume about equal to that of an ordinary *aspirin tablet*. In addition, DNA has a further *property* not shared by any man-made tape: its structure is such that by attracting to itself the relatively simple chemical substances of which it is composed and which are present within cells, it can make a *complementary* copy of itself. Because of its chemical structure and the *spatial* relations between the constituent molecular parts, it is capable of self-*duplication*, correct in every detail.

Of what use is a complementary copy, a mirror image of a molecule? The answer to this question reveals another remarkable property of the DNA molecule. As shown recently by J. D. Watson and F. H. C. Crick, the structure of DNA consists of two chains which are complementary copies of one another. Separate these chains, let each build a mirror image, and you have two molecules of DNA where you originally had one. And the two new molecules are precisely the same in structure!

Self-duplication is, of course, the basis of life. We see it *on a grand scale*[1] by watching the multiplication of living things. But self-*reproduction* must happen within organisms, on a molecular level, as well. The newly-fertilized egg divides over and over again. At each division both daughter cells get a full *complement* of forty-six chromosomes, but the repeated division of these chromosomes does not mean that the chromosomes get smaller and smaller. The process of 'division', or *mitosis*, is actually one of duplication or *replication*. With the possible exception of the first few divisions of the egg, development involves growth—the manufacture of *proteins* and *enzymes*, and the construction of new molecules of DNA. Each of the 46 human chromosomes attracts to itself the material necessary to make an exact *duplicate* of itself—a duplicate whose precise similarity to the original is guaranteed by the chemical structure of the DNA molecule. Only then does the cell divide.

# Summarize the passages (108 - 115), which follow, in your own words without the aid of questions.

## 108

A radical change in the eating habits of the Japanese in the post-war years has been a dominant factor in inducting changes in the country's agriculture, to the mutual benefit of both producer and consumer. Traditionally, the staple diet in Japan was based on rice, fish and vegetables. Today, stimulated by Western ideas about food, and the inadequate supplies of fish resulting from over-fishing in home waters, the Japanese have acquired a taste for a more varied diet, including meat, eggs, milk and dairy produce. It has led to a spectacular expansion of livestock production, and the development of mixed farming, which is more profitable than the former cropping routine of rice, wheat and barley.

In ten years' time the total value of the livestock output in Japan should represent one-third of the total agricultural production, and will be equivalent in value to the production of rice. By then, the demand for meat will have risen to five times the present level.

This vast program of livestock development is based on a policy of pasture improvement concentrated increasingly in the uplands, where rice cultivation cannot be carried out. In a country with little or no experience in grassland management, the difficulties involved in building a new industry to produce meat and milk from grass on such a scale must have appeared truly formidable. However, the Japanese tackled the problem systematically, and with the aid of the UN Food and Agriculture Organization have spent the past six years in intensive study, comparing "cut and carry" methods of utilizing pasture herbage with various grazing techniques, testing local and foreign types of grass and clover, and training technicians and advisory staff. To overcome the limitation imposed by the distance of upland pastures from the villages, and the difficulty of access, the Government has launched a road building program.

Now it seems that there are encouraging prospects of further development of the livestock industry in the plains and the valleys, for the introduction of new varieties of rice which mature in about 100 days instead of the normal 150 will release more land for pasture and fodder crops in areas where formerly only rice was grown.

The small size of the average farm – seven to eight acres – would have been a serious obstacle to these changes in farm practice, but industrialization, with its higher wages and promise of rapidly increasing living standards, is already attracting labour from the rural areas. A 35 – 40 percent fall in the farming population by 1970 is forecast. The resultant economic pressure to form larger farms will therefore favour crop diversification and mechanization.

R.A.Close               ( 450 words)

**(Passages 109 & 110 follow)**

[109]

Silence is unnatural to man. He begins life with a cry and ends it in stillness. In the interval he does all he can to make a noise in the world, and there are few things of which he stands in more fear than of the absence of noise. | Even his conversation is in great measure a desperate attempt to prevent a dreadful silence. If he is introduced to a fellow-mortal, and a number of pauses occur in the conversation, he regards himself as a failure, a worthless person, and is full of envy of the emptiest-headed chatterbox. He knows that ninety-nine per cent. of human conversation means no more than the buzzing of a fly, but he longs to join in the buzz, and to prove that he is a man and not a waxwork figure. | The object of conversation is not, for the most part, to communicate ideas: it is to keep up the buzzing sound. There are, it must be admitted, different qualities of buzz: there is the even buzz that is as exasperating as the continuous ping of a mosquito. But at a dinner party one would rather be a mosquito than a mute. | Most buzzing, fortunately, is agreeable to the ear, and some of it is agreeable even to the mind. He would be a foolish man, however, who waited till he had a wise thought to take part in the buzzing with his neighbours. | Those who despise the weather as a conversational opening seem to me to be ignorant of the reason why human beings wish to talk. Very few human beings join in a conversation in the hope of learning anything new. Some of them are content if they are merely allowed to go on making a noise into other people's ears, though they have nothing to tell them except that they have seen two or three new plays or that they had bad food in a Swiss hotel. | At the end of an evening during which they have said nothing at immense length they justly plume themselves on their success as conversationalists. |

350 words.

"Silence" from "The Money Box"
— Robert Lynd.

[110]

Sport and games are the possession of no one country or race. They belong to all countries from time immemorial. But sport, to use the term in its widest sense, is an older thing in Britain than elsewhere, with a more settled custom and a more generally accepted place in the national life. Because it is ancient it is an almost inevitable part of the average boy's upbringing. Even if he does not like games - and the average boy does like them - he is almost of necessity familiar with them during certain years of his life. Even he gives them up altogether when he grows up the familiarity remains, so that he unconsciously applies to the affairs of work-a-day life expressions which really belong to the language of sport. In fact sport is one of the most obvious features in the general background of life, and of all interests it is perhaps the one which is common to the greatest number of people of all classes. It is said that when the Briton buys a newspaper he turns first of all to the sporting pages. That is not true in times of political anxiety, but it is probably as true as are most generalizations in more easy-going times, and many of the names that figure on those pages are in the nature of household words. This does not necessarily imply any grave lack of a sense of proportion. It does not follow that he thinks sport the most important thing in life or that the man who has made a long score or won a big race is a greater man than the Prime Minister. It only means that he keeps a very warm corner in his heart for sport and that he likes to think about it and talk about it in his hours of ease. It is a definite part of his life which gives him much pleasure and interest, and it is a great and for the moment an absorbing contrast to work: but to say that it is all or anything like all in his life would be utterly unfair. Moreover, I think that modern youth has got in this matter a better sense of proportion than the generations that have preceded it, and has a better notion of the place that sport can justifiably occupy. |

**111**

The first quarter of the twentieth century witnessed rapid progress in breaking down prejudice against the education of women. The liberation of women from ignominy and suffering became an ever increasingly popular mission: Minna G. Cowan wrote in 1912, "One of the most interesting features in India today is the number of women's societies which are springing up, partly in conjunction with European ladies and partly by spontaneous effort." The Bharat Stri Mandal was founded in the United Provinces and Bengal; the aim was to establish a centre where women of every race, creed and political colour could work side by side for emancipation. In Bombay, the Gujrati Stri Mandal devoted considerable energy to the abolition of purdah in order that the women might associate with one another; it also drew up an ambitious programme of education. The Seva Sadan Society, established in Bombay in 1909, did much philanthropic and educational work. The National Indian Association, though administered from London, had many Indian women as Secretaries and committee members at its Indian branches. Perhaps one of its most effective activities was the organization of lectures and meetings to persuade women of the advantages of education. But for all who were actively concerned with these movements the task was a difficult one, especially as the strongest opposition came from the women themselves: G. K. Gokhale remarked in 1879 that a combination of enforced ignorance and overdone religion had not only made women in India willing victims of customs unjust and hurtful in the highest degree, but it also made them the most formidable and most effective opponents of all change and innovation.

Until the First World War, the reforming bodies were successful in bringing emancipation only to their own members. But the outbreak of war gave the movement impetus: hardly a congress or debating society existed which failed to give the problem its attention, hardly an Indian newspaper or journal failed to air the subject. Mrs. Annie Besant, who entered politics in 1914, delivered a memorable series of public lectures in Madras entitled 'Wake up, India!' in which she emphasized the need to abolish child marriage and to give every woman the opportunity of literacy. Later in 1927, she inspired the foundation and shared with Mrs. M. Cousins the leadership of the Women's Indian Association.

The first venture of the Women's Indian Association was to demand the enfranchisement of women. Later, the provisional governments granted women enfranchisement, and subsequently permitted them to enter the legislatures: in March 1921 the Madras Legislative Council passed a resolution which allowed women to be enrolled on the electoral register, and by 1926 every other provincial legislature had done likewise. Dr. S. Muthulakshmi Reddi was the first woman to come to a legislature, and also the first to be elected as the Vice-President of the Madras Legislative Council (1926 – 30).

Out of social revolution came political revolution. The All India Women's Conference entered the political arena in 1928 by pledging its support to the cause for independence, and by calling for equal rights for women, so that they might add their votes to the cause. Mahatma Gandhi encouraged women by saying "I am uncompromising in the matters for women's rights. In my opinion she should labour under no legal disability not suffered by man. I should treat daughters and sons on a footing of perfect equality." During the Second World War, the conscription of men into the military services and the rise in cost of living made it necessary for women to leave their homes to replace or supplement their men as breadwinners. Shocked into a consciousness of social and political reality, they became once again productive members of society. Many entered the women's military services or contributed in other ways to the war effort.

When India attained Independence in 1947, women came into their own. The principle of equality was incorporated into the Objective Resolution of Free India, Later Articles Fourteen and Fifteen of the section of the constitution on fundamental rights, guaranteed this equality: 'equality before law' and 'equality in matters of public employment'.

The major parties encouraged women to participate in politics by securing for them representation in the central and state legislatures. Many women now occupy seats in the state legislatures and both Houses of Parliament. Though the last chapters of the history of the social evolution of women in India have yet to be written, the adoption by parliament of the main sections of the Hindu Code Bill indicates that their completion is within sight.

(880 words)

**(Passage 112 – (2 sheets) - overleaf)**

Men have long known how important the sun is to them. There was a time when they worshipped it as a god. The light from the sun gives us day and enables us to see. The heat from the sun warms us and the earth. Without this heat, the earth would be too cold for us to live on.

The sun helps us to grow crops. The crops need its light and heat in order to grow and ripen. The sun also helps in making rain. Its heat falls on the water in rivers, lakes and oceans and warms some of the water so that it goes up into the air. When this happens, we say that the water evaporates. Although we do not notice this except in the dry season, much water evaporates like this all the time. Later it comes down from the air again as little drops, which we call rain.

Although the sun does all this, much of its light and heat go into the earth and thus get wasted. We can make use of this energy for our own purposes. We need heat to warm our houses, and to cook our food. We need heat to make steam for driving machines, and for making electricity. We need heat in big furnaces for melting metals in factories.

To get all this heat we have to burn some kind of fuel. In villages this fuel is often wood or dung. In factories and electric power stations it is usually coal or oil. Unfortunately many of us, particularly in the tropics, do not have all the fuel that we need. Coal and oil are especially scarce, because of this, men have wondered whether they could use some of the sun's heat instead of ordinary fuel. If we could only trap a little of all the heat reaching us from the sun, we would have all the energy we would ever need.

It is hard to imagine how much heat from the sun reaches us. On a sunny day in the tropics, an acre of ground receives an amount of heat equal to the power needed for running a small factory. In only two days, the whole earth receives from the sun enough heat to equal all the power that we could get from burning all the coal, oil, and underground gas which exists in the earth.

The difficulty is that this heat from the sun cannot be used without some machine to turn it into power or energy. What we therefore want is to trap and use some of this heat. However, this is not easy.

If we take a simple magnifying glass and use it to focus sunlight on to a small spot on a dry leaf, the leaf soon catches fire. This is not because of the suns light, but because of its heat. This heat is in the sunlight, although we cannot see it. The magnifying glass focuses the heat at the same time that is focuses the light. All the heat passing through the magnifying glass is brought to the bright spot where we focus on the leaf. Therefore, the small spot gets much heat from the sun than it would otherwise. In fact, it gets so much heat that it burns.

This is one way of trapping some heat from the sun. By focussing its light on to a single spot we can make things very hot. With big, curved, metal mirrors we can focus sunlight on to boilers containing water. The water then gets increasingly hot, until it boils and turns into steam. We can then use this steam to drive a steam engine. More than a hundred years ago, in 1876, an Englishman built a machine of this kind in Bombay. Thirty years later another such machine was built in Egypt. It had very big large mirrors that turned as the sun moved across the sky, and kept sunlight focused on a boiler. This made the steam intended for driving pumps to take water from the Nile into the surrounding land. Unfortunately this machine was never used. Today a machine of the same kind has been built in Israel.

**113**
The actual course of human evolution before the dawn of history is traced chiefly by the tools and ornaments left by man, but also, though to a much smaller extent, by actual human remains in the shape of bones. Through these latter we know that in the early days of man's existence – the Taungs man-ape, the ape-man of Java, the Heidelberg man, Neanderthal man - all of which have now become sapiens. These extinct men were on the whole more apelike than we and represent so many unsuccessful side-lines in evolution.

From the evidence of tools, especially flint instruments, we can trace man's progress more in detail. First came the crude objects known as coliths – flints serviceable. Then, in the Old Stone Age, they were definitely shaped, but never polished. In the New Stone Age, they were polished too; but though bone was widely used, we get never a trace of metals.

Then began the age of metals, first with bronze and then with iron; and with that we are at the beginning of recorded history. What is interesting is to find that progress becomes more and more rapid as time goes on. We may date the earliest known flint implement at something like half a million years ago. At least three-quarters, probably nine-tenths, of that time had passed before man learnt to polish his flints. The age of bronze started perhaps ten thousand years ago, as apparently did the earliest agriculture. Practically all history is crowded into five thousand years, while the last thousand alone have been responsible for a whole host of fundamental inventions like printing, flying, wireless, and the control over bacterial diseases. From man's first beginnings until the present, the rate of progress has been growing more and more rapid; and there are no signs that it is slackening now. Humanity is biologically still youthful.

Once the human type of mind originated, it brought with it speech and as a result, permanent tradition, first by means of writing and later by printing. Through tradition man comes to differ fundamentally from all other organisms; for tradition provides a new method of inheritance, which stimulates the inheritance of acquired characteristics and makes  passing on to later generations of the results of learning and of training. It is on tradition that the social environment depends, and what we call human progress has almost all been progress in our tradition.

(400 words)

## 114     Dieters' Club'

It is a dieter's favourite fantasy. Puddings and fry-up that aren't either drenched in caloric-packed fats or taste like aerated cardboard; a way to get the rich creamy taste of fats without the associated health and waistline penalties. It's a dream with a price tag of $200m – that's what the food and household products giant Procter and Gamble (P&G) has spent on trying to transform it into a reality and now it looks as though their American division might be about to succeed.

However, there are those who believe that if they do, far from ushering in a dieter's heaven, this could be the beginning of a nightmare. Not only that, but our current fat-phobia has led to widespread and unhealthy confusion about what is and is not safe to eat. Far from promoting health there is plenty of evidence that low-fat foods just make matters worse.

The fat-vanishing trick that P&G hope to pull off is performance by an oil called Olestra which has had its molecules tinkered with so that it passes straight through the gut, leaving not a calorie behind. But because unlike other low-fat products, it actually contains fat molecules, it has the all-important "mouth-feel" of fat and it can also be heated to the high temperature needed for frying without breaking down.

After years of deliberation, the American Food and Drug Administration looks set to grant it an initial licence to be used in savoury snacks – a prospect that fills many nutrition experts, including Myra Karstadt of Ralph Nader's Centre for Science in the Public Interest, with alarm. Earlier, she took the unusual step of sending documents explaining precisely why to UK's ministry of agriculture, which is considering it for approval and to British food campaigning group. "It would be a huge uncontrolled experiment with public health. It is just not worth the risk, she says.

Her concern centres on the way the fat-like Olestra absorbs fat-soluble vitamins and nutrients and then rushes them out of the body. Carotenoids, the nutrients found in vegetables that many researchers now believe boost the immune system and protect against some cancers, are especially vulnerable. "A third of a bag of Olestra-cooked potato chips could leach out 40 percent of your lycopene, which is used by the prostate gland," says Karstadt.

But the real interest of the battle over Olestra is that it raises the whole issue of fat in our diet and whether the lucrative commercial attempts to reduce it aren't a huge mistake.

In food engineering terms, Olestra is a genuine break-through. Reducing fat and keeping food palatable is a tricky business. Most of the low-fat products that beckon to us from the supermarket shelves are produced by tinkering with existing foodstuffs. Something called Simplesse, found in salad-dressings and cakes, consists of concentrated whey protein chopped up into microscopic balls. McDonald's, for instance, uses an extract of red algae in their reduced-fat hamburgers. But none of them is terribly convincing.

This doesn't stop the food engineers from trying. Waiting in the wings for a licence are such delights as Salatrim and Caprenin, both poorly absorbed by the body, so 40 percent less in calories, but both high in harmful saturated fats.

The trouble is that we have no way of knowing what these chemical marvels are doing to us. Karstadt's point about artificial food constituting a public health experiment is echoed by the eminent nutritionist Joan Dyegussow.

"We don't even fully understand what fibre does and we have been researching it since the beginning of the century", she says. "For instance, we think oat bran helps to reduce cholesterol because it has soluble fibre. But rice bran is just as effective, and it has no soluble fibre. So, what hope have we of predicting the effect of food that have only been around for a few years?"

Not only that, but when it comes to helping weight loss, low-fat foods don't seem to do the business. Prof. Barbara J Rolls of the Johns Hopkins University School of Medicine gave healthy volunteers either a high-fat or a low-fat lunch without revealing which was which. They were free to eat whatever they wanted the rest of the day. On low fat days, the subjects had made up the calorie difference by dinner time.

When dieters consciously have something low in fat they feel freer to have a little treat later. In one recent study, dieters who knew that they had eaten a low-fat yoghurt ate more at lunch than those who thought it was an ordinary one. In fact, as researchers at the Chemical Senses Centre in Philadelphia found, the problem with fat-substitutes is that people who eat them still want fat, so as soon as the diet has stopped or their guard is down, it is the full-fat things they turn to. On the other hand, people who cut out both high and low-fat substitute foods and go for naturally lower fat foods such as bread, vegetables and fruit, reduce their craving.

But does fat deserve its unhealthy reputation? Certainly children, major consumers of savoury snacks such as crisps, need it. A recent issue of Nutrition Today warned that avoiding giving certain foods to children because they had a high fat content could lead to nutritional deficits". What's more, a recent study at McGill University in Montreal, Canada, found that reducing saturated fat in the diet to recommended levels may add no more than three extra months to life, and possibly as little as an extra 3.5 days.

A venerable fat heretic, Dr. Malcolm Caruthers, believes the interaction between stress, hormones and cholesterol is far more influential in determining blood-fat levels. "It's not so much a question of what you are eating," he says, "but what's eating you." Yet another perspective comes from Dr. Arteni Simopoulos, director of the Centre for Genetics, Nutrition and Health in Washington.

She has amassed evidence to show that it is your genes that determines whether you need to worry about fat. "If you come from a family with no history of major diseases you should feel comfortable about eating anything you fancy. There is no reason to avoid eggs, butter or red meat, say, providing that you don't become overweight.

(Courtesy: The Times of India)                                          (1,000 words)

## 115

**Report of a Conference** at the National Physical Laboratory, Teddington 26th – 28th June 1961           By Dr. B. Wheeler Robinson

a)     As more people live closer together, and as they use machine to produce leisure, they find that their leisure, and even their working hours, become spoilt by a by-product of their machines – namely, noise. Noise is nowadays in the news; it has acquired political status, and public opinion is demanding, more and more insistently, that something must be done about it. So it was very appropriate that many people professionally interested in noise control should meet to discuss their common problems at a large-scale conference.

b)     In the three days of the Conference at Teddington, 25 papers were presented; and faced with the pile of texts, whose contents range from sophisticated aerodynamics to general comments on the irritation expressed by neighbours, it is difficult to sort out the new ideas which will be active in one's mind six months from now, from the big mass of valuable knowledge and fact which will remain on the shelves for reference.

c) This difficulty was faced by Mr. D.W. Robinson, head of the acoustics work at the National Physical Laboratory. His introduction elaborated the general idea that noise must be considered in relation to the social organism which produces it. Sound becomes annoying noisy only when someone's opinion has made it so. In terms of energy it is an undesired by-product, often an exceedingly small fraction of the main output of the machine or process which produces it, and correspondingly difficult to reduce significantly. (A jet engine converts perhaps only 1/10,000 of its power into sound; to make it acoustically unnoticeable, this fraction would have to become 1/10,000,000) To control noise is going to demand much self-discipline (annoyance arises often from lack of common courtesy and imagination), a sense of proportion (there is usually a conflict of interest if a noise is to be stopped), the expenditure of money (and it is far more economical to do this early rather than late), and, finally, technical knowledge.

d) Technical difficulties often arise from the subjective-objective nature of the problem. You can define the excessive speed of a motor car in terms of a pointer reading on a speedometer. But can you define excessive noise in the same way? The results of several large-scale experiments, involving numbers of vehicles and of listeners, show how difficult it is to fix any instrumental reading as a legal limit in a way which satisfies most of the public, and yet is fair to the vehicle owner. You find, for example, that with any existing simple "noisemeter", vehicles which are judged to be equally noise by a jury may show considerable difference on the meter.

e) A group of papers dealt with noise at the source – the basic origins of noise in gears, internal combustion engines, fans and jets. The prospect of a significant reduction in noise output from jet engines of the future was one of the most important questions discussed at the Conference. Though the ideal cure for noise is to stop it at its source, this may in many cases be impossible. The next weapon in the anti-noise armoury is to absorb it in transit to the ear.

f) It is a common fallacy that a sound absorbent such as glass wool is opaque to sound, and is therefore the best way of diminishing annoying noise from the flat next door. In a normally furnished room, lining a wall with absorbent will have little effect on the noise level built up by reverberation, and will contribute hardly anything to the acoustic opacity of the wall. In a typical factory building, even if all available surfaces are covered with absorbent (a very expensive matter), the noise level is unlikely to drop by more than five decibels. A consultant will often recommend light partitioning, and partial screening round noisy machines, as a more effective and a more economical course.

g)  Domestic noises may perhaps be controlled by forethought and courtesy, and industrial noises by good planning a technical improvement. But, if we are going to allow fast motor-cycles and heavy diesel lorries to pass continuously through residential and business property, the community as a whole must decide on the control it needs to exercise, for in the long run it has got to pay for it. And if a nation is to take a leading part in modern air transport, it must enter into international agreements on the noise control measures it will impose at its airports and here the cost of any real control is immediately to be measured in millions of pounds.

R. A. Close.                                                          (560 words)

# Unit X: Note Making

Making notes is a very valuable exercise for students. You may need to make notes from all kinds of information texts like textbooks, reference materials, journals, magazines, newspapers and so on. In textbooks the information may be more conveniently organized, Notes made from textbooks are valuable for pre-examination revision. However, in other materials the information may not be very conveniently arranged. Learning to read quickly but carefully, identifying the important/ essential points of information, perceiving relationships and connections between these points, organizing these in convenient groups and giving them headings, arranging them in their hierarchy of points and sub-points, or listing and enumerating them are useful skills that help in preparing good notes. These skills will be practised in the exercises that follow.

The summary practise in the units above have already demonstrated and yielded practise in identifying the overall topic of a passage and the main points and related information in it. The skills of looking for patterns of organization and the cohesive signals which cue them have also been dealt with. This should lead us smoothly on to arranging the information in points and in a neat well-organised note form. Thus, the related points need to be numbered and grouped under a heading. Also, if there is a hierarchy of points these need to be systematically numbered and arranged, while an overall title for the whole note should encompass all the subtitles in the note.

Look at the following summary of the 'Laser Light' passage 42 (in Unit IV)

**1 A laser light is more effective than ordinary light because it is coherent. 2 This makes for a concentration of energy at a sharply defined point and tremendous extension of the range of the light source. 3 Three special uses of the laser are that firstly, it can illuminate the surface of the moon with a two-mile-wide circle of light, secondly, it can send a searing pinpoint of light into the human eye to weld a detached retina, and thirdly, it can also weld metals and is useful for precision work in making micro-electronic circuits.**
**(93 words)**

This summary can be presented in note form by grouping and numbering the properties of laser light in Sentences 1 and 2, and the uses in Sentence 3 under separate headings as follows:

<u>Overall Title</u>: *Lasers/ Laser Light*

<u>Sub-Title</u>:   *Properties of Lasers*
A laser light is more effective than ordinary light because of 3 properties
Cohesion
Concentration of energy at a sharply defined point
Extension of the range of the light source

<u>(Sub-Title)</u>: *Uses of Lasers*
Illumination of the moon with a two-mile-wide circle of light,
Sending a searing pinpoint of light into the human eye to weld a detached retina
Welding metals: especially useful for precision work in making micro-electronic circuits.

Note how information conveyed in a sentence or more in the original passage is reduced to 'point' form a) by focussing on the main ideas e.g., Sentences12 &13 of the passage? (i.e., "12 A laser can weld metals as well as retinas. 13 But here, too, its use is for precise work, as in making micro-electronic circuits.") are reduced to point C above and b) by converting important verbs into gerunds/ nouns that become the 'head word' of the point as shown by the underlined words in the following example: "<u>Welding</u> metals: especially useful for <u>precision</u> work in making micro-electronic circuits."

Notice, also, the neat layout with the subtitles in italics and the points under each, numbered and laid out neatly in the same margin. Further sub-points, if any, numbered in a different system, would have to come under a new margin, a little further to the right as shown in the following note on the 'Dolphins' passage (33) in Unit III:
*Kinds of Dolphins:*
River dolphins
Sea dolphins are of two kinds:
smaller common dolphins and
12-feet long bottle-nosed dolphins

Notice the capital letters used for the main points (kinds of dolphins) and small letters used for the sub-points (kinds of Sea dolphins). The numbering, which needs to be systematically used, and the neat layout make the hierarchy clear. Another way of laying this out is in a branching form or a tree diagram as was done for the 'Causes of Disease' passage in Unit VIII. The diagram is reproduced below:

Diagrammatic Representation Of ('Causes Of Disease') Passage 90

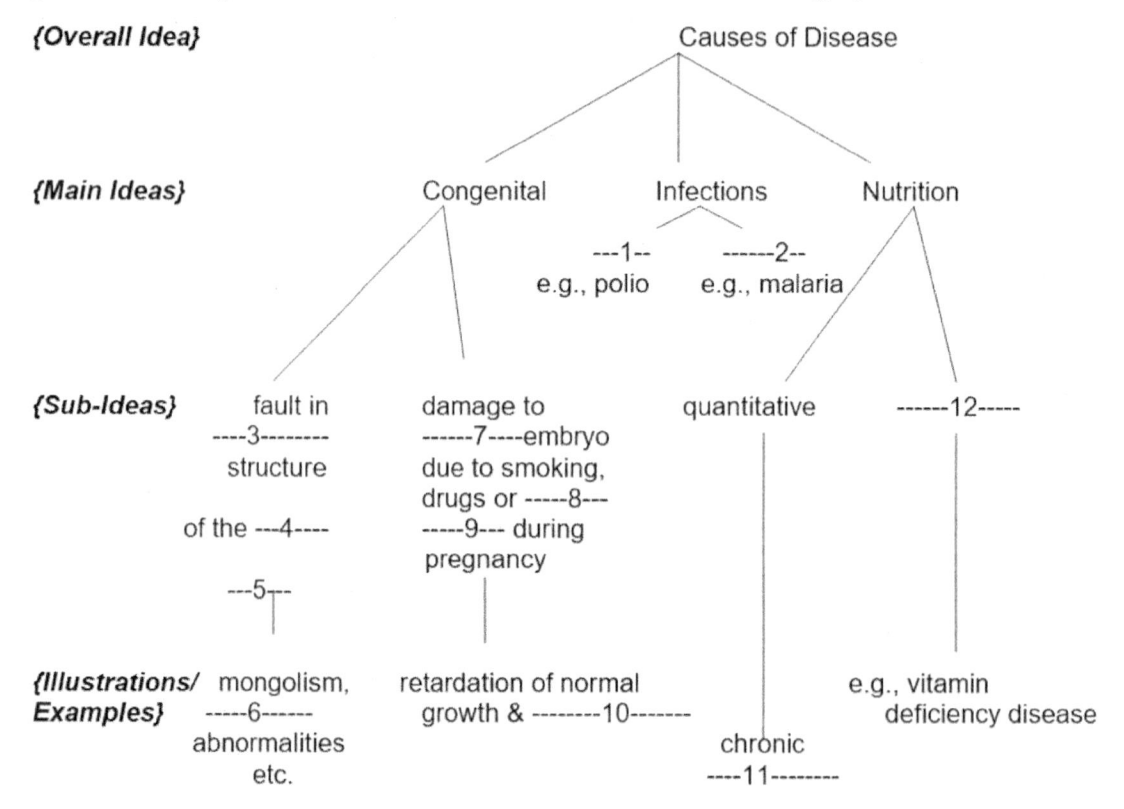

```
{Overall Idea}                                    Causes of Disease
                                                 /       |        \
{Main Ideas}              Congenital         Infections            Nutrition
                                               ---1--    ------2--
                                             e.g., polio  e.g., malaria

{Sub-Ideas}        fault in        damage to          quantitative      ------12-----
                   ----3--------   ------7----embryo
                   structure       due to smoking,
                                   drugs or -----8---
                   of the ---4---- -----9--- during
                                   pregnancy
                   ---5---

{Illustrations/  mongolism,     retardation of normal              e.g., vitamin
 Examples}       -----6------   growth & --------10-------         deficiency disease
                 abnormalities
                 etc.                            chronic
                                                 ----11--------
```

Often, certain texts may contain dense information which may be difficult to remember/ understand. Such information, if it falls into a pattern can be charted onto a table, graph or map and become much easier to remember and retrieve. For example, look at the following passage dealing with population figures, which can be condensed into the chart that follows for better understanding, memory and retrieval:

The population of the world today is about 4,950,000,000. That is an enormous number, yet it is known quite accurately, because there are very few parts of the world which have not carried out a modern census. China was a big unknown quantity until 1953, when a census was carried out. Their population was over 600,000,000.

The important thing is not so much the actual population of the world, but its rate of increase. It works out to be about 1.6 per cent per annum net increase. In numbers this means something like forty to forty-five million additional people every year. Canada has a population of twenty million – rather less than six month's increase in world population. There are about ten million people in Australia. So, it takes the world less than three months to add to itself a population which peoples this vast country. England and Wales have forty-five to fifty million people. This is just about a year's increase in the world population.

By this time tomorrow, and every day, there will be added to the earth about 120,000 extra people – just about the population of the city of New York.

| Populations | |
|---|---|
| World | 4,950 million |
| China | 600 million |
| Canada | 20 million |
| Australia | 10 million |
| England & Wales | 45 million |
| New York | 120,000 |
| World Population Increase per Year | 45 million |

The table makes clear what the passage is trying to say. In other words, we can see clearly that the world adds an England and Wales, or two Canadas or four Australias every year to its population, or a New York every single day!)

## Think About How You Make Notes:

As you read and mark/ underline all the points that seem important/ interesting.

A point would be a phrase or a short sentence.

Skim through the points again trying to pick out the crucial /main/ general points.

Look at the other points and their relationship to the main points. Do they elaborate, i.e. are they

Explanatory?
Examples?
Repetitions/ paraphrases?
Descriptions?
Illustrations?
Statistics?

Or are they branches (sub-points) of the main point?

Can some main points be grouped under a single heading or separate headings? What would be the suitable heading(s)?

Would some headings come under a broad subtitle(s)? (These subtitles are sometimes provided by textbooks).

What would be the overall title for the whole note? Keep in mind that it should encompass all the subtitles in the note.

Try to maintain a systematic numbering (and titling) pattern for the note.

 For example

Title
Subtitle: I, II, III, etc.
Headings: A, B, C, D, etc.
Sub-Headings: 1, 2, 3, 4, etc.
Main Points: (a), (b), (c), (d), etc.
Branch/(sub) points: (i), (ii), (iii), (iv), etc.

Easy Steps to Summary Writing and Note-Making

(All these may not be necessary all the time.  Use only what you need).

Adopt a neatly tiered (layered) layout for the notes as shown below:

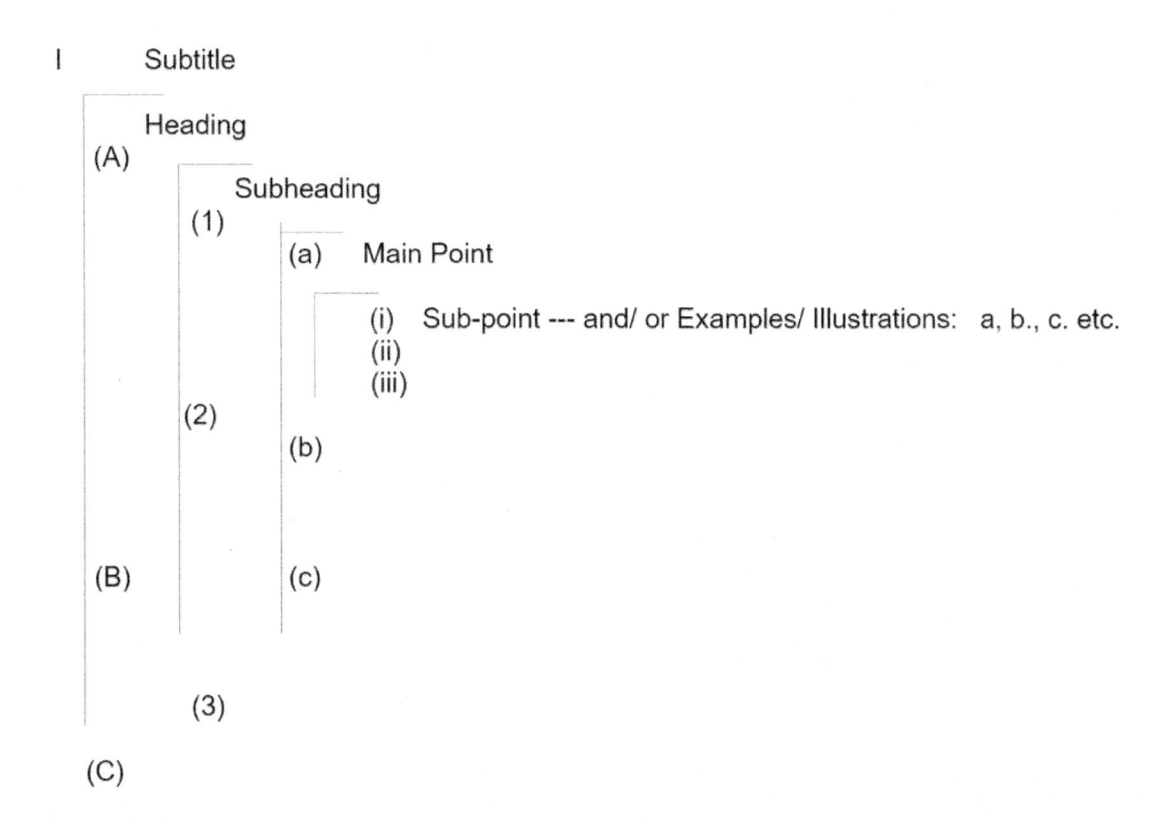

```
I     Subtitle
      Heading
(A)
          Subheading
      (1)
              (a)   Main Point
                      (i)  Sub-point --- and/ or Examples/ Illustrations:  a, b., c. etc.
                      (ii)
                      (iii)
      (2)
              (b)

(B)           (c)


      (3)
(C)
```

10.   Where points are unconnected but could still be grouped under a common heading, asterisks may be used to separate points.  They need not be numbered or ordered.

# Exercises

Below are given a variety of texts including passages from précis/ summary practice books, articles from newspapers, magazines and journals, extracts from textbooks and reference materials. Read each of the following passages (attached) carefully, and then work on the exercises that pertain to it, to gain practice in note making. For further practice make notes on your textbooks and reference reading.

**116**

One of the important methods of improving study habits is to distribute practice, i.e. to devote a number of brief study periods to the material rather than to spend the same total amount of time in a single long study period. There is some evidence that distribution of practice is relatively more important with materials to be learnt by rote, such as vocabulary lists and numerous separate factual details, than with materials that are more meaningful and better organized. Review at various intervals after learning has also proved to be valuable. Such review should be done carefully, for a superficial review may even interfere with remembering. A review should help to organize the material so as to make it more meaningful. Deficiencies in information should be recognized and corrected during the review. It is often a good practice to look over the material, as a whole, first. We may do this by looking at section headings in order to see how the material is organized. We may find it to read a chapter rapidly, perhaps making marginal notes and underlining. Then we can move on to a detailed study of the material. The material may be made more meaningful by deliberately and habitually looking for relationships to other things already known. In studying a psychology, for example, we should actively think about examples from our own experience. Arranging for a good setting in which to study is very helpful. Factors which are well known, but frequently not controlled, include freedom from distractions and interruptions, a comfortable, well-lighted work-place, and adequate reference books, papers, etc. Although these factors are conducive to effective study, they are not sufficient in themselves. Motivation and attitudes are probably the most important factors in effective methods of study. Taking clear and accurate notes is also helpful. Many students take unnecessarily detailed lecture notes and fail to distinguish the important form the less important material. We should write down key ideas, not everything that is said. Afterwards the notes may be edited for readability, checked for accuracy, and otherwise revised to make them more useful.

**Exercises**

I      What is the overall topic of the passage? Formulate an appropriate title for the passage.

II     Read the passage carefully and answer briefly the questions below

A) What are the three important requirements for a good setting?
B) What is the first thing to be done at a study session?
C) What three things does an overview imply?
D) How does a review at intervals of material to be studied help us?
E) Which four actions are recommended for taking clear, accurate lecture notes?

III    There are seven factors mentioned in the passage that help improve study. Write these down in note form and in a chronological sequence (i.e., time order). Your answers to Exs. I & II above could help you in the note.

**117 (follows)**

## 117

A Kitchen Garden as the name as the name implies, is the garden around or near the house. Raising a kitchen garden is a fascinating experience. The greatest satisfaction a family gets from it is dining on the harvest, which means vegetables produced in the home garden are used in their most fresh state. Besides producing food for the family the kitchen garden beautifies the house as it also includes trees, flowering shrubs, creepers, grass and flowering plants The kitchen garden is not a new innovation as even in the olden days and in backward areas families grew some vegetables near the house for use by the family. Anyhow, as modern technology has brought about many improvements in Indian agriculture it has also tried to touch this important aspect of the Indian Home. Agricultural Universities in India have produced a lot of material on kitchen gardening. Kitchen gardening has also been encouraged by the use of other medias such as home science extension education for the villagers. Services of All India Radio, Newspapers, Kisan Divas and Melas are being organised to extend education in kitchen gardening. T. V. is also being used for televising relevant programmes for the people. Among the advantages of having kitchen gardens in India, the most important one is to produce more food for the people on any land available anywhere. To produce food for all the Indians has been the greatest problem baffling the Indian Planners. In spite of our Green Revolution India still has to import food from outside to feed its hungry millions. The most grown things in the kitchen garden are different types of seasonal vegetables used by the family. Most of the Indian families cannot buy these vegetables because these are beyond their means. Moreover, home grown vegetables including lettuce are cleaner and safe to eat. The quality of the soil, water and manure used are better than those used for growing market vegetables'

Exercises

I   Decide which of the following topics are dealt with in detail in the passage. Which of these        serve well as an overall title?
a)   Agricultural Universities
b)   Kitchen Gardens in India.
c)   What is a Kitchen Garden?
d)   Advantages of Kitchen Gardens   e) The History of Kitchen Gardens f) Disadvantages of Kitchen Gardens  g) Improvements in Kitchen Gardening.


II  Complete the following note by filling in the blanks and supplying suitable headings using the relevant topics from those listed above:

_____1_____

The Kitchen Garden is a ____2_____ around or _____3____ the house and produces vegetables and _____4____ for the family's daily use.

_____5_____

a) Kitchen Gardens gives the _____6_____ of dining on a fresh _____7_____ of home-grown fruits and _____8_____.
b) The Kitchen Garden _____9____ the house with flowering shrubs, trees, creepers, etc.
c) It helps to ____10____ more on all _____11_____ land.
d) This can mean ____12_____ food imports.
e) Also, ____13_____ seasonal vegetables for the poorer Indian families.
f) Home-grown vegetables are cleaner and _____14____ to eat because better ____15___, ____16____ and ____17_____ are used.

_____18_____

a) _____19_____ on Kitchen Gardening have been produced by _____20_____ _____21_____.
b) It has been encouraged by other ___22_____ and Home Science _____23_____ _____24_____.
c) The use of various media like _____25____ ___26_____ and _____27_____ help to spread this education.
d) This is also done by the organization of 'Kisan _____28___' and '_____29_____ _____30_____'.


## Exercises   (on 118 overleaf)

I    What is the overall topic of the passage?

II   Write a gist of the first paragraph in about 25 words

III  Which paragraphs list the good and bad results of advertising?

IV   For which three groups of people are the advantages and disadvantages of advertising
Put the entire information into a neatly laid out tree-diagram.


## (Passage 118 overleaf)

Merchants all over the world have advertised their goods for hundreds of years, but modern advertising as a great commercial and social force began less than a century ago. Because it has proved to have an influence on the way in which the people of the world spend their money, it has grown into one of the essential partners of modern commerce and industry.

Advertising can have both good and bad results.

Skilful advertising of a useful product makes certain that a great many people will buy it. This enable the manufacturer to plan ahead, to keep large supplies of materials and machines, to keep his output at a high level, and to sell his product at a much lower price than if he had to wait for the buyers to discover its value slowly. The advantage to the buyer is that of the reduction in price which is made possible by mass production. On the other hand, much the same method may be employed to unload onto the public a product of low quality before any large number of buyers can find out for themselves the poor quality of what they are buying.

Advertising sets standards of quality in the minds of the public and thus prevents the sale of goods of low quality. On the other hand, if a certain product is standardized through advertising, the manufacturer of a new make of the same product which is of still better quality may be unable to spend the large sums of money necessary to overcome that advantage.

Advertising can raise standards of living by making people want better things. On the other hand, it may encourage useless spending on unimportant things.

Advertising helps small shopkeepers, because when they lay in stocks of well-advertised products, they can be more certain of a continued demand for them. On the other hand, if several competing makes of the same product are equally well advertised, a shopkeeper has to keep all the makes in stock.

Advertising can introduce new products; but it can also cause a lot of possessions to be thrown away while they are still useful. For example, many wireless companies and clothing manufacturers try to persuade people that last year's radios or suits are old-fashioned and no longer up-to-date.

Many advertisements educate the public about scientific inventions and discoveries, health, etc.; such as advances in medicine, but others are based on falsehood, to encourage the sale of worthless products.

Newspapers, magazines and the commercial radio are largely supported by advertising. Without it, these agencies of information and entertainment would be ruined. On the other hand, this dependence on advertisers gives these people an undue control over public opinion.

**119** 'The thin plastic carry bags ... ending up in a cow's belly' (passage follows the Exercises)

**Exercises**

I    **A)** Choose the title that is **most suitable** for the passage from the options given below:
a) The Menace/ Danger of Plastics
b) Saving the Environment
c) A Solution to Plastic Waste
d) Biodegradable Wisdom

**B)** For each of the options **not chosen**, indicate the reason for not choosing it by choosing from the alternatives given below:
i. Too broad in scope
ii. Too narrow or Partial
iii. Inaccurate
iv. Incorrect

II    A) Some of the topics that follow are dealt with in the passage. Which of these are not covered with enough detail in the passage?
a) Plastic bags everywhere
b) Recycled Plastics: A Blessing
c) The Thriving Plastic Industry
d) Lessons for Schoolchildren
e) Environmentalists: Trouble mongers
f) Laws in Europe and India
g) Amendments on Recycled Plastic Manufacture and Usage
h) The Mishra Committee Recommendation
i) Miniscule Measures
j) The Problems of Waste Pickers

B)    Which of the relevant topics from the list above would you use to make notes under the following headings:
a. Plastic Wastes in India
b. Miniscule Measures
c. A Wise Approach

III  Make notes on the passage, using the given headings, adding your perspective where necessary. Lay out your notes in a neat point form.

**(Passage 119 & 120 follow)**

|119|

THE thin plastic carry bags can be seen everywhere. They are light, fluffy, and they fly around with the breeze, littering the landscape. They can be found all along railway tracks in the countryside, on high hilltops and even in bird's nests and cow's bellies. They are eyesores and they are toxic for the environment. No wonder the use of plastic bags has driven both nature lovers and environmentalists to passionate activism.

It is fitting that the government has sought to curb the menace through legislation. Not once (first in 1999), but twice (now again in 2003, under the Recycled Plastic Manufacture and Usage (Amendment) Rules, 2003). Henceforth, no plastic bags which are thinner than 20 microns and smaller than eight-by-twelve inches shall be manufactured. The question is, does this then solve the problem of plastic wastes?

The multinational plastic industry in India contributes over two million tonnes of plastic to our waste stream each year. One billion bottles, food packaging, cement bags, medical disposals, all become waste after being used only once. The Rs 25,000 crore "sunrise" industry, growing at 12-15 per cent annually, hates it if anyone even mentions the words "environmental impact". They spend time telling schoolchildren how "essential" plastic is and ways in which it has changed our lives for the better. They avoid talking about issues of livelihood of local potters, basket makers, jute farmers and craftsmen now displaced. They also do not talk about cows who choke on plastic bags, or how incinerating chlorinated plastics like PVC leads to some of the most toxic emissions known to man. They resist any moves by the government to impose a collection or recycling tax on them. In short, they run the show. For them environmentalists are just trouble mongers. Internationally the plastic industry has come under many types of environmental legislation. Laws in Sweden, Norway and Germany have forced packaging manufacturers to collect plastic waste and recycle it. "Producers are responsible," says the European Union. If you make plastic packaging, then ensure that it does not pollute. However, as a contrast, last year when the government's Ranganathan Mishra committee tried to have our plastic industry collect its 15,000 tonnes of bottle waste by setting up 1,000 collection centres nationally and paying a measly Rs 0.25 tax, they raised a hue and cry! Even today no one knows the fate of this directive.

**INTER**VENTION

**RAVI AGARWAL**

So is it enough to say that small thin carry bags are henceforth banned? Instead of taking on plastic as a material, and trying to formulate laws and taxes to manage and minimise the waste from plastic per se, the government is content with this miniscule measure. It is also doubtful if this law itself will work. No small bags? No problem, let's just use larger ones! The rationale for banning small thin bags is that they do not get collected and recycled. Over 800 small bags make a kilo, which fetches the wastepicker a mere two rupees. How will this change with the slightly larger bags? Collection will still take hours, time better spent garnering more lucrative items like bottles, tumblers and plates. It is unlikely that plastic carry bags will even now be collected instead of ending up in a cow's belly.

(courtesy: The Times of India)

[120]

## POPULATION

The total population of the world is estimated to be about 7,000 million. If this number of people were distributed evenly over the whole of the earth's surface, this would give a population density of about six people to the square kilometre. In actual fact, of course, population is not evenly distributed, so that in desert areas, the density is far below six to the square kilometre, and in urban areas far above this figure.

The blank areas on maps, where no centres of population appear, are deserts, uninhabitable because the climate is too severe—either intensely hot or intensely cold. Other areas are sparsely populated because nature there is too hostile and conditions too adverse. High mountain areas are usually sparsely populated because of the ruggedness of the land and because communications are difficult. Some areas in the far north are not inhabited because the soil is poor and the climate harsh. Even in the temperate grasslands, because of distances and poor communications, population is sparse. In tropical climates, impenetrable forests and disease make many areas uninhabitable.

Because of factors of this kind, more than a half of the total population of the world is estimated to live on about one-thirtieth of the total surface of the earth, the bulk of them concentrated in three great areas— Western Europe, the eastern U.S.A. and the area covered by China and India.

In Western Europe and the eastern U.S.A. the climate is temperate, and because of the nature of the soil, it is possible to cultivate a wide variety of crops. In addition, these areas possess good resources of coal, oil, electricity and of the minerals essential for the development of modern industry; transport facilities are also easily available. About 680 million people live in these areas, the bulk of them in the great industrial cities, some of them seriously overcrowded.

In India and China the greatest concentration of population is to be found in the basins of the great rivers, where the fertile soil can support huge numbers of people—1000 million in India and 120 million in China. In some parts of the Gangetic plain the concentration of population is 600 to the square kilometre, although the standard of living of the bulk of the population is not very high.

Population is comparatively dense in the areas surrounding the Mediterranean Sea, where, although there are not many mineral resources, the climate is favourable and the soil in some places is fertile; consequently the principal occupations of the population are farming and cattle raising. Malaya and the islands of S.E. Asia, where the climate is tropical but modified by proximity to the sea, are also densely populated; some areas have a density of 400 to the square kilometre.

(continued overleaf) →

120 (contd)

One of the adverse consequences of over-population is a low standard of living. An over-populated country is one in which natural resources cannot provide a reasonable standard of living for the bulk of the population.

One of the dangers which confront poor countries in which there is a gap between food production and consumption is that of famine in times of bad harvest–in India, for example, if the monsoon fails. Modern equipment and improved methods of agriculture will help to reduce this deficit and the danger of famine.

Two solutions to over-population are migration and industrialization. An industrialised country can export its products and in return import food and other goods to enable it to raise its standard of living. But industrialization in the 19th century also led to over-population in some European countries and this in turn led to migration from these countries to others which were under-populated. Similarly, over-population in India has led to migration East and South Africa and South America. The present effort to industrialise India and China is an attempt to solve the problem of over-population.

The pressure of population is responsible for the efforts being made to develop the under-populated areas of the world. Advances in scientific knowledge and modern equipment have made it possible to grow crops in Siberia, to make life easier in such difficult regions as the Amazon basin by eliminating diseases, to irrigate and electrify areas which until recently were deserts.

An increase in population means both more births and fewer deaths. Increased medical knowledge and facilities by eliminating some diseases have brought a world-wide increase in the expectation of life – in Europe in the 19th century it increased from 50 to 60 years. The death rate in India is still much higher than in Europe; a reduction in the figure will mean an increase in population. But experience in Europe has shown that a rising standard of living brings with it a stabilisation of population.

(840 words)

**Exercises (on 120)** ' The total population ……. stabilization of population' **(above)**

I   Complete the following table by providing the statistical information from the passage as shown in the e.g. in 1 below:

| Area | Density of Population / Sq. Km. |
|---|---|
| 1. World (Average) | 6 |
| 2. Indian Gangetic Plain | |
| 3. South East Asia | |
| 4. Deserts & Mountains | |

II  Complete **the following notes** providing **suitable headings** where necessary:

  a. _____1_____  _____2_____

The World Population of _____3_____ million is not ___4___ distributed.

  b. ___5___ Population

Some areas are not ___6___ populated because of the following factors:
i. ___7___ of rain/ water in deserts
ii. ___8___ because of unsuitable climate i.e., severe heat or cold.
iii. Poor ___9___ in mountainous areas and dense forests.

  c. ___10___ Population
       W. Europe, U.S.A. and S.E. Asia contain ___11___ of the population because of :
i. favourable climate: temperate in ___12___ and ___13___ and tropical in ___14___.
ii. fertile ___15___ yielding a variety of ___16___.
iii. ___17___ resources of coal, oil, etc.
iv. ___18___ Facilities

d. _____19____ of Over Population (i.e., high ____20__ rate of population):

i. __21____ standard of living.
ii. Danger of ____22____ if there is a gap between food ____23_____ and ____24____.

e. _____25_____ to Over Population
i. ____26____ to less densely populated countries such as ____27____ and____28____.
ii. Greater _____29_____ so that _____30_____ could be imported and ____31____ of living raised.
iii Increased _____32_____ knowledge can improve _____33____ and _____34_____ and reduce death and _____35_____.
iv .Improved standard of living checks population _____36_____.

**(Passage 121    'The Safest Blood' follows)**

# The safest blood is your own

No amount of screening can really ensure the safety of blood used in transfusions. Autologous transfusions, where the patient's own blood is stored and used, may just be the solution to the problem, writes
**MEHER PESTONJI**

REPORTS of HIV positive blood being administered to patients made Shobha nervous. Her husband had been thrown off a crowded bus fracturing his hip. Corrective surgery was required to enable him to walk again. She had been told to arrange for two units of blood but while she could well afford to pay for it, she had no way of ensuring that the blood would be safe.

It was a doctor friend who told her about autologous transfusion — a procedure where the blood requirements of a patient planning surgery are anticipated by his doctors and the patient is encouraged to store his own blood at a blood bank for retransfusion as required. Since the blood is his own there is little risk of reaction or infection.

"Anyone who can wait for surgery, who has a normal haemoglobin count and whose blood is not infected (eg. abscess, cancer) qualifies for autologous transfusions," says Dr Chandrika Kudva, who is in charge of the blood bank at Bombay Hospital. "Normally blood donors have to be aged between 18 and 60 with a minimum weight of 45 kg and 12.5 per cent haemoglobin but these criteria can be relaxed when blood is donated for oneself and safety is the primary concern. While 350 cc are normally extracted from an adult blood donor, smaller quantities can be extracted from children. Even 75-year-olds can store blood for themselves.

"Persons whose haemoglobin is slightly low may be administered iron, multivitamins or, in certain cases, a hormone called erythropoetin to stimulate the bone marrow to produce red cells before extracting blood," continues Dr Kudva. "Autologous transfusions are ideal for a person whose body metabolism is normal but who requires surgery anyway, as with orthopaedic fractures, plastic surgery and kidney donors. It is also useful in lung and coronary surgery. Patients with rare blood groups for whom it is difficult to find a matching donor benefit from this technique."

Bombay Hospital stores blood for 15-20 autologous cases each month. Facilities for autologous transfusions exist wherever there are blood storage facilities but as the shelf life of blood is 35 days, only a limited quantity can be stored. As blood is a very good medium for bacteria to multiply in, it must be stored in impeccably sterile conditions with the temperature maintained at 4-6 degrees Centigrade.

"Some years ago it was not uncommon for a patient to be transfused 7-8 units after a major surgery but for modern sophisticated techniques two units are sufficient, though some abdominal surgeries may require more," said Dr K Ghosh of the Indian Council of Medical Research. "A transfusion committee comprising the surgeon, physician and blood bank specialist can estimate the blood requirements of a patient, which varies from patient to patient even if it is for the same type of surgery. When more blood is required, using the leap frog technique, as many as four units of a person's blood can be stored for later use."

In the leap frog technique, the transfusion schedule is spaced out over a month. To begin with, one unit is extracted from the patient for two consecutive weeks. In the third week, two units are extracted and the first unit, which is nearing the end of its shelf life, is returned to the patient. Similarly in the fourth week, two units are again extracted and the second unit is retransfused. At the end of the fourth week, four units of the patient's own blood are available during surgery. Though the leap frog technique is widely used in the West, it is still to catch on in India where the handful of patients opting for autologous transfusions store only one or two units of blood.

"More than 75 per cent of transfusion accidents are the result of clerical errors — wrong entry in registers, wrong labelling — which defeat the purpose of medical research," said Dr Ghosh. "Scrupulous maintenance of records and multiple cross-checks are vital. In the West, separate refrigerators are used to store blood for autologous transfusions, which does not go through the rigorous tests of blood donated for homologous transfusions (donated to others). In some institutions patients are asked to sign their sealed blood bags to avoid the risk of them getting mixed up."

According to FDA regulations, all blood taken from a donor is to be tested for four diseases — HIV, hepatitis B, STD and malaria — although at least eight other infections including the fatal hepatitis C may still be passed on through the blood stream. In autologous transfusion the blood is returned to the donor, so it does not go through this screening process. However, doctors advise repeating the cross-match before the retransfusion to decrease the risk of mislabelling and to ensure that there's been no mix-up during storage. "Even screening does not make blood 100 per cent safe, so transfusions should only be prescribed in essential cases," says Dr Maya Parihar Malhotra of KEM hospital, Bombay. "Unfortunately, too many doctors prescribe them when the patient can easily be treated with medication."

The FDA, which lays down guidelines for blood safety, has yet to establish norms for the age, weight and haemoglobin levels of potential autologous donors. In UK and USA, transfusion medicine has evolved into a highly specialised field commanding an MD degree while India is still trying to catch up with certificate courses. FDA officials, who have no medical background, are ill-equipped to devise norms which should ideally be left to a specially appointed committee of transfusion experts from different blood banks.

## Exercises (on 121 above)

I       Some of the questions answered in the passage are indicated below. Which of these do not directly deal with autologous transfusion?

a)      What fears did Shobha have about her husband's corrective surgery?
b)      What is autologous transfusion?
c)      Who qualifies as a donor for this?
d)      What are the normal (homologous) blood donating conditions?
e)      Which medical conditions make autologous transfusion useful?
f)      What are the conditions for storing blood?
g)      How can blood be stored, how much and for how long in autologous transfusion?
h)      How can transfusion accidents be avoided?
i)      What is screening of blood? Is it required in autologous transfusion?
j)      What is the status of transfusion medicine in India? How would it help the cause of autologous transfusion?

II      Answers to which of the questions above would you consider for inclusion in your notes on the passage under each of the headings below?
1.      Autologous Transfusion
2.      Its Uses
3.      Conditions for Donating
4.      Procedure for Donating
5.      Conditions for Storage

III     Complete the following notes by filling in the blanks suitably:

Autologous Transfusion
Autologous transfusion is a procedure where the blood ---1----- of a patient planning ---2---- are   anticipated and the   ---3--- own blood is stored at a ---4--- bank for ---5----- as required.

Its Uses
a)      Little risk of ---6---- or ----7---.
b)      Ideal for persons with ---8----- metabolism and who require ----9---- or ----10----. Also useful for ----11---- donors and in ---12---- and ---13--- surgery.
c)      Patients with ---14--- blood groups for whom it is difficult to find ----15----- donors.

## Conditions for Donating
1) Those who can ---16--- for surgery.
2) Whose ----17--- count is normal.
3) Whose blood is not ----18---- ( e.g., abscess/ cancer)
4) Whose ----19---- is normal
5) Even -----20---- year-olds can store their blood
6) ----21--- haemoglobin count should be ----22---- with administration of red ----23--- , -----24---- and -----25----- if necessary.

## Procedure for Donating
Stored blood has a shelf life of ---26---- days. In autologous transfusion, if more than two units of blood are required the ----27---- technique is used. The transfusion schedule is spaced over a ----28---. One unit is extracted for two ----29--- weeks. In the third week ----30--- units are extracted and the first unit (nearing the end of its shelf life) is ----31---- to the patient. Similarly, in the ---32--- week two units are extracted and the ---33--- unit is re-transfused. At the end of the four weeks, ---34--- units of blood are available during surgery. The technique is still to catch on in ----35---- where only two units can be stored. Cross ---36--- before transfusion is recommended.

## Conditions for Storage
1. Any blood bank with blood ---37---- facilities.
2. ---38--- quantity can be stored: Shelf life being 35 days.
3. Absolutely ---39--- conditions.
4. -----40---- maintained at 4 – 6 degrees centigrade,
5. No screening required for ---41----- transfusion.
6. Sealed blood bags have to be ----42—and preferably ---43---- by the donor to avoid the risk of getting mixed up.
7. Guidelines for blood safety with the norms for the age, weight and haemoglobin levels of potential autologous ----44--- need to be laid down by the ---45--- in India with guidance from ----45----- experts.

## 122. We Face the Guns from Both Sides
(The Sunday Times, 3rd September 1995)

The exquisite teak and walnut carvings on Kashmir Palace, the four bedroom-luxury houseboats of the six member Wattoo family stand in stark contrast to the patchwork on its weather-beaten roof. The photographs in their albums are of smiling guests and family members, shot in wintry mornings on a frozen Dal Lake or in flower-filled shikaras in spring and summer. The visitors' book with its many entries from persons of various nationalities, is a record of impressions, nostalgia and sentiment made over the years. Both, the albums and the visitors' book, are indicative of the valley's special brand of tourism, where comfort and luxury mesh naturally and beautifully with warm, proud Kashmiri hospitality. They are reminiscent too, of a different time.

The photographs in the newspapers today though, provide a chilling counterpoint: they depict the cruelly dismembered body of Hans Christian Ostro, a Norwegian hostage killed by a hitherto unidentifiable group of terrorists, Al Faran.

In the week we spent at Nagin Lake, the warmth of the Wattoo family was our only cushion against the inescapable deep depression that Kashmir has sunk into. In six years, everything seems to have changed. As we drove in from Srinagar airport, we saw a city under siege: army bunkers at every street corner; glamorous houseboats –

Once the hub of commercial activity – in ruins; school and hospital buildings that had been searched, occupied, vacated and then gutted by the security forces. There are more than 150 of these ruins.

To put it in Abba Wattoo's words, "Inside [pointing to the heart] …. everything's changed. You see that army truck? If something went wrong with my car in earlier times, they would have stopped. Now if there is a breakdown and I am stuck, I will be picked up by the army and roughed up." Then Abba Wattoo made a disarming switch from the specific to the philosophical. *"Agar pyar se bolo to koi bhi suntan hai.* Even my own son. *Dande aur goli ki baat kaun sunega?* (Who needs the language of the lathi or the gun?)"

On the last night of our stay, after the Wattoo's generous and lavish *wazvaan* (banquet), members of our team were kidding 19-year-old Irfan about his commitment to the Jammu and Kashmir Liberation Front (JKLF) and its political aspirations for *azaadi*. He took the jibes good-naturedly for a while, and then he turned angry and deadly serious, snapping, "It is just this condescending attitude of India and Indians that convinces us that your government will never be prepared to talk or negotiate fairly and unconditionally."

Later, Abba Wattoo asked, "Did you hear Irfan, sense how angry he was? That is the anger of the youth. What we say is nothing to them. There must be dialogue very soon. And India has to initiate it. Someone has to help the Kashmiris out of this endless cycle of guns and bullets, killings and funerals. If talks are not held soon all will be lost."

Anger, despair and disappointment with the government of India's response to the Kashmir tragedy was reflected in every conversation with young and old, no matter what their political affiliations, in Srinagar and Charar-e-Sharif.

Back at the houseboat we would talk into the night. Of how burial grounds now dot every street in Srinagar – an everyday reminder of the lives lost, hundreds of thousands of them. Of how the lives of this six-member family (there is Abba and Ammi Wattoo and their four children: Hamida and Wahida, Murtaza and Mustafa, and little Nikhat, a cousin who has been drawn into the family), have changed.

Hamida and Wahida, in their late teens and early 20s, have been forced to drop out of college, and confined to their home. They have no interaction with men and women their own age. "My parents fear for our safety. My father will not let us go outside. There have also been ghastly instances of dishonour. How can we blame our parents for keeping us home? My mother does not even visit her own family, though they live half-an-hour away," said Hamida.

This in a state that, prior to 1989, had the lowest crime rate in the country, with hardly any instances of rape. Where female literacy was, and still is, very high.

All four Wattoo children, like the 20 lakhs youth in J&K, have been witness to gruesome violence. The Wattoo boys, who were 13 and 8 when the politics of violence burst upon them, seem more deeply affected then the girls. And it is about them that Ammi Wattoo is really worried. "*Beta Murtaza*, now in Delhi with his uncle, loves to come here, but in six days or so he is depressed and wants to leave. He cannot face what has happened to all of us, to our Kashmir. His friends all carry weapons now,"

"Whenever I come home, I try to go to my college, see my friends. But it is not safe. For 15-20 days every month, the colleges and schools are closed, examinations in some classes have not been held for over three years," said Murtaza. "When we were young, we used to shiver when we saw our father's hunting pistols. Now, do you know how many *tanzeems* (organisations) there are on campus? For the pettiest squabble over a girl or anything, they pull out a weapon. How can you study in such an atmosphere?

This corrosion of a culture by violence threatens a whole generation of Kashmiris. Fourteen-year-old Mustafa's reaction to any teenage brawl in school is to summon his "gang contacts" (those with weapons). "The boys have been affected the most," agreed Hamida. "What would any youngster, who has been shown heaps of bodies of his friends and neighbours, tortured and shot by army bullets, be expected to do? How would he react?

"We face guns from both sides" said Misral and Gulzara, university students in Srinagar. But why must the Indian army continue to humiliate us?" For the continued presence of the BSF and army in civilian areas – particularly the university, educational institutions and hospitals – is a sore point with all Kashmiris. The ignominy of their forced physical presence is heightened by the humiliation of sudden but frequent searches on civilians – students, doctors and professionals – despite the mandatory possession of identity cards. A weary army commandant confessed that the security forces had overstayed their welcome in the valley but were forced by the government to stay on.

A close and trusted friend of the Wattoos, a woodworker who called one morning, said, "The Indian government has abdicated any responsibility towards a lasting solution to the problem in the valley by reducing us to a permanent state of occupation by our own army. At any time of day, while performing a routine chore like walking to school or shopping or driving, an anonymous BSF *jawaan* can walk up to me, demand that I stop, subject me to a routine or a humiliating search and enquiry. My boys can be picked up any time. It would then be my responsibility to trace them. On the road back to the airport, you will be searched three times. Is this wise or necessary?

One night we drove with Abba Wattoo through Srinagar to share a lavish Kashmiri *wazvaan* with Shabbir Shah, formerly of the People's League, imprisoned for 22 years by the Indian government for is struggle for *azaadi* . The six-course meal was accompanied by an intense political interview. But all the while my host and my escorts urged me to eat faster so we could leave. To be out after dark for a woman, even if escorted, is inadvisable.

Abba Wattoo drove back at a speed born of fear and panic. Not one vehicle passed us. There was no one in the streets. Srinagar and other cities are on self-imposed curfew after dark. As we passed The Mall and were about to turn off, our vehicle was hailed and asked to stop. We drew up alongside the road.

Three or four young men held up an old man gasping for breath. There was no way to get him to hospital. He was a heart patient with asthma in addition. No ambulances ply on the streets of Kashmir anymore. Even if they did, they couldn't be summoned because the telephones never work. Emergency medical services are therefore completely out of reach. So could we please drop him to the hospital which was on our way home? We took him to the hospital. What would he have done had we not passed by? That question stayed with me. As does the image of the Dal and Nagin lakes overrun with weeds. It's a place gone to seed.

## Exercises

I    Can you see a pattern of organization constantly recurring throughout the feature article on Kashmir? What is it? Choose from the options below:
a.    Explanation through details
b.    Cause and Consequence
c.    Statement and Examples
d.    Contrast
e.    Narration
f.    Comparison and Contrast


II    Can you see a pattern in the facts about Kashmir that are being contrasted? What would be the headings if you grouped your points, in the whole article, on the two contrasting sides? To answer choose from the following:
a)    Kashmir for Tourists & Kashmir for Locals
b)    Family Life & Public Life in Kashmir
c)    Kashmir Then & Kashmir Now
d)    Beautiful Kashmir & Ugly Kashmir


III    Fill in the blanks in the following notes on the passage contrasting the aspects related to the beauty of Kashmir:

(A) The Beauty of Kashmir

| Kashmir ___1___ | Kashmir ___2___ |
|---|---|
| 1. Exquisite ___3___ & walnut ___4___ on Kashmir Palace | ___5___ on the weather-beaten roof |
| 2. Beautiful ___6___ & ___7___ Lakes | Lakes overrun with ___8___ |
| 3. Photographs of ___9___ guests & international ___10___ amidst flowers, ___11___ and ___12___. | Newspaper ___13___ of Ostro and other tourists ___14___ by ___15___. |

In similar tables that follow on 'Kashmir Then and Now' the remaining points are segregated under 3 different headings mentioned below.
a)   Governmental Attitude
b)   Public Life
c)   Personal & Family Life

Complete or fill up the missing points in the two columns, and also match the headings given above with the appropriate tables:

( B ) _____

| Kashmir Then | Kashmir Now |
|---|---|
| 1. a prosperous Kashmir with happy friendly people | A city _____ |
| 2. Irfan took jibes good-naturedly | After a while _____ |
| 3. Murtaza _____ | Murtaza now wants to leave |
| 4. Children _____ | Murtaza's friends now carry weapons |

(C) _____

| Kashmir Then | Kashmir Now |
|---|---|
| 1. Hamida & Wahida at college | Mother's visits _____ |
| 2. High _____ | Colleges & schools closed |
| 3. | Forced to drop out of college because unsafe & for fear of dishonour |
| 4. Children shivered at _____ | Youngsters angry & deeply affected by violence |

(D) _____

| Kashmir Then | Kashmir Now |
|---|---|
| 1. _____ | The Army roughs up common people |
| 2. BSF & Army were there to protect Kashmiris | _____ |
| 3. Emergency vehicles & ambulances plied at night | _____ |
| 4. Kashmiris open about India | Frustration _____ |

**123**     'Television is not entirely injurious ... turn on your TV now': (follows)

## Exercises

A) Make notes on the newspaper article, reproduced below, to bring out the debate about TV watching by children. You may list your points on the two sides of the debate in two columns with suitable titles for your columns

(B) Suggest an overall title for the entire note/ article

TELEVISION is not entirely injurious to your health, or that of your child. So says Dr. Anne Colby who toured Delhi and Mumbai recently with such evangelical messages that children would love her. So would harried parents. As director, Henry Murray Research Center of Radcliffe College, Harvard University and a licensed psychologist, Dr. Anne Colby should know what she's advocating. Besides impressive credentials, she has published and presented numerous papers, and co-written several books on child development. She was invited to India by Cartoon Network to talk on Television and Children's Development, a topic of concern to parents, educators and policy-makers, not to exclude children themselves.

There have been over 5,000 studies and according to Dr. Colby, "much of the research is quite reassuring". She proceeds to reassure us some more.

She believes that television can widely assist in a child's intellectual, emotional, social and moral growth, since " study after study has proved that children watch TV actively, not passively. That they look for logical relations and narrative sequences in the stories they watch and connect these stories to their own life experience." And more important, "hundreds of studies have failed to find any deficit in children's attention spans due to watching television."

Happily she continues busting the myths that were drilled into our psyches, thanks to the '50s scholar Marshall McLuhan, after television entered our lives. McLuhan gave us that famous maxim, "The medium is the message". Today, in '90s, that appears to have been just another soundbyte, because according to McLuhan it was the nature of the medium that was more powerful than the message itself.

And so children were turning into couch spuds. We believed that and we still do. Dr. Anne Colby does not. Especially since research in viewing habits has proved him wrong. It was the message - sex, violence, etc. that came across strongly and not just via TV, but via books and films and theatre. We only have to look around and see how many Bachchan wannabes and Naomi Campbell imitations float around to know that McLuhan was wrong. Other media are as culpable in the progress or regress of a child's development as television.

"Children who watch moderate amounts of TV a week show better school performance than those who watch little or no TV," she says. Before we have a collective sigh of relief and reach for the remote, she rises again to its defence, " It is not watching television per se that affects a child's development, but the quality of what they're watching."

Thus violent TV programming leads to increased levels of aggressive activity and unflattering stereotypes, while programmes exemplifying positive social behaviour influence children to imbibe those qualities. "If we think of television solely as entertainment, we're missing an important opportunity." She insists, "It is an exciting source of learning for children and adults alike", she says. As for viewing hours, she suggests parental control. An hour-and-a-half a day seems in order. And regulate what your child watches, make sure it's educative and fun.

That was the good news. The bad news is that there are hardly any such fun, educative programmes. At least not here in India where children's television is not even an issue. In her opinion, it's not so hopeless yet, not while programmes like Big Bag (for pre-schoolers) from Cartoon Network are around. Or, might we add, the Discovery Channel and to a certain extent the BBC. So it's safe to turn on your TV now.

**The next few passages (124 - 128) are each followed by the Exercises you should attempt**

# Bitter Boon

Don't expect a neem-based pesticide to zap the bugs instantly. Such murder and mayhem is better left to crude killers, the synthetic pesticides. Neem is far more subtle. And better at plant protection. While it leaves birds and mammals and beneficial pollinating insects unharmed, it deters leaf-chewers with a battery of chemicals so marvelous that the most ferocious and resistant of pests would rather starve than take a single bite of neem. Intriguingly, Asian goats and camels seem to feed on neem leaves without any ill-effects.

'Neem contains several active ingredients and they act in different ways under different circumstances,' says Dr. Sunil Bambarkar of McDA Agro Ltd, Bombay, 'These compounds are quite unlike the chemicals in today's synthetic insecticides. Neem chemicals belong to a class of natural products called triter penes or limonoids distantly related to steroids and hormones like cortisone, birth-control pills and many valuable pharmaceuticals. They are unique in that they are not outright killers. Rather, they alter an insect's behavior or life processes in subtle ways. Eventually, the insect can no longer feed, breed or metamorphose.

Other plants can absorb some of these chemicals through the soil. The fortified plants are protected internally. Such protection is not washed off in the rain. Nor do you need to spray new growth to protect it Field trails have shown that a single session of soil treatment protected the leaves and stems of wheat, rice, sugarcane and cotton for 10 weeks.

Moreover, nothing happens to those who eat these neem fortified plants. "Indeed, their lack of toxicity to warm-blooded animals may be the neem products' greatest asset,' says Dr. Virendra Chavan, who is managing director of Innovative Laboratory and Workshop, Bombay. He calls neem a supreme example of super-tech in action. Because neem contains so many different compounds, building up of pest resistance becomes impossible. Also, for all their exquisite potency, neem compounds degrade easily – they are broken down by sunlight and acid rain.

However, some scientists like Prof. Steven Ley of Imperial College, London, are trying to improve on nature. They are reported to be 'a bond's length away' from synthesis of azadi-rachtin, a major neem chemical. They are also trying to build more potent or more stable analogues of neem compounds.

'While the scientists may succeed, the new compounds cannot possibly match the holistic effects wrought by nature's bitter pill,' says Dr. Chavan. 'More important, the neo-neems will cost millions of dollars to develop and to test. Why should poor farmers buy them when they have their neem?'
Vithal C. Nadkarni
(400words)

**Exercises**

I    a) State the main point of each paragraph in a sentence and
b) indicate the pattern of organization in each paragraph.

II    Write a summary of the passage in about 130 words by indicating the general advantages of neem and its merits as an insecticide and as a plant pesticide.

III    Suggest an alternative title for the passage apart from the given one. Which title would you prefer and why?

IV    Present your answer to Ex. II above in the form of a tree diagram.



**125** Read the News report reproduced below, carefully, and attempt the **Exercises** which follow:

Easy Steps to Summary Writing and Note-Making

125

## Brazil's new worry: Amazon drying

**KYODO**
RIO DE JANEIRO | OCTOBER 15

1. AN abrasive dry season in the Amazon rainforest in northern Brazil has caused the worst drought in the region in 60 years, isolating thousands of people in remote jungle areas.
2. The severe drought has totally dried or sharply reduced the water volume of local rivers, which are the main route of transportation for ribeirinhos, the river dwelling people in the Amazon rainforest.
3. Brazilian TV networks have been broadcasting shocking images of riverbeds turned into dusty roads that vehicles now ply to transport essential supplies to isolated communities.
4. "The oldest people are scared with what they have been seeing and living along the rivers," said environmentalist Mario Menezes.
5. The Solimoes river, whose traditional depth in October averages at least 12 metres, measured only 92 centimetres on Thursday by the Municipality of Caapiranga, 222 kilometres west of Manaus, the Amazonas state capital.
6. Amazonas, Brazil's largest state has declared a state of emergency in 61 of its 62 municipalities.
7. "There are over 1,200 communities lacking drinking water and food supplies because they live by rivers and lakes which have dried up," said the coordinator of the emergency plan. That authorities have made up to assist the isolated villages.
8. The Brazilian armed forces are using planes and helicopters to reach remote jungle communities in what the army general in charge has called "war operations" because of the difficulties involved in reaching areas deep in the jungle.
9. Authorities have concentrated emergency assistance on getting drinking water, food and medicine to some 132,000 families, according to the state government.
10. Millions of dead fish, which succumbed from lack of oxygen in the river water, polluted the remaining waters sources and pose a major threat of contamination.
11. Above all, medical authorities fear a cholera outbreak because reduced water levels tend to increase the concentration of bacteria and viruses. "This may bring back diseases which were under control," said the chief of the health monitoring foundation, Bernardino De Albuquerque.
12. Fishermen in the neighboring state of Para have told local daily *O Estado De Sao Paulo* they have never seen the Amazon river so dry.
13. "I am 57 years old and I do not remember seeing something like that, not even when I was a child," a fisherman told the daily about the river, which has the largest volume of water in the world and the biggest drainage area of any river system.

*The Sunday Express, 16.10.05*

## Exercises (on 125 above)

I  Choose the correct alternative to complete the statements or answer the questions provided below:

a) The Amazon in the title refers to
i) a town in Brazil.   ii) the rainforest.   iii) the isolated community.
   iv) a river in Brazil.
b) 'Drought' (in Para 1) refers to
i) a famine conditions.   ii) the lack of rains.   iii) the drying up of rivers.   iv) drying up of rainforests.
c) What is the problem for the people in the remote jungle areas?

i) starvation.   ii) wild animals.   iii) lack of transport.   iv) diseases like cholera.
   d) Millions of fish died because of
i) lack of water.  ii) lack of oxygen.   iii) water pollution.   iv) the dried river bed.
   e) The Amazon has been
i) the largest river system in the world.    ii) the longest river in the world   iii) the largest river system
in Brazil   iv) the oldest river in the world.

II   Answer the following questions in a phrase or sentence:
1. What/ Who are the 'ribeirinhos'?
2. How much water is there in the Solimoes rive
3. Which state in Brazil is suffering from the drought?
4. What is referred to as 'war operations'?
5. Why were they needed?
6. How many villages have been affected by the drought?
7. How many families have been helped in the drought?
8. What poses a major threat of contamination?
9. Which disease was under control and may come back again?
10. Who have lost their livelihoods?

III   Fill in the numbered blanks in the following gist of the article:
The Amazon is the ___1___ river system in the world. It drains a widespread ___2___ covered with dense -___3___ . It has been in the news recently because it is ___4___. The people living in the deep ___5___ are now without ___6___ and ___7___. The ___8___ in the state are doing their best in a kind of '----9___ operation' to ___10___ these essential commodities as well as ___11___ to these stranded ___12___ . to prevent or ___13___ the bacterial diseases like ___14___, with the use of planes and ___15___.

IV   State in numbered points (about 10) the problems of the people of the drying Amazon Valley.

## 126  New Roles for Old Neem
(Courtesy: The Sunday Times of India)

*Long revered for its 'miraculous' powers in India, the neem has only recently been rediscovered by modern science. The wonder tree may be the plant's bulwark against global warming and marching deserts and promises to provide safe biopesticides, novel medicines and birth control pills for all mankind.* **A report by Vithal C. Nadkarni**

Salute the neem next time you see the tree. For centuries, our ancestors have been turning to this big, bitter-leafed tree for a variety of products. The list of the neem's virtues and uses is so long that the tree deserves to be called Kalpavriksha, the wish granting tree celebrated in our myths and fairytales.

After two decades of research, western scientists are ready to support that view. Even some of the most cautious researchers are saying that the neem deserves to be called a 'wonder plant'. In a recent report called Neem: *A Tree To Solve Global Problems*, the Washington-based National Research Council says, 'Probably no other plant yields as many strange and varied products or has as many exploitable by-products as the neem'.

'As foreseen by some scientists, "this tree for the 21st century" may usher in a new era in pest control, provide millions with inexpensive medicines, cut down the rate of human population growth and perhaps even reduce erosion, deforestation and the excessive temperature of an overheated globe'.

After saying that the neem may eventually benefit every person on the planet, however, the report adds a caveat – 'that all remains only a vague promise. Although the enthusiasm for neem may be justified, it is largely founded on empirical and anecdotal evidence. The greatest impediment to the neem's commercial development (in the industrialized countries) may simply be a general lack of credibility, or even awareness, of what it is and it can do.

Traditional societies have no such doubts. Native to India and Burma, the tree is a stately cousin of the mahogany and has been venerated since ancient times for its medicinal and fumigant properties. Neem is one of the five 'essentials' that tradition prescribes for every Indian garden; (the others are *amla* (Indian gooseberry), *palash* (flame-of-the-forest), *bilva* (Bengal quince or bael) and *tulsi* (sacred basil).

Ayurveda ascribes amazing curative powers to the neem. This is reflected in the term *'neem hakim'*.

Then there is the neem *panchang*– the roots, bark, gum, leaves, fruit, kernel and oil – which furnishes a variety of antivirals, anti-bacterials, fungicides and other bioactive substances. These have been found effective against a host of ailments ranging from Chagas' disease to malaria.

Countless Indians today use neem twigs, called *datun* in Gujarat, as disposable toothbrushes. This explains why, despite a general lack of toothpaste and toothbrushes, most people in India have white, healthy teeth.
Dried neem leaves are put in stored grain, clothes and books to protect them from pests. Neem leaves are used for skin ailments and in rituals to propitiate the goddess Mariamma of smallpox (which has been eradicated) and to fan the patients. Neem-oil cakes curb pests, improve the soil and serve as a nourishing animal feed.

A survey done in 1959 estimated that India had 14 million neem trees. Since each full-grown neem yields about 50 kg of fruit and some 350 kg of leaves annually, India probably produces 0.7 million metric tonnes of fruit and about five million metric tonnes of leaves every year. Although the neem plantations are unorganized and barely 20 to 25 percent report collection, according to the latest neem update by the Society of Pesticide Science, India, the 141 seed collection and 70 oil-production centres in the country are doing brisk business.

So valuable and adaptable is this tree that Indian immigrants and colonial administrators took it with them wherever they went to Africa, to the Caribbeans, to West Asia. Although it thrives 'almost anywhere' in the lowland tropics, the neem is particularly suited to hot and arid areas, which have the greatest need for tree cover.

In the last few decades, the tree has become well established in over 30 countries. This includes the nations along the Sahara's fringe where the tree provides precious fuel and lumber and is helping to halt the march of the desert. A United Nations report in 1968 called a neem plantation in northern Nigeria 'the greatest boon of the century' to the local inhabitants. A Saudi philanthropist has created what is probably the world's largest neem plantation – 50,000 trees --to provide shade and comfort to the two million Haj pilgrims who camp each year on the Plains of Arafat.

Moreover, unlike other imports like water hyacinth and congress grass which have become a serious nuisance in their host countries, the neem flourishes in a variety of habitats without aggression, in harmony with the native animals and plants.

All this explains why the Africans call the neem *muarubaini* which in Kiswahili means 'forty uses' or 'forty cures.' The Sanskrit name for the neem, arishta, means 'warder-off of evil and pestilence'. Persians have perhaps given the neem its most appropriate name: they called it *Azaddirakht-i-Hind* which literally means 'free tree of India'. From *Azad-dirakhti-Hind* comes the Latinized Botanical name for the neem, *Azadirachta indica*.

It is this remarkable freedom – *azadi* – from pests displayed by the neem which sparked western scientists' interest in the tree. Ironically, Indian scientists pioneered such studies as far back as the 1920s, but their work was little appreciated. At a recent seminar on neem held in Bombay, Dr. R.A. Mashelkar, director of the National Chemical Laboratory (NCL) Pune, described how India had frittered away its early breakthroughs – the structure of the neem's first major bitter principle, the anti-viral nimbin, was elucidated at NCL by Dr. Narayanan way back in 1965. But the country failed to capitalize on the lead.

The renaissance of neem research began with a plague of locusts in Sudan in 1959. A German entomologist, Dr. Heinreich Schmutterer, noticed that neem trees imported from India were the only green things left standing by the locusts. On closer investigation, he saw that although the insects settled on the trees in swarms, they left without feeding.

Subsequent work in labs all over the world uncovered even more amazing power of the neem. For instance, researchers at the US Department of Agriculture have found that the neem is 'by far the best among thousands of plant extracts tested' against a variety of pests which cause billions of dollars of damage annually. In 1985, the US Environmental Protection Agency approved a commercial neem-based insecticide for 'non-food uses', such as in greenhouses. Experts maintain despite the neem's apparent lack of toxicity of environmental danger, getting it approved for use in industrialized countries is an expensive and time-consuming process.

Fortunately for farmers in the developing countries, the neem chemicals are effective even in their low-tech (which is really super-tech; see next page) *avatar*: merely crush the leaves or seeds and soak them in water, alcohol and other solvents. The resulting cocktail of chemicals is dramatically effective, sometimes even at concentrations as minute as one-tenth of a part per million.

In field trials, neem proved as good as standard pesticides like DDT, dieldrin and malathion; while as far as safety and eco-friendliness went, it was incomparably superior. Experts say that while neem won't necessarily knock all the synthetics out of the market, there exists a huge global demand for 'soft' pesticides. This will be worth $813 million annually in 1998 in the US alone, according to a market survey, up from $450 million at present. With all this you will keep hearing about neem in the future. Salute it then.
(1,500 words)


## Exercises (on 126)

I    Complete the following table to list the tributes paid to the 'Neem' through the centuries.

|   | Tribute or title of praise | Tribute by | Reason for tribute |
|---|---|---|---|
| 1 | Kalpavriksha | Our ancestors | Virtues and uses |
| 2 |  | United Nations Report |  |
| 3 | Neem hakim |  |  |
| 4 |  |  | A new era in pest-control |
| 5 | One of the five essentials for every Indian garden |  |  |
| 6 |  | Persians |  |
| 7 |  |  | Forty cures |
| 8 | Arishta |  |  |
| 9 |  |  | Botanical value |

II    Write notes against each of the following landmark dates in the history of modern study and research on the 'Neem' as shown in this example e.g.

1920 – Indian scientists studied the neem for its freedom from pests.
1959

1965
1985

III    Prepare notes in points under the following headings:

a)    Traditional Uses of the Neem
b)    The Neem Abroad
c)    New and Modern Uses of the Neem

## 127        Excerpts from an article in a journal of Food Technology

Interest in nutrition has never been higher. Besides the prevailing interest in weight reduction diets, consumers increasingly desire information on diet and disease relationships. They are asking what they should eat to lower their serum cholesterol; what diet will make them less susceptible to cancer; and if they change their eating patterns, will they live longer. This article discusses the problems in communicating such nutrition information to the public.

### How Informed Are Consumers?

Today people have become more and more aware of nutrition. The 1989 Food Marketing Institute (FMI) Survey of consumer attitudes found that 76 percent of consumers say nutrition is a very important factor in selecting foods, up from 72 per cent in 1988. In the same survey, 27 per cent say fat concerns them most, up from 16 percent in 1987 and 9 per cent in 1983.

People are also making the connection between diet and disease. They accept that what they eat may have an effect on their health. The 1988 Health and Diet Survey by the Food and Drug Administration (FDA) and National Heart Blood and Log Institute (NHBLI) of the National Institutes of Health found that 55 percent of the people surveyed believe that fatty foods cause heart disease (compared to 29 per cent in 1983) and 25 per cent say fatty foods cause cancer (compared to 12 per cent in 1983).

Yet ironically according to the same study, only 34 percent know that fat and cholesterol are not the same. This indicates that there is a nutrition knowledge gap, i.e. what people believe about nutrition and what is scientifically correct vary greatly. This gap makes communicating nutrition very difficult. People typically do not understand complex nutrition concepts which require a background in chemistry and physiology.

Furthermore, consumers want precise dietary recommendations. They want to be told, 'This is the best food, this is the worst food'. Unfortunately, this is difficult for professionals to do, and when they hedge, consumers doubt their credibility and/or knowledge.

Consumers need to know you're offering an opinion based on the current facts. Asking 10 nutritionists to describe the role of saturated fat in the diet will provide 10 different opinions – hopefully all based on scientific fact. It is difficult, however, to communicate to consumers that nutritional issues are not black and while.

Oat bran is a good example of a difficult nutrition issue. How do you explain to the public that there isn't a perfect fibre, that the scientific consensus on dietary fibre is simply not in yet? Soluble fibre probably lowers cholesterol more than insoluble fibre, yet insoluble fibre such as rice bran also lowers cholesterol. While certain fibres clearly play a role in a cholesterol-lowering diet, there are not magic bullets, no cure-alls.

Nutrition information is not readily available to the public. Registered dieticians usually work in hospitals with sick people and it is difficult to get access to them. Although there are dieticians in private practice, most consumers are not willing to pay to have nutrition questions answered.

If consumers have a nutrition question, where do they go?
The two main sources of nutrition information for consumers are the media and food industry advertising.

Problems with the media are time constraints and entertainment value. Because few issues are given more than a minute for coverage on television, it is not possible to provide background to help consumers understand a topic or put the study into the context of all existing studies. Furthermore, the media is here to inform and entertain. Routine results do not help with ratings. No television host wants to talk about moderation and variety as the keys to good nutrition. You need a book like 'Processed Cheese Prevents Cancer' to get on the television talk shows.

Most scientific studies are reported by the media as a definitive answer – they are not put into the context of all existing studies on the topic. This means that consumers may decide to change their food habits based on a nutrition study that contradicts the prevailing scientific consensus. Furthermore, before food professionals can preview and properly evaluate a specific study, it has been reported in all the major newspapers.

Advertising on food products can be equally confusing bout nutrition for the public. If consumers believed everything they heard on daytime television, they would buy a particular brand of peanut butter because it contained no cholesterol, never knowing that no plant product contains cholesterol. They might not purchase shredded wheat since it would take a dozen bowls of shredded wheat to equal the nutrition in one bowl of a fortified cereal. Many consumers believe that 2 per cent milk is extremely low in fat since whole milk must be 100 per cent milk. Thus, even if your intentions are good, it is easy to confuse consumers about nutrition sine they lack an adequate background in the science of nutrition.

## Who should Communicate Nutrition?

People who communicate nutrition information should have the oratory skills of Daniel Webster, the wisdom of Solomon, and the wit of Bill Cosby, noted Dr. Ted Labuza in a recent IFT Nutrition Division Newsletter. Besides they should have an adequate scientific background in nutrition. Anyone can call oneself a nutritionist. We all eat, so we must all know about nutrition. Generally, 'nutritionist' has no legal meaning as profession or course of study.

Registered dieticians have a minimum of a bachelor's degree and some formal on the job training. The American Dietetic Association has strict standards for becoming a registered dietician and maintaining a registration status through continuing education credits.

## Exercises (overleaf)

I   Make a table with the column headings shown below, organizing information on improvement in nutrition awareness among consumers, given in the passage above. An example has also been provided for you.

| Agency conducting the survey | Points of nutrition awareness | Improvement in nutrition awareness over the years |
|---|---|---|
| Food Marketing Institute | Nutrition is an important factor in selecting foods | 72 per cent in 1988 |
|  |  | 76 per cent in 1989 |

II   Indicate briefly the 6 problems that come in the way of giving consumers satisfactory nutrition information. The first one is given as an example.

Eg (i) <u>The nutrition knowledge gap</u>: People cannot understand complex nutrition concepts which require Background of chemistry and physiology.

III   Complete the following diagram to show the problems connected with each of the sources of nutrition information, as shown in the example.

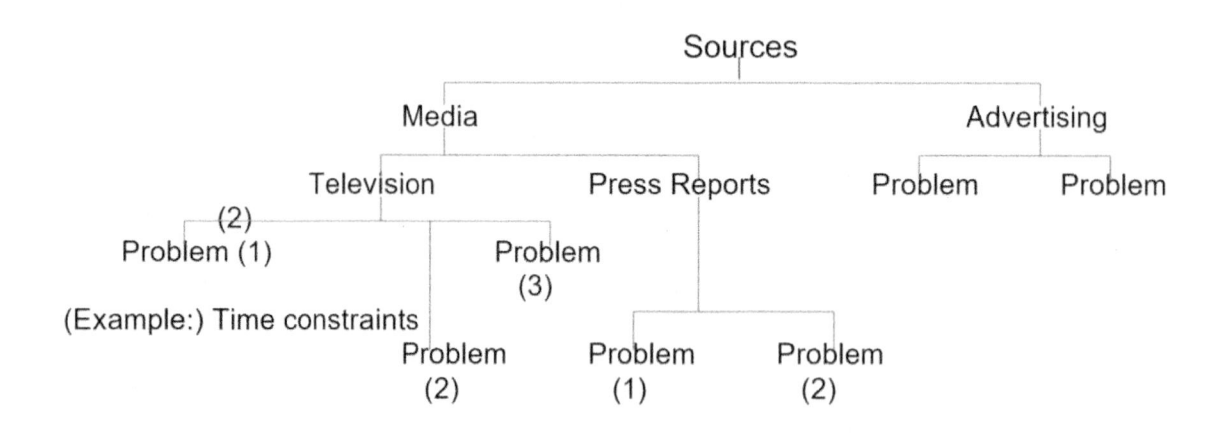

```
                            Sources
            ┌─────────────────┴─────────────────┐
          Media                              Advertising
   ┌────────┼────────┐                    ┌──────┴──────┐
Television        Press Reports        Problem       Problem
   │(2)              │
Problem (1)       Problem
   │                (3)
(Example:) Time constraints
         │         ┌────────┼────────┐
       Problem  Problem  Problem
         (2)      (1)      (2)
```

IV   List the qualities required in an ideal Nutrition Communicator.

**128**  **Concrete Example**
(Courtesy: The Sunday Times of India)

*A revolutionary technique of making concrete from lunar soil without using water, has revived the hopes of scientists of building a colony on the moon, says N. Suresh.*

The dream of building a colony on the moon has now became a reality - thanks to the revolutionary technique of obtaining concrete from lunar soil without using water.

Since the landing of 12 astronauts on the moon between 1969 and 1972, scientists have been obsessed with the idea of setting up a manned station on the earth's natural satellite. For, it could act as the base for further forays into space, especially Mars, the planet nearest to the earth in the solar system.

It has been a difficult task to design a manned station due to the harsh climate conditions on the moon. First, the structure should be able to resist great thermal shocks, as the moon's temperature fluctuates between minus 150 degrees C and 120 degrees C in a 28-day cycle. Moreover, the structure would have to be designed to withstand the vagaries of weather on the satellite which has no atmosphere and gravity which is six times less than that on the earth.

It is precisely for these reasons that it would be impossible to produce conventional concrete, the elements making up concrete – cement, gravel, sand and water – cannot combine in such climatic conditions.

Even if the right technology to make concrete that could work on the moon was perfected, the magnitude of the task of transporting the construction material from the earth to the moon would be insurmountable. To build a lunar base, 40 meters in diameter and 20 metres high, at least 1000 tonnes of cement, 330 tonnes of water (due to lack of water on the satellite), and 300 tonnes of iron would have to be transported there. And the cost could be anywhere near Rs. 190000 crore.

An attempt was made in 1984 when scientists sent a satellite into orbit with the material which could be used for building. Their aim was to test the resistance and durability of this material in conditions comparable to that on the moon. The results, available after six years, were disappointing. Almost all the samples were badly damaged by solar wind radiation and meteorites.

But engineers have now found a way out, according to a report in the French embassy newsletter, *CEDUST*. An American engineer, Dr. T.D. Lin, is the savior of the Lunar Base Project. He mixed 40 grams of lunar soil (collected during various missions) with water and produced concrete. The properties of this concrete were comparable to the best used in the world, and computer studies confirmed that this concrete could withstand the enormous temperature differences found on the moon.

Encouraged by these results, Dr. Lin turned his attention towards devising a technique to make concrete without water so that the operations could be carried out on the moon itself. The revolutionary technique could produce concrete from ilmenite, a rock consisting of iron oxide and titanium oxide available in plenty on the moon.

The technique involved heating ilmenite to 800 degree C using huge solar panels on the moon itself to produce dry concrete. When hydrogen was added to this the chemical reaction produced iron, titanium and water vapour. The mixture injected into the pressurized mould containing the dry-pressed concrete, after a few hours, produced an exceptionally strong concrete, more resistant than the ordinary one mixed with water. The iron was used to reinforce it.

Dr. Lin's technique decreased the cost of building a base by nearly one-fourth. Experts estimate that the base could be built by spending approximately Rs. 40000 crores. Only 100 tonnes of machinery, five tonnes of vehicles and 100 tonnes of drilling equipment would have to be transported.

The plan for the base is now concretized. An eight-nation Lunar Concrete Committee has been set up and promised a budget of Rs. 100000 crores. A French company has been given the task of reproducing a machine-material complex in the field to produce lunar concrete.

India could benefit immensely if the technology could be used to make durable concrete, for, the conventional concrete made by government agencies has been unable to stand the stress caused by overloaded vehicles on the country's crowded roads.
(800 words)

## Exercises

I   (a) Which phrase in the first paragraph indicates the subject (theme) of the article?
    (b) Is the title a clue to the subject? Explain your answer.

II  Fill in the blanks in the following notes on the passage:
The new concrete making technique would be helpful to mankind in
Setting up a _____1___ station on the moon.
Building a _____2____ there.
Promoting exploration of _____3____, especially of ____4_____, the nearest planet.
A structure for a manned station could not be built on the moon because
it had to resist _____5____ shocks (e.g., temperature fluctuations between ___6___ and _____7____ in a _____8_____ cycle).
ii)  it had to withstand the absence of _____9_____ and a _____10_____ that was one –
sixth that of the earth.
The cost of _____11____ the materials ( _____12____ tonnes of cement, ____13____ of water and _____14_____ on the moon would have been about Rs. ____15_____ .

III  Make your notes in points on the article using the following headings:

A Revolutionary Technique & Why.
 Dr. Lin's experiment
 Features of the New Concrete
 Plans for the Lunar Base Project
 Future Scope of Space Research
 Possible Use of the New Concrete in India.

IV  Write a summary of the article using your answers to Ex. III above.

## Sins of the flesh

*SHANTI B RANGWANI explodes the myth about the importance of animal proteins and makes a fresh case for vegetarianism*

A RECENT article in the American magazine Health Science states that animal protein rather than fat, is what is increasing blood cholesterol levels. Cut down the animal protein and the cholesterol level automatically goes down. This is really why the cholesterol levels in China are so low.

In a study in Italy, people with high cholesterol levels were put on a low-fat diet. Cholesterol levels dropped, but only from 290 to 270. Next the protein in the diet was switched from animal sources to plant sources, and the cholesterol levels went all the way down to 200. Continuing the research, while the cholesterol levels were way down, they put animal protein back in the diet – although still a low-fat diet – and the cholesterol levels started to rise.

"This clearly establishes that consumption of animal protein increases cholesterol levels. There is a tremendous reluctance on the part of the scientific community to even consider the adverse effects of animal proteins on disease processes."

That the intake of protein, especially the difficult-to-digest animal proteins, leads to a tremendous increase in strength, is another myth. This is absolutely unscientific. Dietician Chittenden has observed that a reduction of protein actually results in an increase of physical and mental energy, a capacity to work for long periods without getting tired, and reduced susceptibility to disease. In fact, an experiment was conducted on a group of German athletes in the early '50s. One part of the group under training was kept on vegetarian food and the second on a non-vegetarian diet. Of course, it was the first group which turned out superior in both endurance and stamina. The more protein one eats, the more vital energy will be spent in digesting it, and the less the energy available to the body for its other functions.

Most medics, however, still consider proteins the most essential of the food groups, refusing to accept that meat is essentially toxic, and throws an unnecessary and harmful burden on the kidneys and liver, which have to purify the blood of extra toxins.

Besides, most farm animals and poultry have been bred from a small common stock – genetically 'murdered' – to ensure greater yields of fresh and other animal products. Consider, also, the elaborate poultry-farming techniques, where broiler chicks are pumped with artificial and often carcinogenic growth hormones and vaccines.

Of course, pesticides also exist in vegetables. But when we consume animals what we get is the concentrated effect of fertilisers, pesticides and all those artificial hormones pumped into fatten the animals, not to mention the sodium nitrate and nitrites which are extensively used to give meats an attractive red colour as well as to preserve them.

For a normal person to digest cooked food requires anything from 4 to 7 hours, depending on how it is cooked, what food group it belongs to, and what it is eaten with. And even then, there is a considerable residue leftover, undigested, which has to be pushed out of the body. The situation is worse in the case of flesh foods which require anything between 25 and 30 hours to pass through the entire gastro-intestinal tract, the food decomposing in the abdomen for a further day or two, at a temperature of 38oC, and acted upon by a variety of acids and enzymes.

According to Leonardo Blanche, author of Cancer and Other Diseases from Meat Consumption: "Cancer of the stomach forms nearly one-third of all cancers, and is almost directly attributable to the fact that if flesh foods are not broken up, decomposition results, and active poisons are thrown into organs not intended for their reception."

One of the biggest frauds in modern nutrition is the excessive emphasis placed on the importance of protein in diet. We must take protein, but not half as much as we tend to. The human body recycles as much as 70 per cent of its protein wastes. It loses only about 20 gm. of protein under normal circumstances, through faeces, hair, urine, perspiration and dead skin. But most of us eat far too great an amount of protein to compensate for this small loss.

All the extra protein absorbed by the body gets stored and adds to your weight. If the body cannot muster enough energy to eliminate these added excesses, it starts to degenerate and weaken. According to Dr Hindheed, the former food administrator of Denmark: "When too much protein enters the bloodstream, it gets converted into nitric, sulphuric and phosphoric acids. The body is then forced to use up large amounts of alkaline minerals to neutralise these acids. The result is a deficiency of minerals in the bones, hair and nails."

Acids such as uric acid cause so much damage to the liver and kidneys that in some cases they may even prove fatal. Excess meat-eating causes erythrocytes and albumin in the urine, increasing manifold the chances of infection. Over consumption of protein has been linked to cancer of the breast, liver and bladder, and to a spiralling increase in the incidence of leukemia and Bright's disease.

But even if you would like to have more than the prescribed minimum of 60 gm. of protein a day, you would be better advised to switch to vegetable foods rich in protein. After all, where do the animals themselves get all their nutrients from? Plants, yes. Try to include primarily raw fruits and vegetables in your diet , and if you have to cook them, make sure you don't deep fry or cook them for long periods so as not to destroy them completely.


## Exercises

I     Indicate which of the following statements are 'True' or 'False' according to the passage or 'Not Indicated' in it:
a)     Animal fat and not animal proteins increase cholesterol levels.
b)     Animal proteins have an adverse effect on disease processes.
c)     They do not throw a harmful burden on the kidney and liver
d)     They are better than plant proteins
e)     Animal proteins are the most essential of the food groups
f)     They lead to increased physical strength and energy
g)     They can add to our weight

II     (A) Complete the following statement by choosing the correct alternatives from the options that follow:

Plant proteins are better than animal proteins because
a) They are digested easily and quickly.
b) They do not cause cancer.
c) They give protein which can be stored in the body.
d) They reduce more cholesterol.
e) They contain no toxins.
f) They do not contain pesticides
g) They leave more physical and mental energy.
h) Extra plant proteins can be eaten safely
i) They are recycled

(B) Of the statements **not chosen from the above**, say whether each one of them is
i. incorrect,
ii. inaccurate according to the passage
iii. unstated in the passage

III (A) Complete the following statement by choosing the correct alternatives from the options that follow:
The <u>dangers of excessive intake of proteins</u> are
a) Extra protein gets stored and adds to our weight.
b) Extra proteins are lost through faeces, urine, hair, perspiration and dead skin.
c) Excess protein increases the cholesterol level.
d) When not eliminated they degenerate and convert to nitric sulphuric and phosphoric acids.
e) The alkaline minerals become deficient in the bones, hair and nails.
f) Plants and vegetable proteins are not easily digested.
g) Uric acid damages the liver and kidneys.
h) The urine with erythrocytes and albumin becomes vulnerable to infection
i) Several types of cancers are caused.
j) We require only 60 gms. of protein.

(B) Of the statements not chosen, say whether each one of them is
a. incorrect,
b. inaccurate
c. irrelevant.

IV   Make notes from the newspaper article under the headings given below. You may use the points given above adding information, brief explanations or examples wherever necessary.
1. Myths about Proteins
2. Research on Plant Proteins versus Animal Proteins
3. Superiority of Plant Proteins over Animal Proteins
4. Hazards of Excessive Protein Intake

**Exercises   (on Passage 130 'I Felt Like God Had Died' which follows)**

I   (Comprehension Questions)

1. How widespread is child abuse in India and abroad? Are the figures given good indicators of the extent of the occurrence of the crime?
2. What are the four reasons mentioned for most cases going unreported in India?
3. List the four categories mentioned of abnormal molesters. Are there normal people also who commit such crimes? What is the reason?
4. What has been the role of the mother and the family in most cases of child abuse?
5. What has the attitude of Indian society been towards child abuse?
6. In what ways have the victims of child abuse been wronged? (You may also use the information in the box which follows the article)

II   By using your answers to the Comprehension questions above (Ex. I), make notes on the article, grouping your points under suitably worded headings.

## "I felt like God had died"

Barely one in ten cases of child abuse is reported to the police. But recently several such crimes have come to light, including one in a school in Bombay which outraged concerned parents. CHAND B RANGWANI reports

*THREE children, aged from three to six years, were sexually abused by a 24-year-old youth in a Bombay crèche recently. The youth is the son of the owner of the crèche.*

*Police have arrested the prosperous owner of a dairy in Delhi on charges of raping his 12-year-old daughter. Having raped his elder daughter almost every day for six years till the trauma led to her eventual suicide, he then turned his attention to the younger one, first molesting and then raping her.*

*In Hyderabad, urchins and runaways in the eight to 15 age-groups are abused regularly by auto rickshaw drivers, porters and other menial workers who sodomise them paying a meagre Rs 5 for each occasion.*

*Police charged a 32-year-old man with the rape of a 11-month-old infant in North Delhi. Police said the accused was a neighbour who knew the victim's parents.*

*An 8-year-old was admitted to a hospital in Chiplun, Maharashtra, with swollen labia and severe rectal bleeding. The rapist was her grandfather.*

*Are these incidents random aberrations? Or do they occur more frequently than many of us would like to think?*

It is estimated that of every four rape victims, three will be minors. And last year in Delhi alone, there were an estimated 400 cases of sodomy of minors. Add to these cold statistics the fact that there are currently an estimated 500,000 child prostitutes in our country.

To make matters worse, the low incidents of police complaints not only undermines the scale of the malaise but also motivates the abuser to perpetrate further crimes against kids, whom they now consider easy meat. According to a crime branch official

in Bombay, barely one in ten cases of abuse gets reported. The social stigma attached to the loss of virtue in girls in a culture which fetishizes female virginity, the absence of the necessary channels of communication between parents and their children regarding sexual matters and the immediate trauma of the experience, all contribute to the horrific silence of acceptance. But the most common cause for this silence is the fact that the molester is often a member of the family.

Mothers will often support their men in their efforts to cover up abuse once it has come to light. At times mothers may even be active participants with their men and a number of incest survivors speak of being held down by their mothers while a male relative carries out the sexual act.

According to Dr Rohini Gavankar, who was on the sub-committee of the now-defunct National Commission on Child Abuse, "More than 50 per cent of the offenders happen to be close male relatives of the child. And in almost all the other cases, the offender was known to the family. So many of the child molesters appear to be such nice and normal people. I believe such incidents are nothing more than an accident in the man's life. I don't really know what else could make them behave like this."

Psychiatric research into the sexuality of offenders however reveals that the molester is an emotionally immature person whose pathological preoccupation with sex makes him turn to children for gratification. Many abusers are also latent homosexuals with a repressed fear of women. Another category of abusers are those in advance stages of venereal disease who believe that having sex with a virgin will cure them. Unfortunately, the prevalent myth about child abuse in India is that it is more a sociological issue than a psycho-pathological issue, and that it is perpetrated only within deprived families. But this is not true here, or abroad. According to a U.S. Dept. of Justice release, one girl in three and one boy in seven will be sexually molested before the age of 18. And the typical American paedophile will abuse 380 children in a lifetime.

Prema Purav feels their pain. As the secretary of Annapurna, Bombay's well-known women's organisation, she has rehabilitated over 800 abused girls to date, helping them redeem their self-worth by employing them in her organisation and even getting many married to progressive men from good families. "The poor have very few choices," she says. "Many raped girls are by their families and are forced to go into prostitution at the tender age of ten or eleven." "Once a girl is raped, the mothers would generally cry and moan about it for a while, but they won't go to the police or the courts. Many don't wish to take them back, for fear that the whole family will be 'spoiled'. Only once did the girl go back. She had been raped by her father, had a baby as a result, and had come to us for protection. A few months later her mother came and pressurized her to return, saying that going ahead with the complaint would jeopardize the future of her other four kids and that she herself would have to fend for them by going into prostitution. The girl agreed to go home, and the case fizzled out. That is what poverty does."

But just who else is there to take up cudgels on behalf of such traumatized children? There are few children's advocacy groups, given that they aren't part of the electorate. "And it's definitely not the government." says Dr Gavankar. "Their entire exercise in appointing the commission was pure tokenism."

As regards the judicial process, "there is a great deal of trauma involved for the abused child in going through an elaborate court procedure," says Purav. "How can she say exactly what happened? And the lawyers can get so vicious and insensitive. I think, there is a need to save the child from the rigours of lengthy cross-examination."

Noted Bombay-based criminal lawyer, Adhik Shirodkar, feels otherwise: "What is really required is some sensitivity-training for the judiciary and the police since they are woefully desensitized and maladapted for handling such cases. Otherwise, the current procedure and the strict standards of proof are quite adequate. If the child has been molested for the first time, the medical evidence will show it clearly. If the child is strong and tried to resist, it would imply that there would be marks. The principle is that we go not by the quantity of evidence but its quality." Indeed, given the high incidence of false accusations in such cases, perhaps a simplistic procedure is something we need to guard against. Because child molestations are so abhorrent, mere suspicion can ruin lives. Remember Michael Jackson? But what is desperately required are post-trauma support services for the children and their families. Says Purav, "Where is the emotional security of the child when the mother is silently acquiescing in what the father is doing?"

"Over the years we teach them to be economically and mentally independent. We tell them that their past hurts are of no consequence today, that whatever happened wasn't their fault, that it was just an accident which they couldn't have helped. And after sometime, they too start to think that way."

The sad fact however is that only a small fraction of those abused ever get the love or reassurances required to heal the psychic scarring. Most abused children will grow up and themselves become abusers or criminals. In fact, a survey of female offenders in prison shows that as many as 67 per cent of them had been raped as children.

Much as we would like to think otherwise, there are some scars which can never heal. As one incest survivor, raped by her father and brother for seven years, put in: "They were my family. When they started it on me, I felt like God had died. I have to cope with it every single day even now. How can I forget when I can never forgive?"

# Child abuse: some after-effects

*A Bombay-based psychologist shares some of his findings with NARENDRA PANJWANI*

GIVEN that paedophiles – adults who strongly prefer to have sex with children – seem as common in India as in the US and elsewhere, what happens to these child victims when they grow up?

Do they also become paedophiles? Do the psychic scars of their childhood heal in later years, or are they traumatised for life? If so, in what way? Is trauma not perhaps an extreme term for all types of adult-child sex, considering that it often occurs among kin, at 'home', and doesn't always involve rape?

One psychotherapist and sexologist, based in Bombay, who has been probing these questions for some years now is Dr Girish Sanghavi, who also writes a weekly column in the city' oldest Gujarati-language newspaper *Bombay Samachar*. "Just taking my patients and stray remarks from one's peers into account, I'd say that at least ten per cent of all children have been molested by the time they are 18. At least mind you: the true figure may be closer to 20."

"Secondly," adds Sanghavi, "The majority of child molestations involve genital fondling or oral sex, Vaginal or anal penetration is not so common, in comparison."

When caught in the act, paedophiles (who usually tend to be males) sometimes apparently offer drunkenness as the reason, saying, in effect, that they are not normally given to acts of this kind. Through this ruse the paedophile seeks to convince the doctor that instead of punishment, psychotherapy or rehabilitation, he simply needs to stop getting drunk.

But what sort of scars does molestation in childhood leave on the adult? Responds Sanghavi, "That's something you discover gradually, often unexpectedly. The symptoms people come with have no apparent connection with it, but as the case unravels you sometimes find that his/her problem today is rooted in childhood sex. Take for instance this case of 28-year-old housewife who refuses to have sexual intercourse with her husband. She will allow him to fondle and caress her, but that's about it. Her husband was very frustrated because no form of persuasion would work, and so he brought her here."

"It turned out that this mental block had to do with sex over a few years with her 40-year-old uncle who would fondle her when she was 11 years old. She came to believe that the sex act began and ended with such stimulation and was terrified of the violence of intercourse."

"Another married middle-class woman suspected all men, including her husband. She withdrew from all contact with men as far as possible. The reason: her father had abused her sexually. Not rape, just genital fondling. But the damage had been done, and it took a lot of work to restore her trust, slowly."

# ANSWERS

## Unit I A
**I**
A    Passage 4 – The Zodiac; 5 – Photosynthesis; 6 – Tides; 7 – At the Planetarium; 8 – Lightning.
B    Passage 10 - What is the Sun Made of? 11 – How a Bird Flies/ How Does a Bird Fly? 12 – What was the Apollo? 13 – What is a Kitchen Garden?
C    A-2; B-3; C-6; D-1; E-5; F-7; G-4.

## Unit I B
**I**    (A) 1-d, 2-e, 3-b, 4-c, 5-a.
(B) 1: -a-i, b-v, c-ii, e-iii; 2: a-ii, b-ii, c-v, d-iii; 3: a-i, c-v, d-i, e-ii; 4: a-I, b-ii, d-iv, e-iv;
5: b-iv, c-iii, d-v, e-iii.

## Unit II
**Passages: 18** <u>First & Last</u> Sentences; **19** <u>Implied</u>: *The fuel crisis has several effects*; **20** <u>Last</u> Sentence; **21** <u>Last</u> Sentence; **22** <u>Implied</u>: That morning everybody got their gifts but my stocking was empty; **23** <u>Implied</u>: There was a terrible storm with lightning and thunder. **24** Sentence 6 ('But there is no doubt …… is diminishing'). **25** <u>Last but one</u> Sentence.( 'Up in this high …. Lightness of heart'). **26** <u>Scattered</u>: Fear of juvenile delinquency and an increasing conflict between parents and children. **27**: <u>Last but one</u> sentence ('Still in your formless …. unfathomable future').

## Unit III
**I**
(A) feeble, visible, hopeful, angry, cheerful, unlucky, clumsy, cool, increasing, probable.
(B) easily, harmoniously, tidily, accurately, gently, merrily, quickly/ fast, ably, disgracefully, neatly.
(A) mumbling, economy, display, approach, disembarkation, crawl, denunciation, acceleration, stroll, strut.

**II**
(A) 1 accelerate; 2 approach; 3 strut; 4 denounce; 5 disembark; 6 display; 7 economize; 8 mumble; 9 stroll; 10 crawl

(B) 1-cloudless, 2-deadly, 3-sandy, 4-luxurious, 5-delicious, 6-neat, 7-shrill, 8-winding, 9-brilliant,
10-sore.

**III**
(A) 1- knuckle, 2 - wrist, 3- sole, 4-ankle, 5-forehead, 6 -nape, 7-thigh, 8 -chest, 9- -eyebrow, 10-stomach, 11- knuckles, 12 -under-arm.
(B) 1-matron, 2-jockey, 3-sculptor, 4-purser, 5-plumber, 6-ambassador, 7-mason, 8-professor, 9- architect, 10-caddie.
( C ) 1-Pliers, 2-corkscrew, 3-scales, 4-thermometer, 5-telescope, 6-tin-opener, 7-spanner, 8-bulldozer, 9-tongs, 10-tractor.
(D) 1-E; 2-H, 3-C, 4-L, 5-I, 6-K; 7-D, 8-F, 9-A, 10-G, 11-B, 12-J.

**Passages:**
**29** Overall Title: <u>Science & Population Control</u>
Main Idea: Advances in medical & ancilliary sciences have helped decrease death-rate.
    Illustrations: The D.D.T. experiment in British Guiana.
**30** Overall Title: <u>Our Sleep Needs</u>
Main Idea: Research has improved the means of neuro-physical measurement & developed better methods of evaluating human performance & behaviour.
    Illustrations: Behaviour studies & experiments on the effects of sleep.
**31** Overall Title: Tarantula &Tarantella
Main Idea: A connection between the dance and the spider: (The vigorous dance was supposed to work out the poison of the tarantula from the body.)
    Illustrations: Examples to show that this was a fiction/ myth.
**32** Overall Title: Coal & Energy
Main Idea: The burning of the atoms in the coal releases far greater energy than the coal itself.
    Illustrations: Examples quantifying the energy generated

# Unit IV
**(A)**
**34**
I    The main distinction is between animals which hunt by night and those which do so by day.
II    *Repetitions*: at night; at night; In the daytime; at night; diurnal (day-active). *Transitional signals*: This is because; The chain then; a second tier; it may be less easy; but it may be.
III    a) The moist night air helps animals without waterproof skins to avoid drying up and even dying during the daytime. E.g., slugs, snails, woodlice, centipedes.

b) Some animals feed on smaller nocturnal animals. E.g., hedgehogs, mice, toads.
c) Some animals avoid large diurnal birds of prey like eagles and buzzards. E.g., foxes, badgers, stoats, owls, rabbits.

**IV** Many animals hunt by night for different reasons. Animals without waterproof skins benefit from the moist night air so as to avoid drying up to death during the daytime e.g., slugs, snails. Some animals feed on smaller nocturnal animals e.g., hedgehogs, mice and others hunt by night probably to avoid large diurnal birds of prey like eagles and buzzards e.g., foxes, badgers, etc.
(50 words)

## 35
**I**  A : 2, 3;   B : 1, 3.

**II** The owl is an effective night hunter because the large window in front of the eye allows maximum light and the rounded lens produces a bright image helping the owl to judge the distance from the prey accurately. The fringes on his feathers help eliminate the noise of air rushing over the wings as the owl swoops down on his prey.
(58 words)

## 36
**I** a) to remove turbidity caused by solid particles suspended in the water
b) to remove colour that may be due to iron salts
c) To remove taste and odour from the water
d) To remove algae which may grow in a reservoir
e) To remove contamination by pathogens from sewage

**II** Coherence Signals:
First there is ...
Then there is ....
... should also ...
.... and it may be necessary ..
Then the most important of all.....

**III** Water should be purified by treating it to remove turbidity, colour, taste and odour, algae and pathogens.

## 37

**I**    *True*: b, d & e.      *False*: a & c

**II**    a) b, d & e.    b) Parts of sentence 2 and sentence 4

c) Transitional Signals: '... though ... never...' (in Sentence 2)
      '... probably ... but ...not actually control' (in Sentence 4)

**III**    a) i) presence of sunlight; ii) presence of chlorophyll in the plant; iii) supply of carbon dioxide and water.    b) In the middle of Sentence 4    c) Tr. Signals: '... other factors ...probably .... not actually control.'

**IV**    Photosynthesis or synthesis of carbohydrates occurs in all green plants and depends greatly on the presence of sunlight, of chlorophyll in the green plants and on the supply of carbon dioxide and water

## 38

**I**    a) Coherence of laser light means that the individual light rays are all of the same wavelength or colour and move at the same rate as each other.
      b) Sentence 2    c) yes. In Sentence 3.

**II**    a:
i) The light waves do not dissipate and their energy is, therefore, concentrated. (Sentence 5)
ii) The energy is concentrated to a sharply defined point. (S. 6)
iii) The range of the light source is tremendously extended. (S. 7)

b) 'The reason...' (S.5); 'This makes ...' (S. 6); 'It also ...' (S. 7).

**III**    a)    i) The light can illuminate the surface of the moon because the light does not dissipate and the range is tremendously extended
ii) Because the energy is concentrated at a sharply defined point it can send a searing pinpoint of light into the human eyeball to weld a detached retina.
iii) Because of the intense energy it can weld metals and is useful for precision working making micro-electronic circuits.

C) 'Because its light ..' (S. 9); 'Because its energy ..' (S. 10);And since its radiation ..' (S. 11)

**IV** A laser light is more effective than ordinary light because it is coherent. This makes for a concentration of energy at a sharply defined point and tremendous extension of the range of the light source. Three special uses of the laser are that firstly, it can illuminate the surface of the moon with a two-mile-wide circle of light, secondly, it can send a searing pinpoint of light into the human eye to weld a detached retina, and thirdly, it can also weld metals with precision in making micro-electronic circuits.
( 88 words)

**B) Famous Lives**
**I**  A – 2; B – 3; C - 1; D – 3; E – 4.
**II**  A) 1 – b; 3 – c; 4 – b.  B) 1 – d; 2 – d; 4 – c.  C) 2 – a; 3 – d; 4 – e.
  D) 1 – a; 2 – d; 4 – d.  E) 1 – e; 2 – d; 3 – d.

## Unit V

### (A) Analysis

**Passage**

47  *Pattern*: Classification  *Coherence Signals*: underlined;

There are three kinds of book owners. The first has all the standard sets and bestsellers ---- unread, untouched. (This deluded individual owns wood-pulp and ink, not books.) The second has a great many books --- a few of them read through, most of them dipped into, but all of them as clean and shiny as the day they were bought. (This person would probably like to make books his own, but is restrained by a false respect for their physical appearance.) The third has a few books or many --- every one of them dog-eared and dilapidated, shaken and loosened by continual use, marked and scribbled in from front to back. (This man owns books.)
(115 words approx.)

*Summary*: The true book owner is the one who loves reading his few books again and again even if they are falling apart. Another kind of book owner keeps the *standard sets* more *for display* while the third kind may dip into his many books but likes to keep them clean and shiny rather than *to read* them.

(50 words)

**48**   *Pattern:* Classification   *Coherence Signals:* underlined

<u>Most insects</u> start life as eggs. <u>The baby</u> insects that hatch out have no wings <u>and often</u> look very *different from adults.* <u>Butterflies</u>, for example, go through a caterpillar stage <u>and young bluebottles</u> are maggots. <u>The big change</u> of the adult stage takes place in the pupa or chrysalis. <u>Young earwigs</u> and grasshoppers, <u>on the other hand</u>, *resemble the adults* quite closely. <u>They</u> gradually acquire wings as they grow up.
(70 words approx.)

*Summary:* Most insects like butterflies and bluebottles start life as eggs and look very different from adults. However, young earwigs and grasshoppers resemble adults quite closely
(30 words)

**49**   *Pattern*: Process   *Coherence Signals*: underlined

<u>A tree</u> in the forest, old with too many springs (= years), is conquered by flourishing fungal parasites; on a day of high wind it falls. The <u>saprophytes</u> slowly devour the log's tissue. <u>Gradually</u> they themselves decay <u>and become</u> food for other saprophytes. <u>The bacteria then</u> take over. <u>There are</u> many linked species, <u>each reducing the dead</u> stuff <u>to forms</u> more elemental. <u>At last</u>, the nitrifying bacteria, <u>both by their</u> living <u>and their</u> multitudinous dying, release nitrates into the soil. Rain and soil water <u>dissolve them</u>. <u>The roots</u> of bracken, spring <u>where the old tree grew.</u> They absorb the nitrates, <u>and they are life again</u>.
        (110 words approx.)

*Summary*: The <u>old tree</u> in the forest <u>is attacked</u> by saprophytes <u>which decay</u> and become food for other saprophytes <u>and later</u> bacteria. <u>Through a chain</u> of linked species the dead stuff is reduced <u>to more elemental forms</u>. <u>Thus, at last</u>, nitrifying bacteria release nitrates into the soil where rain and water <u>help new roots to spring</u> and grow into trees <u>and start the chain of life again</u>.

**50**   *Pattern*: Para 1: Cause & Consequence; Para 2 - 4 Sequence of Ideas (Time Order)

*Coherence Signals*: much more ancient. .... As early as 7000 BC. .... Even a thousand years before .... Tens of thousands of years before ... the first civilizations .... These prehistoric people ....... But the very first signs .... Are older still .... Over two million years ago.

*Summary*: Contrary to the Irish man's conclusions about the beginning of life placed at 4004 BC, the first signs of human beings are over two million years old. Evidence of tools made of wood, bone and stone is dated tens of thousands of years before the first civilizations. Jericho and the Middle East civilizations thrived as early as 7,000 BC.
(56 words)


51      *Pattern*: Sequence of Ideas (Space & Time Order)

*Coherence Signals*: Some centuries after the rise ...... narrow valley ...... dozens of bustling villages and towns grew up .... Over the years .... Vast system of dams ... river ... reliable link ... hundreds of kilometres .... Around 3100 BC. ... In the centuries that followed ... powerful Egyptian civilization ..... flourished .... For two thousand years.

*Summary*: The Sumerian states after some centuries grew into a great civilization of bustling towns and villages. The Nile river served as a highway and the dams and canals irrigated the lands After 3100 BC. The Egyptian rulers became powerful and the splendour of Egypt flourished for two thousand years.
(58 words)


52      *Pattern*:  An Idea & its Component Parts
*Coherence Signals*: That man ... who .... That his body ... whose intellect ... whose mind ... one who is full of fire .... But whose passions ... who has learned to love all beauty.

*Summary*: A man with a liberal education is one who has trained his body to serve his will which in turn is controlled by a sharp and powerful intellect and a mind stored with the knowledge of the fundamental truths of Nature. He is a lover of beauty, art and goodness and is full of life and fire but has passions that are tuned by a tender conscience.
(65 words)

**53**   *Pattern: Sequence of Details / Description*

Coherence Signals: And the rain now .... Before the rain ... but now .... until the whole ... In the train .... In the ditches .... flood water .... into a fine trickle ....swallowed up altogether.

*Summary*: The rain seemed to intensify the heat. Earlier the perspiration evaporated but now the steam rising from the wet landscape of the Deccan Plateau felt like a gigantic Russian bath. The train windows closed to keep the suffocating heat out and the flood water in the ditches diminished to a trickle by the heat of the sun and left the red earth hot and greedily thirsty.

(The remaining answers may be discussed with the teacher or a friend)


## B) Support

**62**   *Pattern*: List of Examples

*Coherence Signals*: In medical research ... T. G. Morton ..... Theobold Smith .... Equally important .... Dr. Walter Reed ... the founding of the Rockefeller Institute .... Investigation ... preventive work ... in every part of the world ............ the headquarters ... war against disease.

*Summary*: America has made a noble contribution to research. T. G. Morton gave suffering humanity the boon of anaesthesia, Theobold Smith was the first to discover the role of insects in spreading infectious diseases and his discovery of toxin-antitoxin conquered the scourge of diphtheria. Dr. W. Reed identified the species of mosquito that spread yellow fever. America also founded the Rockefeller Institute which has organized and financed preventive work and medical research all over the world. The headquarters of the war against disease is in the United States.
(100 words)


**63**   *Pattern:* Idea & Specific Details

*Coherence Signals*: In contrast with ... however, we are now beginning ... We are instituting ... We are making .... We are fighting ... We are improving ... We are providing ... Our factory legislation ... While our laws ... All of these ... together with a rapid advance ... and.

*Summary*: Our earlier indifference to the high death rate in society has changed. Free hospital and dispensary services and medical attention in public schools, uncontaminated water supplies, improved housing and factory conditions, supervision of the general health of the nation and protection of food supplies has helped save lives. Factory legislation and laws against child labour, the regulation of dangerous occupations, rapid advances in sanitary sciences and vast improvement in the standards of living of the people has reduced the death rate in the city.
(110 words)


**64**    *Pattern: Cause & Consequence*

*Coherence Signals*:... and women who used to ... Yet she can't ... The boredom ... Moreover ... The better ... the less reason ... The department stores ... Meanwhile efficient mending ... and left women – still at home -. Coherence Signals: Women complain ... Little babies

*Summary*: The loneliness, boredom and the lack of stimulation that women complain of is due to various factors. The family is out for the major part of the day and the gadgets at home are her only company. Modern apartment living and constant moving has reduced neighbourhood ties. Better electric equipment and organized home tending has reduced her chance of gossip at the corner store. Ready-made clothes and efficient mending services has taken sensible work out of women's hands and relegated them to the pastime of radio and television,
(105 words)

(The remaining answers and those for Units VI and VII may be discussed with the teacher or a friend )


**Unit VIII**

**90** *Diagrammatic Summary*: 1- viruses; 2- bacteria; 3- chromosomal; 4- fertilized; 5- egg    6-heat; 7-deformities; 8- German; 9- Measles; 10- drugs; 11- chronic starvation; 12- vitamin deficiency.

*Model Summary*:    1- disease; 2- be; 3- fertilized; 4- egg; 5- womb; 6- smoking; 7- retardation;    8-viral; 9- malaria; 10- third; 11- diet; 12- deficiency.

**91**
**I**
**Paras 2 & 3:**
A) – g & h.
B)    a)- ii;   c)- iv;   d)- ii;   e)- ii;   f) – iv;   g) – iv.

**Paras 4 & 5:**
A) – c & f
B) a – iii; b–iv; d- ii; e– iv.

**II**    1 common /numerous /many; 2 tightly; 3 porous; 4 under; 5 sunlight /light; 6 soil; 7 bodies; 8 manure; 9 burrows; 10 roots.


**92**
**I**
**Para 1:**
A) – a.    B) b – iii;   c - ii;   d - ii; e- iv.
**Para 2:**
A) - d.    B) a- iv; b- ii; c-iv.
**Para 3:**
A) - d.    B) a- ii; b- iii; c- ii; e- iv.

**II**    1- carbon; 2- tightly; 3- shaped; 4- base; 5- diamonds; 6- earth /ground; 7- pressure;   8- man.


**93**
**I**    A) - b, e, h, i and n. B) a- iii;   c- iv;   d- iv;   f- iii;   g- ii; j- i;   k- ii;   l- iv;   m- ii; o- ii; p- i.

**II** 1 - game; 2 - sport; 3 - Mountaineers; 4 - dangers; 5 - Mountaineering; 6 - rules; 7 - methods;   8 - groups; 9 - themselves; 10 - till /until; 11 - practise; 12 - enjoy.


## 94
**I** A) –a & e.    B) b- iv;  c- ii   d- ii;  f- iv;  g- ii;  h- ii;  i- iv;  j- iv.

**II** (Older residents maintain that Lalbagh was named after a 14th century dargah of a Muslim pir named Lal Syed Shah) and not after the Lalbaug Mansion which was built by Pestonji Wadia in 1792.
(42 words)


## 95
**I** A) a, c, d, g ,l, n, & p.        B) b – iv; c – iii; e –i; f – iv; h – i; i – iv; j – iv; k – iv;  m – iv,  o – i.

**II** Traditionally, children were brought up on a mother's instinct and homely advice from the mother and mother-in-law. Today, parents have multiple sources of information in books, counsellors, classes and cyberspace. They have to make complicated choices about how much and how early to teach the children and how much to indulge them with TV watching etc. Though more responsive to the times, parents often tend to expect too much from their children.

(71 words)


## Unit IX

## 96
**I** The prophecies about the introduction of railways were proved false. In the opening sentence
**II** The remaining sentences.   Both paragraphs.
**III** <u>Para 1</u>:Wrong negative expectations. <u>Para 2</u>: Positive  economic advantages

**IV** *Summary*:
The prophecies about the introduction of railways were proved false because, contrary to their expectations, the farming classes prospered through improved agricultural communication, cheaper lime, coal and manure and no decrease in milk production. There was no pollution from smoke, no fires in farmyards and farm animals remained unaffected. On the contrary, railway lines were in greater demand so that properties which had attracted compensation, now fetched higher prices. There was a clamour for sidings and accommodation near railway stations was in greater demand as land sales advertisements showed.

**V**     A– a).  B. b) – iv; c) – i; d) – iii.


97
**I     Para 1**
1) Yes, Sentence 5;        2) Ss 1-3;     3) An illustration;
*Pattern*: Statement & Explanation.
*Summary*:
Children approaching adulthood and their parents view each other as representatives of a hostile group because of the rebellious spirit of their children.

**Para 2**
Ss. 6 & 7;     6) Afterwards in Ss.8 & 9;   7) S. 6 links the ideas in Paragraphs 1 & 2;
8)     *Pattern*: Statement & Explanation.
*Summary*:
Children want to assert their emancipation. Parents, not realizing that this is a normal and temporary phase, try to contain/ control this tendency. This hostility is strongest in small communities where parents get stricter because teenagers deeds get magnified under the watchful eyes of their neighbours.

**Para 3**
9) S. 10;            10) No, because it is only an illustration.
11) *Pattern*: Statement, Explanation & Example.
12) *Summary* of Para 3:
The adolescent is not as demonstrably affectionate and appreciative as he was as a child but is more openly critical. However, with maturity his appreciation of his parents returns as Twain confirms.
        (32 words)

13) Summary of the Passage:

Children approaching adulthood and their parents view each other as representatives of a hostile group because of the rebellious spirit of their children. Parents, not realizing that their children's desire to assert their emancipation is a normal and temporary phase, try to contain/ control it more strictly in small communities because teen-agers deeds get magnified under the watchful eyes of their neighbours. To the disenchantment of his parents, the adolescent is also not as demonstrably affectionate and appreciative as he was as a child but is more openly critical. However, with maturity his appreciation of his parents is restored as Mark Twain's observation confirms.

(105 words)

II    A - b);    B: a) – i; c) – iii; d) – ii.

## 98
I    Para 1: Problem, Solution & Evaluation of Solution    Para 2: Statement & Explanation    Para 3: Purpose/ Cause & Result.
III    A. - b)    B. a) – i; c) – iii; d) – ii.

## 99
I    Para 1 – a); Para 2 – c), d), h) & i); Para 3 – a), c), f), g) & h).
II    Philip tried not to disturb the silence of the Reference Library. But as he climbed down the ladder with a book on photography, it slipped from his grasp and fell to the floor with a loud crash. The lady assistant reprimanded him and asked him not to disturb the readers again. Her tone however was kinder when she realised that the 13-year-old had shown interest in reading at the library which was for the use of people above the age of fourteen.
III    A – b);    B a) – ii; c) – iv); d) – iii).

## 100
I    The author loved horse racing and had ridden in many international races. He was inspired to participate in the village race when his host offered to lend his horse and the neighbour challenged him to beat his beautiful racehorse. Eight riders participated and at halfway the neighbour was in the lead and the author third. But soon the neighbour's horse seemed to tire and slow down. The author now improved his position and in the third lap his horse shot forward to victory. He had won the race.

II    A – d);           B a) – v; b) – i; c) – iii.

## 101
I    We expected to reach the town across the hills to find a bed for the night. But it was soon dark and cold and it started to rain reducing visibility. The car, too, ran out of petrol and the town was nowhere in sight. We consumed the little food we had and resigned ourselves to spending the night in the car. But John, walking to the top of the hill, saw the lights of the town. We unloaded the car and pushed it too the top of the hill; then reloaded it to reach the town and find a hotel quite easily.
II    A – c).       B a) – i; b) – v; d) – iii.

## 102
1. b.    2. a-i; c-iv; d-iv.    3. S. 2.    4. a.    5. b.
6. Certain birds like to be near man.
7. Of the birds that like the society of man the robin is the most popular.
8. The robin is popular in England because of his striking personality.
9. Ss. 1-3 can help formulate a topic sentence.
10 Ss. 4 – 7.
11. bold.
12. His strong personality is revealed in the boldness of his fearless strutting movements, his colourful dress and the joyful forthrightness of his song which is free and exulting but with a beautiful under-song. His boldness endears us so that we can feed him with worms and befriend him.

13. robin, nest, anywhere, freckled, eggs.
14 'anything from a tin kettle to a hole in a tree or a bank', 'white in ground colour, with freckles of light red', 'of dead leaves, grass and moss interwoven with hair and a few feathers'.

15 He lays freckled eggs in a rough nest which he builds almost anywhere. (13 words)
16. Pattern: Statement & Elaboration/ Explanation.
17. Check with answer to 18

18.1- man's/ human; 2- popular/ intimate; 3- striking; 4 – boldness; 5 - movement/s; 6– attitude; 7 – thoughtful; 8 – character; 9 – eggs; 10 - anywhere.

## 103
1.- d
2. a – v, b – iv, c-iii.
3. i) War is a terrible evil --- Sent.1; ii) War is sometimes necessary----Sents. 2-9.
4. i) Slavery ----'however' (transitional device);
   ii) Oppression under a foreign yoke ---- 'again' (tr. dev.);
      iii) Invasion of the country ------ 'Finally, ...; When.....' (tr. dev.)
5. Pattern: Para 1: Statement (War is an evil);   Para 2,3 & 4: Contrast (But war is sometimes necessary) & Classification (of situations where war becomes necessary)
6. 'evils'

7. Preventive war
8. Love of peace

9. Laziness, indecision and shirking (neglect or avoidance) of responsibility
10. Assisting the weak and oppressed.

11. Because there is no selfish gain and no material advantage.
12. See answer to !4.

13. Paragraph 2: "man of courage and spirit", "submit to a foreign yoke", "admitting an invader to our shores", "murderer or burglar ... ", "no matter what the odds" etc. (Sentences 2-4)
Paragraph 3: "knocking at our gates", "innate love of peace", "excuse for indolence" etc. (Sentences 5-6)
Paragraph 4: "remain unmolested", "no storms looming ahead", "signal crime or wickedness", "gird on our armour and go forth like the knights of olden times in defence of the weak" etc. (Sentences 7-8)

14.1) slavery, 2) greater, 3) Fighting, 4) sometimes, 5) attack, 6) excuse,
  7) freedom, 8) weak, 9) cost, 10) causes /wars.

## 104

**I**      Para 1: Classification;      P. 2 & 3: Statement & Explanation

**II**     There are two kinds of popularity, intimate and long-distance. Intimate popularity is preferred because, often, the man who enjoys long-distance popularity is disliked at close quarters. The man who is intimately popular, in spite of his defects, if any, i) gives pleasure to others while ii) he himself enjoys their society. Iii) He expects to find good company in others and is ready to take risks in social intercourse. Iv) He is always sanguine and hopeful rather than despondent about human mature. v) He thus fills others with his own vitality. vi) He is not an egotist but a hedonist. vii) His easy instinctive liking of others is a virtue because he makes people happy rather than miserable.

## 105

**I**      Topic: Plastics.          Title: Plastics
**II**     Para 1: Last Sentence;     P. 2: Last Sentence; P. 3: First Sentence
**III**    P. 1: Definition & Explanation;    P. 2: Process;    P. 3: Classification.
**IV**    The paradox about plastic materials is that in the manufacturing process, under the heat and pressure the material is flowing and mouldable, but restored to normal conditions the moulded plastic product retains its shape permanently and is not 'plastic' and mouldable any more. The process of moulding is carried out in special presses so that the mould can be heated and the plastic pressured into shape. After the moulding it is cooled. Two broad categories of industrial plastics are thermo-plastic materials which can be softened and re-softened with heat and pressure, and thermo-setting materials which undergo a chemical change under the intense heat and cannot be re-formed further.

## 106

**I**      Topic: The earth's interior. Title: The Structure of the Interior of the Earth.
**II**     Para 1: Statement & Evidence;     P. 2, 3 & 4: Description
**III**    P.1: Implied & indicated with brackets in Answer IV;        P. 2: Sentence 2      P.3: Sentence1;     P. 4: Implied: The crustal layer is composed of a light kind of rock, while with the core comes a different denser rock of a basic silicate variety.

**IV** (Our planet comprises material that is not inert but is frequently subject to changes) which show in earthquakes, volcanoes and even the very origin and evolution of life. The spherical ball consists of a core and a mantle. The core, extending to 3450 of the total radius of 6350 kilometres from the centre of the earth, is made of dense stuff, which at the centre is 13 times as heavy as ordinary water. The thin outer crust of the mantle is composed of a light kind of rock with a density of 2.7 times that of water. Below the crustal layer and right down to the junction with the core comes a different denser rock of a basic silicate variety

**107**
**I** Topic: Chromosomes; Title: The Structure and Functions of the Chromosomes
**II** P. 1 & 2: Description; P. 3: Explanation; P. 4: Process & Explanation.

**III** An extra ordinary substance called DNA (Deoxyribonucleic Acid) is the important constituent of 'chromosomes' which were recently discovered to be the carriers of heredity. The fibre like molecules of DNA are structured and packaged in such a way as to carry the code for all the vital functions performed in living, growing and dividing cells. Its incredible efficiency is shown by the fact that all the chromosomes in the fertilized eggs of the original human being from whom the two and a half billion people of the world have descended would occupy a volume equal to that of an aspirin tablet. A further property of the chromosome is that by attracting to itself the simple chemical substances of which it is composed, and which are present within cells it can make a complimentary copy of itself. This leads to a third property of DNA, demonstrated by F.H.C. Crick and J. D. Watson, that the two chains of the DNA molecule, which are complementary copies of one another, can separate, each build a mirror image and present two new molecules, in place of the single original, having precisely the same structure.

This self-duplication is the basis of life. In self-reproduction within organisms the fertilized egg divides over and over again. Both daughter cells get a full complement of 46 chromosomes. After the first few divisions of the egg, development involves growth – the manufacture of proteins and enzymes and the construction of new molecules of DNA. By attracting the material necessary, the structure of the DNA molecule also ensures that a duplicate whose precise similarity to the original is guaranteed and only then does the cell divide.

**108** A radical change in the Japanese diet from the traditional rice, fish and vegetables to a more varied fare including eggs and dairy produce has led to a transformation in Japanese agriculture. This was due to the influence of Western idea of food and to depleting fish resources. This in turn resulted in phenomenal livestock production and changed methods of farming. Livestock development was based on improved pasture in the uplands, a combination of "cut and carry" methods and various grazing techniques and a road building programme to transport pasture herbage from the uplands. The cultivation of new varieties of rice with better and faster yields helped dedicate more of the plains to the livestock industry. Also, industrialization creating jobs for the rural populace, the increase in the average farm size meant that larger farms could favour crop diversification and mechanization.
(155 words)
*Title*: The Transformation of Japanese Agriculture.


**109** Silence is unnatural and fearful to man, for all through life he tries to make noise. He even makes conversation to break silence, and feels ashamed if he cannot chatter ceaselessly, though he knows his chatter is mainly nonsense. The aim of conversation is mainly to make a buzzing noise, and everyone would rather buzz and keep quiet. Most buzzing is pleasant to the ear and mind, but he would be foolish who entered conversation only when he had a wise thought. Very few people enter conversation to learn anything but merely to make a noise, the weather being sufficient topic. Even so, after talking nothing all evening, people boast of their conversational powers.
(103 words)
*Title*: Silence and Man


**110** Sports and games have been a universal activity from time immemorial but its oldest known place is in Britain The average boy whether he liked games or not was made to play them in a certain period of his life so that he developed a familiarity with and interest in sports. All classes of people in Britain, therefore, in normal times show interest in the Sports Page of the newspaper and absorb its terms and ideas in their routine life. This does not mean that sports and games override all other interests in life or that they are disproportionately emphasized. The modern British youth give sports an appropriate place in life.
(107 words)

*Title*: Sports in Britain

**111**   The prejudice against the education of women in India began to break down in the early part of the twentieth century. The release of women from ignominy and suffering became the mission of several women's groups. Some women's societies were started in collaboration with European women such as the National Indian Association. Others were spontaneously started like the Bharat Stree Mahamandal in the United Provinces and Bengal and the Seva Sadan Society of Bombay, which worked for the abolition of purdah and for other philanthropic work. Their most effective activity was the promotion of women's education. It was, however, not easy because the strongest opposition came from the women themselves, who because of their enforced ignorance were mired in hurtful and unjust religious customs and resisted all change and innovation.

The outbreak of the First World War, however, gave an impetus to women's emancipation with newspapers, congresses and debating societies drawing attention to the subject and with Mrs. Annie Besant clamouring for the abolition of child marriages and encouragement of female literacy. The Women's India Association demanded enfranchisement of women leading to enrolment of women in the electoral register and women being elected to the provincial legislatures. Dr. Muthulakshmi Reddi was the first woman elected as Vice President of the Madras Legislative Council (1926-1930). Mahatma Gandhi also insisted on perfect equality between men and women. With the Second World War women were leaving their homes to replace or supplement their men as breadwinners and even entered the military services. Later, the principle of equality was incorporated in the Constitution of India and the Hindu Code Bill hoped to achieve the completion of the social evolution of women.
(300 words approx.)

*Title*:  The Flowering of Women's Freedom in India
*Or*    Fifty Years of Social Evolution among Indian Women

**112**   Sun has been important to us because its light helps us to see and its heat warms us and the earth and **sustains** life.
But most of the light and heat, which could provide us much needed energy, goes into the earth and is wasted.  The heat received by the earth in only two days is enough to provide the power we would get from burning all the coal, oil and gas in the earth.

This heat if properly trapped and stored could provide valuable energy especially when wood, coal and oil are becoming so scarce. By focusing sunlight, with big curved metal mirrors, on boilers containing water, steam can be generated to drive steam engines. Such solar engines have been built in Bombay, Egypt and Israel. Solar furnaces for melting iron have also been set up in France, Egypt and America. The sun's heat can also be used for solar cooking by day and for heating houses at night, by passing the hot water through a system of pipes. The heat can also be used to drive a cooling machine and solar refrigerators could prove more useful than solar cookers. However, these **processes** are all very expensive.

By reflecting the light of the sun on a special material containing silicon and allowing the current to flow in the silicon, photo-electricity can be **generated**. This has been very valuable in space research to drive the radio transmitters carried by satellites to send information back to earth. While electrical batteries on the satellite would not last long, the solar cells make photo-electricity, when the sun shines upon them. Solar cells can also be used for home radio receivers and for **empowering** country telephone lines as has been done in America. When solar energy can be tapped cheaply, tropical countries will always have all the power they will ever need.

(310 words approximately)

> *Title*: The Taming of the Sun
> *Or*: Solar Power Tapped and Untapped.


**113** The first traces of human evolution were found chiefly in tools and ornaments and fossil bones. The beginning of man's progress is marked by the first coliths or serviceable flints – crude and unpolished. Of the half million years since then, nearly three quarters had passed by in learning to cut and shape and polish these. Thus the initial progress was very slow. With the age of metals began recorded history which is all crowded in the last five thousand years. The last thousand have witnessed a tremendous spate of scientific and technological progress and the pace cannot slacken now. Tradition, which includes the inheritance of acquired characteristics and the results of learning and training is a new medium of mankind's speedy and accumulating progress.

(124 words)

*Title*: The Course of Human Evolution

**114**     Olestra is a fat-free oil, that behaves like regular oil in taste and function, seemed to be a realization of the dieter's dream of gorging on puddings and fry-ups. But several researchers fear that this oil, which has had its molecules tinkered with, could be the beginning of a nightmare.

Nutritionist Myra Kardstat views the American Food and Drug Administration's decision to license its use in savoury snacks with alarm as it would be a huge uncontrolled experiment with public health as fat-like Olestra absorbs fat-soluble vitamins and nutrients and then rushes them out of the body. Carotenoids, found in vegetables, which boost the immune system against some cancers are especially vulnerable. Also the whole issue of reducing the fat in our diet is a mistake. Some other products on the same lines, like Salatrim and Caprenin are forty per cent less in calories but high in harmful saturated fats.

Joan Dyegussow also echoes doubts about what these chemical marvels may be doing to us. Even fibres, which have been researched much longer, have not been fully understood by us. Prof. Barbara J. Rolls' study showed that volunteers on a low-fat diet, when allowed to eat whatever they wanted for the rest of the day, made up the calorie difference by dinner time. Researchers in the Chemical Senses Centre in Philadelphia found that the people on fat substitutes indulge themselves to full fat things when their guard is down whereas those who cut substitute foods and go for naturally low fat foods, like bread, vegetables and fruits reduce their craving. The journal Nutrition Today warns that denying children high fat foods can lead to nutritional deficits and a study at the McGill University (Canada) found that reducing saturated fat in the diet may add at best no more than 3 months to life. Dr. Malcolm Caruthers believes that the interaction between stress, hormones and cholesterol is far more influential in determining blood-fat levels than the fats you consume. Dr. Artem Simopoulos of the Centre for Genetics, Nutrition and Health has amassed evidence that it is your genes which determine whether you need to worry about fat.

(370 words)

*Title*:  Does a Chip a Day Keep the Doctor Away?
*Or*        Olestra – A Boon?

**115**  Noise, which is only a by-product of the machines we use, has acquired political status and public opinion is insistently demanding that we control noise. The conference at Teddington has collected a huge mass of knowledge and fact on the subject. Sound becomes noise when someone's opinion makes it so. Most of the noise is a small fraction of the main output of the machine and is, therefore, difficult to reduce significantly. The ways in which this is possible are:
Making it acoustically unnoticeable
Much self-discipline
Expenditure of money
A sense of proportion when it involves a conflict of interests
Technical knowledge
Some problems and solutions are:
Vehicular noise is difficult to measure by an instrumental reading like speed can be measured.
The noise of engines, fans and jets is best controlled at the source or during its transit to the ear.
Sound absorbant materials in walls etc. can reduce only five decibels of noise.
Domestic noise can be controlled by forethought and courtesy.
Noise control in modern air transport must be worked out at the international level and will be extremely expensive.
(160 words)

*Title:* The Control of Noise


## Unit X
**116**
I     The overall title & topic: 'Improving Study Habits'
II    A) a) freedom from distractions/ interruptions; b) a well lighted workplace; c) adequate reference    materials & stationery.
B)The first thing to do is to arrange for a good study setting.
      C) An overview of the material to be studied, implies:  a) looking at section headings;
b) understanding; c) making marginal notes/ underlining.
D) Review at intervals:    a) needs to be done carefully, b) deficiencies in information need to be corrected
E) For taking clear lecture notes: a) write only key ideas; b) edit for readability; c) check for accuracy; d) revise the notes.

**III** Study habits improve with;
i) Motivation and attitudes are important.
ii) good setting for study requiring: a) freedom from distractions/interruptions, b) a well-lighted workplace; c) adequate reference materials & stationery.
iii) An overview of the whole material implying: a) looking at section headings, b) understanding   c) making marginal notes.
iv) Distributing practice especially with factual details & rote learnt materials.
v) Looking in the studied materials for relationships with known knowledge.
vi) Review at intervals   a) needs to be done carefully, b) deficiencies in information need to be corrected.
vii) For taking clear accurate notes:   a) write key ideas b) edit for readability, c) check for   accuracy, d) revise the notes.

## 117

**I**   b) provides a good overall title; c), d) and g) are dealt with in detail.

**II**   1- What is a Kitchen Garden? 2 - garden; 3 - near; 4 - fruits; 5 - Advantages of Kitchen Gardens; 6 - satisfaction; 7 - harvest; 8 - vegetables; 9 - beautifies; 10 - grow; 11 - available; 12 - reduced; 13 - cheap; 14 - safer; 15 - water; 16 - soil; 17 - manure; 18 - Improvements in Kitchen Gardening; 19 - Materials; 20 - Agricultural; 21 - Universities; 22 - media; 23 - Education; 24 - Extension; 25 - radio; 26 - newspapers; 27 - television; 28 - 'Divas'; 29 - 'Kisan'; 30 - 'Melas'.

## 118

**I**   Advertising.

**II**   Because modern advertising influences the people of the world spend their money it has become an essential partner of commerce and industry today.

**III**   The last seven paragraphs.

**IV**

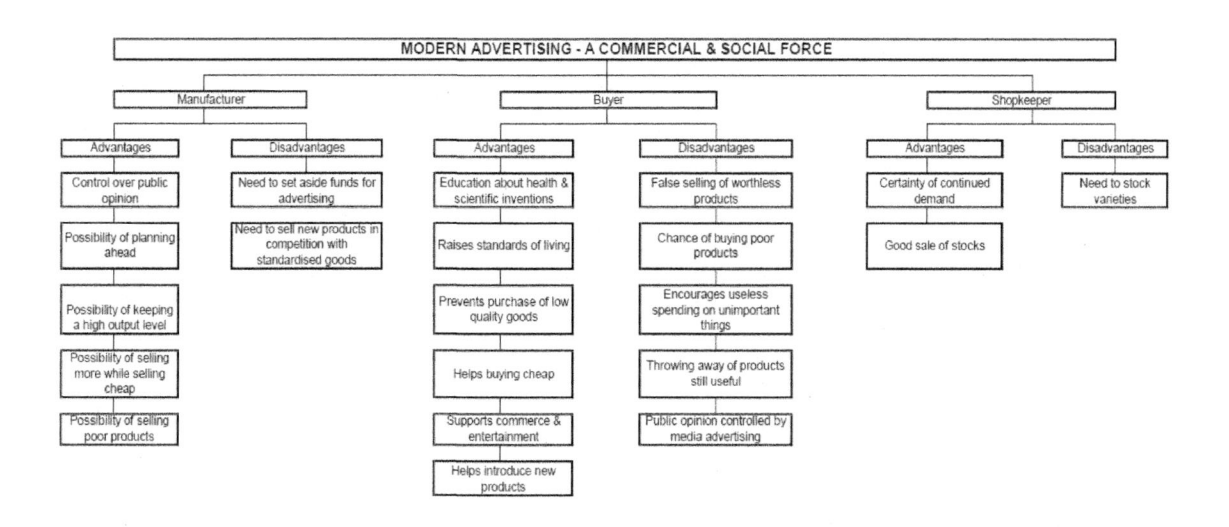

```
                    MODERN ADVERTISING - A COMMERCIAL & SOCIAL FORCE
           ┌──────────────────┬──────────────────────────┬──────────────────┐
                Manufacturer              Buyer                 Shopkeeper
           ┌────────┬─────────┐    ┌──────────┬─────────┐   ┌─────────┬─────────┐
          Advantages Disadvantages Advantages Disadvantages Advantages Disadvantages
```

| Manufacturer | | Buyer | | Shopkeeper | |
|---|---|---|---|---|---|
| **Advantages** | **Disadvantages** | **Advantages** | **Disadvantages** | **Advantages** | **Disadvantages** |
| Control over public opinion | Need to set aside funds for advertising | Education about health & scientific inventions | False selling of worthless products | Certainty of continued demand | Need to stock varieties |
| Possibility of planning ahead | Need to sell new products in competition with standardised goods | Raises standards of living | Chance of buying poor products | Good sale of stocks | |
| Possibility of keeping a high output level | | Prevents purchase of low quality goods | Encourages useless spending on unimportant things | | |
| Possibility of selling more while selling cheap | | Helps buying cheap | Throwing away of products still useful | | |
| Possibility of selling poor products | | Supports commerce & entertainment | Public opinion controlled by media advertising | | |
| | | Helps introduce new products | | | |

## 119

**I**   A – d.    B    a – ii;   c – iii;   b– i.

**II**   A) – b, e & j.    B)   1 – a & c; 2 – g & I; 3 – d, f & h.


**III**   Plastic Wastes in India
i.   Plastic bags everywhere
ii.   Rs. 25,000 crore plastic industry growing at 12 – 15 % annually
iii.   Contributing two million tonnes of plastic waste each year (including bottles, food packaging, cement bags & medical disposals)
   Miniscule Measures
a)   Two legislations (1999 & 2003) under the Amendment on Recycled Plastic Manufacture and Usage: No plastic bags thinner than 20 microns & smaller than 8 x12 inches to be manufactured
b)   Not effective as bigger bags are still strewn around to pollute – waste-pickers collect more lucrative items like bottles, tumblers & plates
   A Wise Approach
a)   Avoid educating children on "essential plastics"
b)   Rather discuss their disadvantages: i)  lost livelihood of potters, basket makers, jute farmers & craftsmen now displaced
ii). cows choking on plastics & other environmental pollution hazards.
iii) emissions from incinerating chlorinated plastics.
c)   Industry should cooperate with any serious measures the Government proposes.

## 120
I   2 - 600;   3 – 400;   4 – below 6.
II   1 – World; 2 – Population; 3 – 7,000; 4 – evenly; 5 - Sparse; 6 - densely; 7 - Lack; 8 - Uninhabitable; 9 - communication; 10 - Dense; 11 - most; 12 - U.S.A.; 3 - W. Europe; 14 - S. E. Asia; 15 - soil; 16 - crops; 17 - Good/ Abundant; 18 -Transport; 19 - Effect; 20 - growth; 21 - Low/ Lowered; 22 - famine; 23 - production; 24 - consumption; 25 - Solutions; 26 - Migration; 27 - U.S.A.; 28 - Europe; 29 - industrialization; 30 - food; 31 - standard; 32- scientific; 33 - communication; 34 - health; 35 – disease; 36 - increase/ growth.

## 121
I   a,d & f.   II   1 – b; 2 – e; 3 – c; 4 – g; 5 – h, i & j.
III   1 – requirements; 2 – surgery; 3 – patient's; 4 – blood; 5 – retransfusion; 6 – reaction; 7 – Infection; 8 – normal; 9 – orthopaedic; 10 – plastic; 11 – kidney; 12 – lung; 13 – cardiac; 14 – rare; 15 – matching; 16 – wait; 17 – haemoglobin; 18 - infected; 19 – metabolism; 20 – 75; 21 – Low; 22 – corrected; 23 – iron; 24 – multivitamins; 25 – erythropoetin; 26 – 35; 27 – Leap Frog; 28 – month; 29 – consecutive; 30 – two; 31 – returned; 32 – fourth; 33 – second; 34 – four; 35 – India; 36 – matching; 37 – storage; 38 – limited; 39 – sterile; 40 – Temperature; 41 – autologous; 42 – labelled; 43 – signed; 44 – donors; 45 – FDA.

## 122
I   – d) Contrast   II   – Kashmir Then & Kashmir Now.
III (A)1 – Then; 2 –Now; 3 – teak; 4 – carvings; 5 – patchwork; 6 – Nagin; 7 – Dal; 8 – weeds; 9 - smiling/ happy; 10 – tourists/ visitors; 11 – comfort; 12 – luxury; 13 – photographs; 14 – killed; 15 – terrorists.
   (B)   – Personal & Family Life. 1.- a city under siege;   2.– after a while the jibes were snapped at;   3.- Murtaza loved to visit from Delhi;   4.- Children shivered at the sight of pistols.
   (C) - Public Life 1.- Mother's visits to her own family stopped;   2.- high literacy in Kashmir; 3.- hardly any rape; 4.- lowest crime rate

(D) – Governmental Attitude. 1. The Army helped common people (e.g., stranded passengers); 2.- Their forced physical presence everywhere and frequent unwanted searches humiliates the Kashmiris; 3.- Wattoo's only vehicle becomes useful for a gasping patient; 4.- frustration with the Indian Government among young & old.


## 123
## Television Watching

| Good for Children | Bad for Children |
|---|---|
| A: Dr. Ann Colby (Licensed Psychologist, Harvard University) 5,000 studies | Marshall McLuhan (scholar of the 1950s) |
| B:<br>TV assists children's intellectual, social, emotional & moral development.<br>　Children watch TV actively (and not passively) & connect narrative sequences with their own experiences.<br>　No deficit in children's attention span due to TV watching; TV watching makes an exciting source of learning<br>　Children watching a moderate amount of TV do better than those watching little or no TV. | Children turn into couch spuds<br>Violent TV leads to aggressive activity and unflattering stereotypes<br>　TV solely an entertainment medium |
| C: The message (sex & violence) comes strong through books, films, theatre & TV | The medium is the message |
| D:<br>It is not TV watching per se but the quality of what they watch that matters<br>　Parental control of children's TV watching important: 1 ½ hours of TV enough<br>　Programs available on Cartoon Network, Discovery Channel & BBC | In India children's TV is not even an issue |

<u>Overall title:</u> Television Watching for Children.


## 124
I　　Paragraph 1: Neem is a subtle and better plant pesticide than the synthetic ones

Pattern: Statement with Elaboration.

<u>Para 2:</u> Neem is unique because it does not kill the pests like synthetic chemicals do, but changes their life processes in subtle ways.

Pattern: Explanation by Comparison & Contrast.

<u>Para 3:</u> Other plants around are protected internally, without the spraying of pesticides (e.g. wheat, rice, sugarcane etc.)

Pattern: Explanation with Examples.

<u>Para 4:</u> Further advantages of neem's non-toxicity to warm-blooded animals and the biodegradability of neem compounds.

Pattern: Explanation with Examples

<u>Para 5:</u> Synthesis of a super-tech 'azadi-rachtin' from a major neem chemical by scientists.

Pattern: Elaboration through further Evidence.

<u>Para 6:</u> Home grown neem a boon to poor Indian farmers who would not afford the neo- neems'

Pattern: Statement of Conclusion.

**II** The neem-based plant pesticide is subtle in that it does not crudely kill the pests but renders them unable to feed, breed or metamorphose, without harming birds, mammals and pollinating insects. Other plants absorb the neem chemicals through the soil and this protection is neither washed off by rain nor is there need for spraying the new growth. The neem-fortified plants are not toxic to warm blooded animals. The multiple compounds in neem make impossible the building up of pest resistance. Also, the neem compounds being biodegradable, the holistic effects make the shade giving neem tree the poor Indian farmer's best friend while not needing to buy the expensive super-tech neem compounds being built by scientists round the world.

(120 words)

**III** Alternative Title: Neem – The Indian Farmer's Super Hero.

## 125

**I** a -iv; b – ii; c – ii; d – ii; e – i.

**II** 1) a river dwelling people of the Amazon rainforests. 2) 92 centimetres. 3) Amazonas 4) Using planes & helicopters to reach the jungles with food, water and medicines. 5) Because of the remoteness of the communities in the dense jungles. 6) Sixty-one. 7) 132,000 .8) the dead fish in the drying rivers. 9) Cholera (&other diseases). 10) Fishermen

.

**III**  1 – largest, 2 – valley, 3 – rainforest, 4 – drying, 5 – jungles, 6 – food, 7 – water,  8 – authorities, 9 –war, 10 - transport/ deliver, 11 – medicines, 12 – tribes, 13 – cure,  14 – cholera, 15 – helicopters.

**IV**  Problems of the people of the Amazon valley:
1.River drying up;  2. Isolation;  3 Lack of water & food supplies;  4 Density of the jungles;  5 Polluted river water;  6 Dead fish spreading contamination;  7 Fear of cholera breakout;  8 Threat of return of bacterial/ viral diseases through contamination;  9 Loss of livelihood for fishermen;  10 Trauma for the old inhabitants to see the aftermath of the biggest river system in the world drying up

# 126
**I.**

| Tribute or title of praise | Tribute by | Reason for Tribute |
|---|---|---|
| 2. The greatest boon of the 20th century | United Nations Report | For halting the march of the desert in Nigeria |
| 3. *Neem hakim* | Ayurveda | Amazing curative powers |
| 4. *Neem: A Tree To Solve Global Problems* | Washington-based National Research Council | A new era in pest control |
| 5. One of the five essentials for every Indian garden | Traditional society | For its medicinal and fumigant properties |
| 6. *Azad-dirakht-i-Hind* | Persians | Useful free tree of India |
| 7. *Muarubaini* | Africans | Forty cures |
| 8. *Arishta* | Sanskrit (Ayurveda) | Wards off evil and pestilence |
| 9. Azadirachta Indica | Latinized botanical name | Botanical value |

**II.** 1959: A German entomologist Dr Heinreich Schmutterer discovered the resistance of the  neem tree to locusts.

1965: Dr Narayanan elucidated the structure of the neem's first major bitter principle, the anti-viral nimbin.

1985: US Environmental Production Agency approved a commercial neem-based insecticide for 'non-food' uses.

**III.**
(i) *Traditional Uses of the Neem:*
- a variety of antivirals, anti-bacterials, fungicides and bioactive substances yielded by the roots, bark, gum, leaves, fruit kernel and oil.

- cures for a host of ailments from Chagas' disease to malaria.
- neem twigs used as datun (or a disposable toothbrush).
- dried neem leaves used to protect stored grain, clothes and books from pests.
- neem leaves used for skin ailments.
- used in rituals to propitiate the goddess Mariamma of smallpox.
- neem oil cakes curb pests, improve soil and serve as a nourishing animal feed.

(ii) *The Neem Abroad:*
- The neem tree provides precious fuel and lumber and is helping halt the march of the desert in the nations along the Sahara desert.
- used in hot and arid lowland tropics for tree cover.
- neem plantations provide shade and comfort to Haj pilgrims on the plains of Arafat.
- it flourishes in a variety of habitats without aggression, in harmony with native plants and animals in foreign lands.
- used for curative properties by Africans and Persians.
- resisted a plague of locusts in Sudan in 1959.

(iii) *New and Modern Uses of the Neem:*
- resisted locusts in Sudan.
- proved best among plant extract pesticides by the US Environmental Agency.
- aromatically effective pesticide in its low-tech form.
- as good as standard pesticides like DDT, dieldrin and malathion.
- superior to them on counts of safety and eco-friendliness.
- foreseen to reduce population growth and perhaps even reduce erosion, deforestation and the excessive temperature of an overheated globe.

**127**

**I.**

| Agency conducting the survey | Point(s) of Nutrition Awareness | Improvement in Nutrition Awareness over the years |
|---|---|---|
| 1. Food Marketing Institute | a. Nutrition is an important factor in selecting foods | 72% in 1988<br>76% in 1989 |
|  | b. Fat is an important factor in food selection | 9% in 1983<br>16% in 1987<br>27% in 1989 |
| 2. Food and Drug Administration (FDA) and National Heart Blood and Lung Institute (NHBLI) | a. People believing that fatty foods cause heart disease | 29% in 1983<br>55% in 1988 |
|  | b. People believing that fatty foods cause cancer | 12% in 1983<br>25% in 1988 |
|  | c. People who know that fat and cholesterol are not the same | 34% in 1988 |

**II.** (ii) Consumers want precise dietary recommendation
(iii) Professionals find it difficult to make these due to scientific reservations. Because of this, their knowledge and/or credibility is doubted by the consumers.
    (iv) Different nutritionists may not commonly agree on specific nutrition issues.
    (v) No access to dieticians who are all usually registered with hospitals.
    (vi) Consumers are unwilling to pay dieticians in private practice for the information.

**III.**

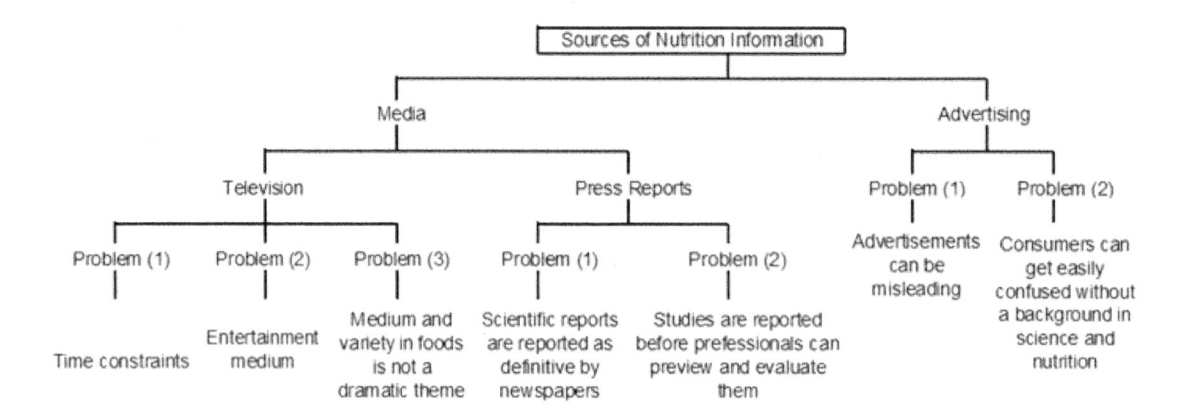

```
                        Sources of Nutrition Information
         ┌──────────────────────┴──────────────────────┐
         Media                                    Advertising
    ┌──────┴──────┐                            ┌──────┴──────┐
 Television   Press Reports                Problem (1)   Problem (2)
    │             │                            │             │
  ┌─┼─┐         ┌─┴─┐                    Advertisements  Consumers can
  │ │ │         │   │                      can be        get easily
Prob Prob Prob Prob Prob                  misleading    confused without
(1)  (2)  (3)  (1)  (2)                                 a background in
                                                         science and
                                                         nutrition
```

Problem (1) Time constraints
Problem (2) Entertainment medium
Problem (3) Medium and variety in foods is not a dramatic theme
Problem (1) Scientific reports are reported as definitive by newspapers
Problem (2) Studies are reported before prefessionals can preview and evaluate them

**IV.** Qualities required in an ideal Nutrition Communicator:
  (i) Oratory skills
  (ii) Wisdom
  (iii) Wit
  (iv) Adequate scientific background in nutrition.

# 128

**I.** (a) 'The revolutionary technique of obtaining concrete from lunar soil.'
   (b) Yes. It mentions the word 'Concrete'.

**II.** (a) (i) Manned (ii) structure (iii) space, Mars
   (b) (i) thermal shocks (minus 150oC and 120oC, 28-day).
       (ii) atmosphere, gravity
       (iii) transporting, (1000 tonnes, 330 tonnes and 300 tonnes), Rs 1,90,000 crore.

**III.** A. A Revolutionary Technique:
       - Heat ilmenite to 800oC to produce dry concrete.
       - Add hydrogen to produce iron, titanium and water vapour.
       - Inject mixture into pressurised mould containing the dry pressed concrete.
       - Result: Exceptionally strong concrete, more      resistant than the ordinary one.
   B. Dr Lin's Experiment:
       - Mix 40 grams of lunar soil with water to produce concrete.

C. Attractive features of the New Concrete:
   - Can withstand lack of atmosphere and reduced gravity.
   - Can withstand enormous temperature differences found on the moon.
   - Reduce the cost of building a lunar base to one-fourth
     (Rs 40,000 crore instead of Rs 1,90,000).
   - Entailed less transportation of materials and machinery
     (only 200 tonnes instead of 1,630 tonnes)
D. Plans for the Lunar Base Project:
   - An eight-nation Lunar Concrete Committee set up.
   - Rs 1,00,000 crore promised as budget.
   - Machine-material complex production allotted to a French company.
E. Future Scope of Space Research:
   - Setting up a manned station on the moon.
   - Further forays into space.
   - Exploration of Mars, the nearest planet.
F. Possible use of Concrete in India:
   - Technology to be used for a more durable concrete for busy Indian roads to take the
     stress caused by overloaded vehicles.

**IV** A revolutionary technique of obtaining concrete from lunar soil without using water is helping scientists realize the dream of setting up a manned station on the moon to further our forays into space and Mars. A structure built with conventional concrete would not resist the thermal shocks caused by temperature fluctuations on the moon between the minimums of 150 and 120 degrees in a 28-day cycle. It would also have to withstand the absence of atmosphere and a gravity that is one-sixth that of the earth. The cost of transporting materials (1,000 tonnes of cement, 330 litres of water and 300 tonnes of iron to the moon would have been about Rs.1,90,000 crores. Dr. Lin's revolutionary technique of heating to 800degrees centigrade , the ilmenite (or lunar rock containing iron and titanium oxides) by using huge solar panels on the moon itself produced a dry concrete. When hydrogen was added to produce titanium and water vapour and this mixture injected into a pressurized mould for a few hours it produced an exceptionally strong concrete more resistant than the ordinary one mixed with water. The cost of building the lunar base was reduced to Rs.40,000 crores. If the French company produced lunar concrete is made available to India, it could replace the conventional concrete of our roads to withstand far better the stress our crowds and overloaded vehicles.
(225 words)

Title:   A Super Lunar Concrete

## 129                  Sins of the Flesh

I     True: b, g.     False: a, c, e & f.     Not Indicated: d.

II    A) Correct: a, c, d, g & i.
       B) Incorrect: e & f;    Inaccurate: h;           Unstated in the Passage: b

III   A) – a, b, d, e, g, h & i.     B) – Incorrect: c; Inaccurate: f; Irrelevant: j.

IV   <u>Myths about Proteins</u>
1. Animal fat and not animal proteins increase cholesterol levels.
2. Animal proteins have an adverse effect on disease processes.
3. Meat is not toxic or harmful to the kidney and liver.
4. They are better than plant proteins.
5. Animal proteins are the most essential of the food groups.
6. They lead to increased physical strength and energy

<u>Research on Plant Proteins versus Animal Proteins</u>
a) *Health Magazine* published an article that animal protein rather than fat increased cholesterol levels. Cutting animal protein helped.
b) An Italian study showed:
      i. Low fat diet reduced cholesterol from 290 to 270
      ii. Cutting animal protein from the diet reduced it further to 200
     iii. Adding animal protein produced a rise in cholesterol.
c) An experiment in Germany showed that athletes on a vegetarian diet were superior in endurance and stamina than those on a non-vegetarian diet.

<u>Superiority of Plant Proteins over Animal Proteins</u>
a. Plant proteins are digested in 4 – 7 hours where flesh foods require 25 – 30 hours to pass through the gastro-intestinal tract.
b. They reduce more cholesterol as the studies mentioned above show.
c. They contain fewer toxins. Flesh foods have to be acted upon by a variety of acids and enzymes.
d. They leave more physical and mental energy because less energy is spent on digesting plant proteins more vital energy is available to the body as the German study shows.

e.    Plant proteins may contain pesticides, but animal foods contain much more: a concentration of fertilizers and pesticides as well as the artificial hormones (used to fatten animals) plus the sodium nitrates and nitrates used for preservation and for an attractive red colour in the meat.

Hazards of Excessive Protein Intake
Our standard protein requirement is 60 grammes per day and extra proteins if taken should be in vegetarian form preferably uncooked but certainly not fried. Too high an intake can be harmful because:
a)    Extra protein gets stored and adds to our weight.
b)    Excess protein increases the cholesterol level.
c)    When not eliminated the stored proteins degenerate and convert to nitric sulphuric and phosphoric acids.
d)    The alkaline minerals in the body are used to neutralize the acids and become deficient in the bones, hair and nails.
e)     acid damages the liver and kidneys.
f)    f) The urine with erythrocytes and albumin becomes vulnerable to infection.
g)    Several types of cancers are caused. Cancer of the stomach results from flesh foods being broken up and active poisons are thrown onto organs not intended for them. Excess proteins are linked with cancer of the breast, liver and bladder and also to increase in the incidence of leukemia and Bright's disease.

**130**
**II    Notes**
   **A.** The Spread of Child Abuse
   *Statistics:*
•    400 cases in a year of sodomy of minors in Delhi
•    500,000 child prostitutes in the country

But this is only the tip of the iceberg as only one in ten cases of abuse get reported according to a Crime Branch official in Bombay
.
American statistics, on the other hand are more realistic;
•    One girl in 3 and one boy in 7get molested before the age of 18.
•    A typical American paedophile abuses 380 children in a lifetime.

**B.** Reasons for Non-reporting of Child Abuse in India
a)    Social stigma attached to loss of virtue in girls

b)   Female virginity is a fetish in Indian culture.
c)   Absence of the necessary channels of communication between parents and children regarding sexual matters.
d)   The immediate trauma
   All these contribute to the horrific silence of acceptance.

### C. Categories of Molesters
1. Paedophiles
2. Emotional Immaturity: a pathological pre-occupation with sex.
3. Latent homosexuals with a repressed fear of women
4. Those in advanced stages of venereal disease who believe that having sex with a virgin will cure them.
5. Among the 'normal' people are close male relatives of the child who in a male dominated society often get away with anything they do (sometimes in complicity even with the mother of the child).

### D. Mother's/ Family's Role
a)   A temporary reaction of bemoaning on the part of the mother.
b)   Quiet acceptance because of the social stigma.
c)   Often, active collusion/ participation with the dominating male in the family.
d)   Refusal to go to the police or the courts.
e)   Refusal to take the molested child back into the home for fear of the 'spoiling' of the family.

### E. Social Attitudes
a.   The indifference and neglect of the families.
b.   Very few childrens' advocacy groups or social service organizations like Annapurna.
c.   No governmental initiatives in rehabilitation of victims of child abuse.
d.   Appointing of the National Commission on Child Abuse is only a token action.
e.   Elaborate court procedures.
f.   Insensitive police, lawyers and judiciary.
g.   No emotional security or rehabilitation of traumatized children

### F. The Wrongs of Child Abuse
a)   The trauma for the child
b)   No emotional security when the mother and family abandon her due to the social stigma.
c)   Rationalization with the child that the past be forgotten as an accident.

d)     The psychic scar is never healed and the children grow to become abusers themselves.
e)     Paedophiles go unpunished or untreated because they plead that they were drunk during the act of molestation.
f)     Even rehabilitated children show inadequate sex relations or fear of sex in their later married lives.

# ACKNOWLEDGEMENTS

I would like to express my gratitude to the references listed below for the extracts from books, newspapers, magazines and other writings, which have been used in this book, helping beautifully with the analysis, exemplification  as also in providing practice tasks for the various skills of summary writing and note making for the prospective readers/ learners who use this book.

**References**
Abbas Zaffar
Agar Herbert
Barzun Jacques
Bellare Nirmala 1984. Towards Designing A Study Skills Course for Home Science Students. Unpublished Dissertation. C.I.E.F.L., Hyderabad, India.
Bellare Nirmala 1997. Reading and Study Strategies Books 1. O.U.P. Mumbai.
Bellare Nirmala 1998. Reading and Study Strategies Books 2. O.U.P. Mumbai.
Bellare Nirmala 2001. An Investigation of Text Processing by Students While Reading for Summarizing. Unpublished Ph. D. Dissertation. University of Mumbai.
Broomfield Louis
Brown Harry M. 1997. The Contemporary College Writer: Patterns in Prose. Van Nostrand Reinhold Co., New York.
Bruce Bill (ed) 1981 Piccolo Explorer Encyclopedia. (Contributors: Michael Chinery, Christopher Maynard, Ian Ridpath & Jonathan Rutland) Piper Books Ltd., London.
Carson Rachel
Charlton James M. ( ) Fifty Precis Exercises worked with Model Solutions. James Broodie Ltd., London.
Close R. A. ( ) English We Use for Science
Coleridge Samuel Taylor
David Le Roi in Thornley
Dickens Charles
Dinesen Isak
Dubos Rene
Dwivedi Sharada
Eiseley Loren
Fitch Robert Eliot
Fromm Erich
Hoyle Fred

Huxley Thomas
India Today (Weekly Magazine)
India Today (magazine) 14 July 1997. 'Dyeing to Live' by Stephen David & 'Toxic Terror' by Shubhadra Menon & Smruti Koppikar. Living Media India Ltd, Delhi.
India Today (magazine) 29 March 2004. Living Media India Ltd, Delhi.
India Today (magazine) 14 June 2004. Living Media India Ltd, Delhi.
Kerrod Robin 1978. The Question and Answer Book of SPACE. Sackett & Marshall Ltd., London.
Knight & MacAlpine
Lynd Robert
McGrath Patrick J. &G. Allen Finley. "Measurement of Pain" in Annales Nestle (1999:57) pp. 13-20 Denges, Switzerland.
Mead Margaret
McGrath Patrick J. & G. Allen Finley (1999) Measurement of Pain in Anneles Nestle
Mukherjee Meenakshi (ed.) 1975. Let's Go Home and Other Stories. Orient Longman. Mumbai.
N. Suresh
Nadkarni Vithal
Odham's Child's First Encyclopaedia in Colour (1959) Odham's Press Ltd., London.
Outlook (magazine) 28 July 2003 (Volume 29). Hathway Investments Pvt. Ltd., New Delhi.
Piccolo's Explorer Encyclopedia (1981) Piper Books Ltd London, U.K.
Purie Aroon
Ray Williams
Robinson Wheeler B.
Russel Bertrand
Sen Satyendranath & Sisir Kumar Das 1955. An Introduction to Economic Theory. Bookland Ltd., Calcutta.
Simply Mumbai (magazine) April – June 2004. Living Media India Ltd., Delhi.
Smart Walter & Daniel R. Lang (1965) Smart's Handbook of Effective Writing. Harper & Row, New York.
Steffens Lincoln
Stephens J. H.
Thomas Dylan
Twain Mark
Thornley G. C. 1972. Further Scientific English Practice. Longman Group Ltd., London.
The Sunday Review 10 Sept. 1995 ( Sins of the Flesh by Shanti Rangwani & Weight Wise by Kalpana Deuskar)

The Sunday Review 15 Oct. 1995 ( I Felt Like God had Died by Chand Rangwani & Child Abuse: Some After Effects by Narendra Panjwani)
The Sunday Review 25 Nov. 1995 (Danger Zone by Kalpana Deuskar)
The Sunday Review 14 Jan. 1996 (The Safest Blood is Your Own by Meher Pestonji).
The Sunday Review 8 July 2003 (
The Times of India July 2003 (Biodegradable Wisdom by Ravi Agarwal)
Time (magazine) 14 Sept. 2004
Ulanov Barry
Vinson Kenneth
Wallace & Dobzhansky
Wertembaker Thomas
Weyl W. E.

A few extracts may remain unreferenced as I was unable to trace the copyright-holder. I shall be grateful to hear from anyone who recognizes their material and who is unacknowledged. I shall be pleased to make the necessary additions/corrections in future editions of this book.

Printed in Great Britain
by Amazon